The Foreign Aid Business

To our wives
Lotte and Ilse

The Foreign Aid Business

Economic Assistance and Development Co-operation

Kunibert Raffer

University of Vienna

H.W. Singer

Institute of Development Studies
University of Sussex

Edward Elgar

Cheltenham, UK • Brookfield, US

Published by
Edward Elgar Publishing Limited
8 Lansdown Place
Cheltenham
Glos GL50 2HU
UK

Edward Elgar Publishing Company
Old Post Road
Brookfield
Vermont 05036
USA

British Library Cataloguing in Publication Data
Raffer, Kunibert
The foreign aid busines : economic assistance and development co-operation
1.Economic assistance 2.Developing countries – Economic conditions
I.Title II.Singer, H.W. (Hans Wolfgang), 1910–
338.9'1

Library of Congress Cataloguing in Publication Data
Raffer, Kunibert, 1951–
The foreign aid business : economic assistance and development cooperation / Kunibert Raffer, H.W. Singer.
p. cm.
Includes bibliographical references and index.
1. Economic assistance. I. Singer, Hans Wolfgang. 1910– .
II. Title.
HC60.R19 1996
338.9'1—dc20 95–49829
CIP

ISBN 1 85898 406 8 (hardback)
1 85898 446 7 (paperback)

Typeset by Manton Typesetters, 5–7 Eastfield Road, Louth, Lincolnshire LN11 7AJ, UK.
Printed and bound in Great Britain by Biddles Limited, Guildford and King's Lynn

Contents

Tables and figures

Tables

Figures

Acknowledgements

In writing this book we have received valuable comments, suggestions and help with regard to literature on special topics. We would like to thank all our friends and colleagues who have kindly contributed with their advice.

We are particularly indebted to our friend Paul Streeten, whose influence can be seen in more than one chapter. With regard to the chapter on Japan we are most grateful to Agata Masahiko, Goto Kazumi and Yamada Keizo for helpful remarks, as well as for the less easily accessible literature. We are grateful to Bruno Gurtner, who discussed the Swiss example mentioned in Chapter 10 in detail with us and sent us useful material on it, and to John Toye for his help with regard to the Aid and Trade Provisions.

While expressing our gratitude we should also like to point out that the usual disclaimer applies: none of the above should be held responsible for our arguments and conclusions.

We are also indebted to Caroline Pybus for her secretarial support.

Abbreviations

ACP	African, Caribbean, Pacific
ADB	Asian Development Bank
AfDB	African Development Bank
AID	(US) Agency for International Development
ASEAN	Association of South-East Asian Nations
BWIs	Bretton Woods Institutions
CEECs	Central and Eastern European Countries
CFF	Compensatory Financing Facility
CMEA	Council of Mutual Economic Assistance
CTTs	Countries and Territories in Transition
DAC	Development Assistance Committee
DFToT	Double Factoral Terms of Trade
ECOSOC	Economic and Social Council (of UN)
ECOWAS	Economic Community of West African States
EDF	European Development Fund
EU	European Union
FAO	Food and Agricultural Organisation
FDI	Foreign Direct Investment
FRG	Federal Republic of Germany
GATT	General Agreement on Tariffs and Trade
IBRD	International Bank for Reconstruction and Development ('World Bank')
IDA	International Development Association
IDB	Inter-American Development Bank
IFAD	International Fund for Agricultural Development
IFC	International Finance Corporation
IFI	International Financial Institution
IMF	International Monetary Fund
JEXIM	Japan Export Import Bank
LLDC	Least Developed Country
MFA	Multi-Fibre Arrangement
MITI	(Japan's) Ministry of International Trade and Industry
NBToT	Net Barter Terms of Trade
NGO	Non-Governmental Organization

NIC	Newly Industrializing Country
NIS	Newly Independent States
ODA	Official Development Assistance
OECD	Organization for Economic Co-operation and Development
OECF	Overseas Economic Co-operation Fund (of Japan)
OOF	Other Official Flows
OPEC	Organization of Petroleum Exporting Countries
SADC	Southern African Development Community
SC	Southern Country
SSA	Sub-Saharan Africa
TNC	Transnational Corporation
ToT	Terms of Trade
UN	United Nations
UNCTAD	United Nations Conference on Trade and Development
UNDP	United Nations Development Programme
UNHCR	United Nations High Commission for Refugees
UNICEF	United Nations International Children's Emergency Fund
UNIDO	United Nations Industrial Development Organization
USDA	United States Department of Agriculture
WFP	World Food Programme
WHO	World Health Organization
WTO	World Trade Organization

PART ONE

Aid – What is it?

1. Aid and help – a necessary distinction

ALL AID SHORT OF REAL HELP?

While the words 'aid' or 'donor' suggest altruism and generosity in everyday English, this relation does not necessarily hold for 'development aid' or 'development assistance' as it is called more formally. These are purely technical terms in development economics and to avoid those wrong perceptions shrewd language wants to create, a book on 'aid' must clarify this at the very start. Of course these terms were coined intentionally to imply help, altruism and generosity. Actual 'aid', however, is not necessarily helpful nor altruistic, although it might be so or it might be motivated by enlightened self-interest. Quite often though interest groups in donor countries have helped themselves rather than the South's poor, and occasionally aid, or 'development aid', has come in handy to finance wars or military coups.

At present the club of Western donors organized in the Development Assistance Committee (DAC) of the OECD, defines official development aid or Official Development Assistance (ODA) as:

> those flows to developing countries and multilateral institutions *provided by official agencies*, including state and local governments, or by their executive agencies, each transaction of which meets the following tests:
> a) it is administered with the *promotion of the economic development and welfare of developing countries as its main objective*, and
> b) it is concessional in character and contains a *grant element of at least 25 per cent.*
> (OECD 1985, p. 171; emphases as original)

A donor is someone who effects such payments. Resources crossing the North-South divide – such as export credits, direct investments by transnational corporations (TNCs), or commercial bank loans – which cannot be subsumed under this definition adopted by the DAC in 1969, are presently called 'flows'.

Initially the North regarded any flow to the South as 'development aid', based on the philosophy that whatever emanates from the North must be good for the South. This perception was in line with both neoclassical and orthodox Marxist approaches to development and their strong, if not virtually exclusive emphasis on physical capital accumulation. Myrdal (1970, pp. 315ff) pointed out that the distinction between ODA and 'flows' made in official

DAC statistics was regularly and systematically blurred. Economists, experts, officials, journalists, everyone equated 'flows' with 'development aid' – a malpractice tolerated and occasionally supported by the DAC 'by some of the titles of tables and comments on the tables' (Myrdal 1970, p. 316).

This generous presentation of one's own generosity produced puzzling results: 'In the DAC statistics petty fascist Portugal year after year is given the place of honor as having the largest "flows" to underdeveloped countries in comparison to its gross national product' (Myrdal 1970, p. 324). The explanation was simple: Portugal, one of the poorest European countries and itself an 'aid' receiver at that time, had a low GNP and fought a protracted colonial war in Africa. As wars are costly, substantial flows of resources to Angola and Mozambique were recorded.

Myrdal's critique contributed greatly to a change of perception and to a clearer definition of ODA. Nevertheless the DAC has never totally dropped the notion that flows across the North-South divide are always conducive to development. The recent uncritical enthusiasm about increases in private flows, including highly volatile, speculative capital, which quickly evaporated after the Mexican crash in 1995, seems to derive from this deep-rooted conviction.

The DAC's present ODA definition deserves close scrutiny. Although it is generally accepted, it must be recalled that it is a definition by one group of donors, not by recipients. ODA figures produced by each member state are reviewed by other DAC members. No recipient is involved in this process of control. Other groups of donors in the South, such as India, China or OPEC members, and the USSR and Eastern European countries as long as they were donors, have apparently accepted the DAC's definition and statistics, including data on their own flows. At least neither OPEC nor the former communist countries have ever tried to present their own figures in a comparable way, which does not make an objective assessment easier. Thus all internationally quoted data, including those of Southern donors are published by the DAC.

Strictly speaking test (a) in the definition of ODA is not a test at all. People disagree on what 'welfare' or 'economic development' means, and there is even more disagreement on what measures promote them. However an actual increase in welfare or an actual promotion of development is not necessary – the intention suffices. Therefore (a) applies automatically, unless the donor's intentions to the contrary (for example doing harm or having another main objective) can be conclusively proved, which is next to impossible. Activities pointedly referred to as 'lethal aid' by Brigitte Erler (1985), a German ODA critic, fall within the definition of ODA if the main (not even exclusive) objective is to promote welfare and development. There is no logical reason not to include military activities if soldiers shoot or kill mainly to promote welfare and economic development. Possibly as a result of Myrdal's remark on Portugal, 'any kind of military assistance is excluded' officially according to the DAC (OECD 1985, p. 171). However the IBRD (1990, p. 253) cautions: 'Although this definition is meant to exclude purely military assistance, the borderline is sometimes blurred; the definition of the country of origin usually prevails.'

Military assistance is not always excluded officially either. In 1990 the US started to include substantial amounts of military debt cancellations (1990: $1.2 billion; 1991: $1.86 billion; OECD 1992, p. 109) in its ODA statistics. The US forgave Egypt military debts because the country fought Iraq with the Americans in the Gulf War. The DAC agreed to review the appropriate recording of debt forgiveness, particularly of military debt and non-ODA export credits. These debt reductions were accepted as ODA, although with 'appropriate footnote indications and further explanations where required' (OECD 1992, p. 86). The DAC recorded them as ODA for members reporting them but did not include military debts in the DAC total. Thus the sum of ODA by all members was bigger than the DAC total – one had one's cake and ate it.

During the review it was argued that military debt forgiveness was not military aid; if undertaken in the context of supporting effective policy programmes, its economic effect was said to be similar to programme aid. Finally the US attempt to have military debt reductions recognized as ODA within the DAC was unsuccessful. The DAC confirmed that forgiveness of military debt was:

> a new and separate transaction dissociated from the purpose of the original transaction, that the inclusion as ODA is based on the development motivation of the act of forgiveness, that this logic is also the basis for including as ODA forgiveness of debt arising from export credits and that therefore both types of debt forgiveness should be treated statistically in the same way.
> (OECD 1992, p. 86)

Although military debt reductions are therefore ODA according to the DAC, it was agreed not to record them as ODA in the future 'in deference to concerns expressed over public opinion impacts' (ibid.) while forgiveness of non-ODA export credits is now recorded as ODA. The fact that donors encourage Southern Countries (SCs) to reduce military expenditures and arms imports was also seen as a reason why recording military debt reductions as ODA would be inappropriate. There is, however, another convincing point not raised by the DAC. If debt forgiveness for military aid were accepted as ODA, any such transaction could easily be transformed into ODA by 'selling' arms first 'on credit' and 'forgiving' these debts afterwards. Finally there is one important distinction between military and other loans which justifies this differentiation. In practice export credits would quite often have been recorded as ODA if the grant element had been sufficiently high, naturally so if the goods had been given as grants. Thus the differentiation between military and non-military debts is justified, even though the latter need not actually promote development.

In its *World Development Report 1990*, the IBRD (1990, pp. 127f) concludes: 'Many "aid" programs in donor countries cover an assortment of activities (including commercial and strategic initiatives) which often have, at best, a tenuous connection with development.'

The *Human Development Report 1994* (UNDP 1994, p. 72) documents that high military spenders received much more aid per head than other SCs. Until 1986 this first group received five times as much as low military spenders from bilateral sources. In 1992 they were still getting two and a half times the amount. In extreme cases this relation is even much more pronounced. As strategic allies, Israel and Egypt received from the US 100 times and 37 times respectively more aid per head than Bangladesh. In the case of multilateral donors, military spending seems to make little difference in the distribution of funds. As money is fungible, more aid to countries with high military outlays means that non-military aid too frees resources for military spending, money which would otherwise have to be used for urgent purposes now financed by aid.

HELPING DONORS THEMSELVES: AID AND COMMERCIAL INTERESTS

Northern politicians openly stress employment effects of ODA to their constituencies. The Federal Republic of Germany (FRG) even introduced a law demanding that employment effects in Germany must be proved for each German project (Erler 1985, p. 85). Commercial pressures on aid are not new but – as the DAC itself acknowledges – they 'have been growing in recent years' (OECD 1995, p. 28). In defence against Republican plans to slash aid substantially, US-AID 'distributed fat folders of documents showing that nearly 80 percent of its budget is recycled to the United States' (*Time*, 29 May 1995).

Nevertheless there seems to exist only one case where doubts regarding the intentions of a donor were loudly and officially expressed by the DAC itself. Austria, a small country, which had routinely reported substantial amounts of export credits as ODA, had reached 0.53 per cent of her GNP in 1982, thus placing herself well above the DAC average. In a review of her performance in 1984, the DAC downgraded Austrian ODA, which had been reported on a commitment rather than on the agreed disbursement basis, to 0.35 per cent, and expressed strong doubts about the 'development orientation' of these flows (OECD 1985, p. 172; 1988, p. 69). However while it is easy to prove that these export credits were of benefit to Austrian exporters, it is impossible to prove that they had not been administered with the main objective to promote welfare and economic development. It should also be noted that mixed credits or 'associated financing' combining ODA and export credits proper have always been tolerated by the DAC (OECD 1985, pp. 243ff).

The Aid and Trade Provision (ATP), a controversial part of the British bilateral aid programme (cf. Toye 1994, on whom this passage is largely based), illustrates the problems of combining aid and commercial gain very clearly. In essence it represents a form of subsidized exports. For this reason most development economists would argue that it represents trade promotion rather than aid, and should therefore be charged to the budget of the Department of Trade and Industry rather than the aid budget administered by the Overseas Development Administration. The supporters of ATP argue that it is necessary as a retaliation against export subsidies given by other industrial countries in order to put British firms exporting to SCs on a 'level playing field'. It is also argued that this benefits British firms, creates employment and thus helps to make the aid programme more acceptable, increasing popular and parliamentary support for aid.

The critics reply that this is essentially a beggar-thy-neighbour form of competition between donor countries and that it would be better to abolish such export subsidies by international agreement. This would increase the value of aid to SCs because they would not be limited in their sources of procurement. Moreover the critics question the benefits to the British economy and to employment by pointing out that in fact ATP is concentrated on a small group of very large firms. This is certainly confirmed by the ATP statistics which show that over the last few years 55 per cent of ATP money has gone to five large firms. While these firms may benefit, this will be at the expense of their competitors and at the expense of the taxpayer, with the result that there will be no net welfare gain for the British economy.

Another criticism borne out by statistics is that ATP aid is given mainly to better-off middle-income countries, and thus diverts aid from poorer SCs. In the 1991–92 period 68 per cent of British aid other than ATP went to the 50 poorest countries, while the corresponding percentage for ATP was only 51 per cent. The figures for preceding periods consistently tell the same story. In relation to this, Africa received only 27 per cent of ATP money in 1991–92, as compared with 38 per cent of other non-ATP aid; this goes against the declared intention to concentrate the aid programme increasingly on Africa as the poorest continent.

Another criticism of ATP aid is that it takes place in an atmosphere of lack of transparency and lack of proper examination. The request for ATP money comes from a private firm which has fonnulated the project for the purposes of increasing sales and profits, and negotiated it with a governmental or government-designated private agency in an SC.Thus these projects have not been subjected to the normal scrutiny for impacts on the environment, on poverty, for the observation of human rights, or other criteria governing the aid programme. It is true that theoretically the officials of the aid agency (in the UK case the Overseas Development Administration) can examine the request and refuse ATP money if the proposal does not conform to aid criteria. In practice however it has been the UK experience that private firms present the aid agency with a *fait accompli*: a prior commitment has already been made to the government or an agency in the recipient country and the firms will plead that lengthy examination will jeopardize the whole project. This puts aid officials under pressure. In the notorious case of the Pergau Dam in Malaysia, which has moved ATP into the centre of public debate, it was found that the examination of this project from the point of view of the guidelines which should apply to the British aid programme was not sufficiently lengthy or sufficiently detailed under the pressure of the argument that the contract would otherwise be lost. There is certainly no element of competitive tendering and insufficient publicity given to the way ATP money has been allocated in the past.

In the light of this criticism one would wish that ATP be removed from the aid programme or radically reformed, preferably by way of international agreement. The only agreement reached so far is the so-called 'Helsinki Package' aimed at avoiding trade distortions by the use of tied aid and associated financing as well as at ensuring that aid credits do not substitute viable commercial financing (OECD 1995, p. 30). Naturally an escape clause exists, enabling donors to proceed with projects not conforming to the agreement: 'a letter to the Secretary-General of the OECD, outlining the overriding, non-trade related national interest that forces this action' (ibid.) is all that is needed. In 1992 this escape clause was used for 10 of the 28 projects considered commercially viable by the controlling Consultation Group. For 1993 this source declines to give figures.

ODA is often used to open markets to domestic products, subsidize one's own firms, (especially those in problem regions), or to fight unemployment, even if products are delivered on actual – in contrast to merely technical – concessional terms. In such cases the donor is able to shift part of the costs of domestic economic policies onto SCs. This is apparently one reason for the popularity of tied aid: loans are only provided if the SC agrees to spend the money in the donor country, or to use special, sometimes more expensive carriers for transport. Aid might thus be subject to double or triple tying.

In creating multiplier and accelerator effects as well as leading to additional purchases (for example spare parts), aid exports have beneficial repercussions on Northern economies. It was estimated that every dollar of tied aid results in an increase of $2–$3 in the (developed) donor's GNP (Shihata

1982, p. 4). As tying restricts the number of possible suppliers to very few firms, it promotes overcharging (Bhagwati, 1970). Erler (1985, p. 85) claims that the German practice of tying ODA increases prices by 20 per cent on average.

The possibilities of using ODA to the donor's own advantage have often been criticized. In the 1960s and 1970s demands were voiced to replace bilateral ODA (given from country A directly to country B) by multilateral concessional flows (channelled via international organizations such as the UN or the IBRD). The rationale was that greater international publicity, international tendering and mutual control by donors would eliminate the worst shortcomings of bilateral ODA, also reducing the possibilities of single donors to exert political influence (Balogh 1970). In the meantime the notion that multilateral is necessarily better than bilateral aid has become very debatable. As the closer scrutiny of the records of multilaterals such as the IBRD has shown, these institutions have often been extremely careless, unwilling to take the interests of 'beneficiaries' into account, and have very often exerted political influence on SCs. Projects violating human rights have been financed by them, as well as by bilateral donors. In spite of international tendering, Northern countries are keenly calculating ratios between contributions and money flowing back. Big and powerful industrialized countries, such as the US, have reason to be particularly content. The hope that multilateralism might improve aid records was thus not vindicated.

THE GRANT ELEMENT – MEASURING 'CONCESSIONALITY'

In contrast to test (a), the grant element of at least 25 per cent is a more objective measure of ODA. The present value of an actual loan (aid does not necessarily mean grant) is compared with the present value of a loan carrying 10 per cent interest. The figure of 10 per cent is a conventional figure supposed to reflect the donors' opportunity costs or their costs of raising capital. The OECD (1985, p. 172) quotes the following examples of loans where grant elements just surpass the threshold:

- 4 per cent interest, seven years maturity, including three years grace (no repayments during the first three years)
- 5 per cent interest, 11 years maturity, including four years grace
- 5 per cent interest, 15 years maturity, no grace period.

If the interest rate charged is not below 10 per cent, the grant element of a loan is zero. Obviously an outright gift has a grant element of 100 per cent. In all cases the whole loan rather than the grant element – which would be the actual subsidy according to the DAC's reasoning – is recorded as ODA.

As the grant element simply measures the difference between conditions of repayment it need not imply a gift or subsidy at all. For example if a firm from the donor country charges the recipient double the price which would be paid on the world market, the loan will also double. A 5 per cent official loan with 15 years maturity would yield a grant element of just above 25 per cent, qualifying this transaction as ODA although the recipient has been heavily overcharged. The more excessive the overcharge the higher the recorded ODA and, in consequence, the more 'generous' the donor.

As Yeats's (1990) analysis of iron and steel trade showed, overcharging of African countries was the rule during the period 1962–87, with biennial averages of up to 70 per cent and over for these quite homogeneous products. Apparently for a shorter period Portugal overcharged by over 120 per cent(!) on average. There is no reason to suggest that exports declared as ODA were necessarily always at better prices. The less homogeneous the exports, the easier overcharging becomes. Bundling whole turnkey plants with management, marketing or transfer of technology contracts (a rather popular ODA practice) yields a package deal which often cannot be compared with similar arrangements, especially for a buyer with the information resources of a small SC. Market studies, project analyses or the formulation of tenders by donor-financed experts also allow donors to cut out competition by foreign suppliers. Gerster (1989, p. 28) documents the example of a plastic products plant in Togo, sold at nearly 300 per cent of its 'fair market price' according to a 'high official of the World Bank in Togo'. Such examples document that surcharges of at least 34 per cent necessary to make one's 'generosity' commercially profitable could easily be accommodated.

Gerster's example itself was most probably not recorded as ODA, because the author would certainly have mentioned this. However to the extent that the Swiss government was involved via a public export risk guarantee, it qualified at least as 'other official flows' in DAC terminology, increasing the transfer of resources to SCs in DAC statistics.

The constant 10 per cent assumption offers donor countries with sufficiently low domestic rates of interest another option of profitable charity. If the rate at which the government can issue bonds at home is, for example, 6 per cent (historically not unrealistic) it could give a 7 per cent ODA loan, thus combining earnings with philanthropy, at least as long as the domestic rate of interest does not rise to or above 7 per cent and the recipient is able to service the loan. To qualify as ODA the loan would have, for example, 30 years maturity and 11 years grace, or 22 years maturity and 16 years grace. Using the grant element formula presently applied by the DAC, interested readers can calculate different ODA options yielding immediate financial gains to the 'donor'. To discourage such ODA, DAC Terms of Recommendation specify a minimum grant element of well over 80 per cent on average. This however is only recommended and the profitable loans above would still qualify as ODA by DAC standards.

All ODA figures should thus be read with appropriate caution. To illustrate the volume of aid one might quote Rosenstein-Rodan's (1981, p. 4) comparison that the US spends on aid about 'as much as is spent on Kleenex'. Appendix A.1 gives some concrete examples of what has been recorded as 'aid'.

THE PARTICULARLY PRECARIOUS DATA SITUATION OF NON-DAC DONORS

DAC figures on non-DAC donors have occasionally been criticized in the past and justify doubts about their reliability. Nevertheless these donors have never tried to provide statistics comparable to those of the DAC. As will be shown in Chapter 4, close analysis of DAC figures on Soviet ODA by Kaiser (1986) exposed so many contradictions and irregularities that politically motivated manipulation is the most plausible explanation. Of course the fact that neither the USSR nor its allies did ever provide reasonable information – as repeatedly requested by both the OECD and the G77 (OECD 1985, p. 118) – certainly does not speak in their favour either. The practice of non-DAC donors to withhold information, and the resulting precarious database, must be severely criticized too.

Criticism of the DAC's presentation of OPEC ODA was voiced by Shihata (1982, pp. 5f) amongst others and is presented in detail in Chapter 9. He points out that the possibilities of tying OPEC aid are extremely limited. Exporting mainly oil, OPEC countries cannot use ODA for export promotion in the way traditionally done by the North. It should be added that multiplier and accelerator effects hardly exist within the big OPEC donors because of their extreme concentration on oil. A substantial part of OPEC money has thus been used to finance imports from the North.

The former Soviet bloc apart, other donors exist. Non-DAC members, such as Greece, Iceland and Israel give ODA on a relatively small scale. But more important: the DAC has repeatedly stated that a 'growing number of developing countries' (for example OECD 1985, p. 119; 1988, p. 91) have given development assistance. These flows are logically at odds with the prevailing Northern perception of aid as help for the South by the North. They are however fully compatible with the DAC definition of ODA. The flows are not even documented in a way comparable to OPEC's. According to the DAC the availability of data is bad, and there have apparently been no serious attempts to improve it sufficiently. The quality of South-South ODA is no worse than North-South aid, as the OECD's (1985, p. 119) extremely favourable opinion of Chinese aid proves (see Chapter 9).

WHO GETS AID AND WHY?

As the recipient of ODA must be a 'developing country' by DAC definition, a liberal use of this term increases the amount of aid and flows. The DAC has always been eager to extend the group of potential receivers, including the EU member Greece and, not so long ago, Portugal and (until 1982) Spain. Also included are Malta, Cyprus, Turkey (both member of NATO and Group B, the industrialized countries in the UN), and Israel, traditionally the major US aid receiver. During 1986/87, for example, 15.8 per cent of US ODA went to Israel (OECD 1988, p. 219). Yugoslavia, a non-aligned country which has seen itself as part of the South rather than the West, was also included.

Colonies and dependencies are naturally 'developing countries', even if they are legally part of the donor. Costs of regional policy or colonial administration may thus turn to aid. In the late 1950s when the list of recipients was initially made, this was not felt to be controversial. Meanwhile however 'the question of propriety of including as ODA contributions made by a Member country to territories with which it has a constitutional relationship has been debated by the DAC' (OECD 1985, p. 171).

Nevertheless such flows continue to be included. In the case of France, whose ODA to its overseas departments and territories (DOM/TOM) is particularly large, two separate aid figures are shown. In the case of the Netherlands, the UK and the US not even this precaution is taken. Therefore we find Reunion, French Polynesia, the Netherlands Antilles, the Virgin Islands, the Falklands, Crown Colonies such as Hong Kong and the Caymans, and the US Trust Territories all on the list of aid recipients. The US Pacific islands have traditionally been among the major recipients of US aid. Reunion, Martinique and French Polynesia usually occupied the top ranks of French ODA during the 1980s, receiving more than one fifth of total ODA. In 1980/81 for example, they received nearly 30 per cent (Reunion and Martinique alone 24.7 per cent) according to the OECD (1988). All DOM/TOM received nearly one-third of French aid at the end of the 1980s. The Netherlands Antilles have usually been among the top three or four recipients of Dutch ODA, which makes British ODA to Gibraltar, St. Helena and the Falklands look comparatively modest.

For obvious reasons Eastern Europe was excluded from this list 'designed for statistical purposes' (OECD 1985, p. 171) during the Cold War. The present change in global politics, the demise of the partition of Europe together with Western interest to channel money there, have quickly prompted the idea to include these countries. After some discussions on whether to include the former Eastern bloc, a compromise was agreed not to do so (see Chapter 14). Some of the former Soviet republics were included in the list of ODA beneficiaries, but the OECD has recently initiated a special chapter on financial assistance to the former Eastern bloc. If the East had been included in the list of recipients, this would have boosted ODA; furthermore declining flows to SCs could have been statistically compensated by increased resources to the East.

Through analysis of the regional distribution and concentration of aid, the major political interests and their shifts can be clearly discerned. According to the 1963 Clay Report '72 per cent of total (military and economic) assistance appropriations' were concentrated on 'allies and other countries at the Sino-Soviet border'. After criticizing dispersion of aid to an excessive number of countries, the report claimed that economic assistance to some non-allied countries was beyond that 'necessary for our interests' (Ohlin 1966, p. 21). In the 1950s and 1960s South Korea and Taiwan were major recipients of US aid, as well as India, which the US tried to lure away from Soviet influence. During the period of the Vietnam War Vietnam occupied top ranks, accounting for more than 10 per cent of total US aid in some years. In 1992–93 Israel (13 per cent) and Egypt (10.5 per cent) received nearly one-quarter of US aid, followed by El Salvador, Somalia, the Philippines and Colombia (OECD 1995). In 1991–92 Egypt, participating actively in the Gulf War, received 29 per cent of total US ODA, far ahead of Israel's 9.9 per cent (OECD 1994).

The same interest pattern can be discerned with all other donors. Old colonial ties are still clearly visible. Commonwealth countries, particularly India, receive most of British aid. Francophone countries enjoy significantly more financial sympathy from Paris than others. Burundi, Rwanda and Zaire have been Belgium's biggest recipients. Over 50 per cent of Portuguese ODA went to Mozambique in 1992–93, 24.1 per cent to Angola, Cape Verde, Guinea-Bissau, Sâo Tome and Principe and Brazil. All other major recipients received less than 0.01 per cent of Portuguese aid (ibid.). Historic continuity also exists in the case of Germany – Turkey, where the German Empire had imperialist interests, is still a major recipient.

Aid by non-DAC donors also mirrors political and economic interests. Arab aid has been highly concentrated on Arab and Muslim countries. For obvious reasons the handful of developing CMEA members, most notably Cuba, had traditionally received an extremely heavy chunk of Soviet ODA as long as CMEA aid existed.

QUANTITATIVE TARGETS

Quantitative targets were set and accepted for both ODA and all flows. In 1968 the Second UNCTAD adopted a decision demanding the North provide annual net flows (aid and other flows) to the South of at least 1 per cent of their GNP, picking up an idea initially introduced in a less precise form by the World Council of Churches (OECD 1985, p. 135). In this context, 'net' means that repayments or repatriation of assets in connection with previous flows are deducted from gross inflows. ODA is also measured on a net base. The 1 per cent norm mirrors the postwar idea that any flows of resources to the South could only be welcome. It was endorsed and accepted – but not necessarily implemented – by DAC members. Better known nowadays is the famous 0.7 per cent target for ODA, whose history and origin will be described in Chapter 4.

In 1980 finally, a separate sub-target on behalf of least developed countries (LLDCs) was introduced by the International Development Strategy for the Third UN Development Decade, and confirmed by the UN Conference on LLDCs in Paris 1981. The sub-target was 0.15 per cent of GNP for the first half of the 1980s and should have risen to 0.2 per cent afterwards. With the exception of New Zealand, Switzerland and the US, all DAC donors accepted this target before 1986.

MULTILATERAL AID AND 'DEVELOPMENT FINANCE'

ODA targets include both bilateral aid and contributions to multilateral organizations. A vast number of multilateral institutions exist, such as the IBRD group (or World Bank, as the IBRD prefers to call itself) and regional development banks (see Chapter 3). In contrast to the recognition of bilateral ODA on the basis of actual payments (disbursements) rather than mere pledges (commitments), contributions to multilaterals have not been judged equally severely. In 1980 DAC members agreed to record capital subscriptions to multilaterals on a deposit basis, that is when a note encashable on demand is deposited, rather than on an encashment basis. Before 1980 both methods of recording had been used. To illustrate this point: when the IBRD was established only 10 per cent of capital subscriptions were actually paid in. The remainder was on call, forming part of the Bank's assets and improving its standing in credit markets. When its capital was doubled in 1959 members did not have to pay any funds at all, the increase was simply added to the unpaid portion. Nevertheless deposit-based statistics record a net flow of resources in favour of SCs.

These imputed 'flows' are calculated as ODA for OECD countries. But SCs contribute to multilaterals too. A logical problem emerges: are SCs granting ODA and, if so, to whom? To themselves? According to the DAC anyway it is not to those countries of the North that are (unlike Greece) not included in the list of ODA recipients.

Contributions to multilaterals are recognized as a DAC member's ODA even if the activities of those multilaterals cannot be qualified as ODA, which is mostly the case with development banks. These banks lend at terms much too tough to qualify as ODA. The OECD (1985, p. 172) quotes a grant element of only 3 per cent for normal IBRD lending in 1984. Naturally the grant element depends on the going market interest rate. If it is comparatively low, the grant element is higher. Most helpfully the DAC coined the term 'official development finance' in order 'to recognize the developmental value of lending by multilateral development institutions' (ibid., pp. 172f). It should be noted that bilateral loans with similarly tough conditions are not qualified with equal benevolence. Also there is no objective criterion to measure this alleged developmental value or even to prove that it exists at all. Thus it may appear that another positive sounding expression was created by DAC members, who hold the majority of shares in international development banks such as the IBRD.

In the 1980s the IBRD succeeded in gaining a leading role as an aid co-ordinator, and successfully invited bilateral donors to participate in IBRD projects by financing parts of them. The problem of aid co-ordination is highly ambivalent. On the one hand there exists much scope for doing so, as for example Kenya's water supply documents where 18 different makes of water pumps were supplied by a variety of donors (Cassen et al. 1986, p. 318). Diversity though might be a good or a bad thing. If pump types are chosen according to geological differences this might even be optimal. If donors' export interests are the driving force, pumps inappropriate to the specific circumstances might be brought in. Co-ordination, on the other hand, makes the country face a unified front of donors, which results in an enormous amount of leverage on the recipient's decisions, especially so in some very poor countries that are literally kept going by aid disbursements. Supposing that Kenya's diversity of pumps does not merely result from inefficiency but may derive from deliberate export promotion by donors, the problem of diversity might not be cured by co-ordination.

Actual experience of co-financing between bi- and multilateral donors does not dispel such fears. The official Three Years Programme of Austrian ODA by the Ministry of Foreign Affairs (1989, p. 39f) states with utmost clarity that co-financed projects (with the IBRD) are judged not only by developmental criteria but also by whether they lead to Austrian exports. After listing some projects the Ministry writes: 'The *actual realisation of projects now depends on whether Austrian industry will be able to obtain the contracts*...' (our emphasis and translation). Such practices are not restricted to donors expressing their intentions so bluntly (OED 1989, pp. 52f).

Regarding leverage, Cassen et al. (1986, p. 155) remark quite frankly: 'Individual donors are rarely effective in promoting economic reform through non-project assistance. They should therefore work in concert with other donors and the international financial institutions.' As the experience of the 1980s has shown, (programme) aid has been increasingly used to force SCs to adopt economic policies according to donors' perceptions, even though donors themselves do not necessarily adopt these policies. The IBRD and the IMF have made SCs adopt the economic policies of the Reagan-Bush administrations, which have led the US economy into crisis. Currently donors have started to focus on a new form of conditionality.

NEW TRENDS IN CONDITIONALITY

In perceptible contrast to the decades of the Cold War, North-South relations have become characterized by an increasingly strong emphasis on good governance, democratization, participatory development, transparency and accountability. In spite of their obvious importance these demands, directed at the South by Northern donors, had not been emphasized in an even remotely comparable way for quite a long time. For decades the most corrupt torture-regimes have benefited from strong support by the West, such as Baby Doc in Haiti, Nicaragua's Somoza family and Zaire's Mobutu, because they were considered bulwarks of the 'Free World'. Or in the famous words of a US president describing one of the Somozas: 'He is a son of a bitch, but he is our son of a bitch.'

After the Cold War human rights or good governance are suddenly manifestly present both in bilateral and multilateral development co-operation, adding a new dimension of political conditionality to the traditional instrument of so-called 'economic conditionality'. Seeing both need and scope to strengthen market mechanisms, the donor community shows a growing interest not only in principles of good management (governance) by public institutions but also – at least rhetorically – in the observation of human rights. Regarding economic aspects these principles include sensible economic and social policies, financial accountability and the creation of a market-friendly environment. Aid is said to have become increasingly conditional on appropriate observation of these new, political demands. But donor practice does not live up to donor rhetoric. Furthermore demands directed at SCs may go beyond what Northern governments themselves practise. This new trend in development co-operation will be discussed in more detail in Chapter 12.

NON-GOVERNMENTAL DONORS

Foreign aid is not the exclusive domain of states. Voluntary, Non-Governmental Organizations (NGOs), which are discussed in Chapter 9, are also engaged in development co-operation (Gordon Drabek 1987). Grants by private voluntary agencies from DAC countries amounted to slightly less than 10 per cent of ODA during the second half of the 1980s. 'Well over 2000' (OECD 1985, p. 151) NGOs in OECD countries were active in development assistance, relief and development education about a decade ago and their number has increased dramatically since then. NGOs are diverse, ranging from religious to non-denominational institutions, from self-taxation groups and NGOs raising their own financial resources to mainly (or wholly) government financed NGOs. As 'non-governmental' is the only common denominator of NGOs, the term covers a wide variety of organizations from altruistic volunteers or experts and NGOs with reasonable or small overheads to sectarians who offer food for conversion and private enterprise activities in the charity market. Occasionally secret services are said to have used NGOs for their purposes.

Criticism of ODA, especially of official predilection for gigantic projects and its adverse results, and successes of dedicated NGOs and their ability to reach down to grass-roots level have increased their importance. The OECD (1985, pp. 153f) gives credit to Northern and Southern NGOs for pioneering approaches, such as primary health care or rural development, but also sees Northern NGOs as 'perhaps the strongest domestic constituency or lobby' for ODA in industrialized countries owing to their advantages over huge bureaucracies in implementing small grass-roots or community self-help projects. Participatory development co-operation with affected locals is a strong principle of NGO projects. To some extent NGOs might also be seen by aid officials as a way to use funds without having to find projects themselves.

NGOs have formed national and international umbrella organizations and several official donors have established institutional contacts to NGOs, such as the NGO Liaison Committee of the EU or the UN Non-governmental Liaison Service.

AID UNDER CRITICISM

From its early years aid, particularly official assistance, has been criticized and evaluations of its usefulness have been made. Examples are Cassen et al.(1986), Lipton and Toye (1990) and White (1993). Contending that there is no good evidence that aid is beneficial for growth, White argues that there exists no good evidence to the contrary either. Thus he thinks that results are not sufficiently sound to justify radical policy conclusions such as the reduction or abolition of aid. As he is able to produce evidence that aid does indeed increase investment, a rather unflattering conclusion of the general effectiveness of aid follows logically: it may boost investments that do not result in growth. This does not imply of course that each single aid project failed.

Interestingly criticism came from such divergent poles as Milton Friedman (1970), P.T. Bauer (1976) and Gunnar Myrdal (1985). The reasons though were quite different. Friedman argued that the market would do better anyway with regard to development, and that aid should be restricted to achieving political purposes. Myrdal on the other hand saw ODA as mainly self-serving, as well as supporting 'corrupt, exploiting cliques' in the South. Therefore he advocated discontinuing any aid except in three cases: emergency aid, support for the very few countries where governments actually cared for the population (he specifically mentions the 'liberated' Nicaragua of the Sandinistas, and Tanzania under Nyerere), and to help dissidents within SCs.

Aid fatigue has become a widespread phenomenon. The UNDP (1994, p. 72) contends that it has even been growing in the South. Answering critics who argue that aid has failed altogether and call for a total stop, the UNDP (1994, p. 69) states that 'legitimate criticism should lead to improvement, not despair'. In spite of disenchantment on both sides, donors and recipients, it claims that 'the development process – along with foreign assistance – has had more successes than its critics usually concede' (ibid.). Thus it sees the end of the Cold War as a 'rare opportunity to make a fresh start' (ibid.), calling for a restructuring of aid to become more participatory and people-centred to benefit genuinely the poor – something it has hardly done so far.

Appendix 1 Recorded examples of aid or development finance

The Broadening Interpretation of ODA

The OECD (1995, p. 118) points out that while the definition of ODA has not changed for over 25 years, 'changes in interpretation have tended to broaden the scope of the concept'. This means that administrative costs, imputed costs of students from SCs (since 1984) and aid given to refugees from SCs in the North have been included successively as ODA. Aid to refugees has been increasingly reported as ODA since 1991, although available for some time. This help to refugees in the North, while laudable and necessary, does not promote economic development at all. If donors had not decided to increase the coverage of activities subsumed under ODA, their present performance would be noticeably worse.

Administrative Costs Within Donor Countries

The DAC has included administrative costs since 1979 to avoid understating the value of aid provided. This argument is defensible, although these sums are, strictly speaking, not flows to the South. Technically it is possible to increase aid by spending more money on one's own civil servants.

Students from SCs

After some debate the DAC agreed to record 'indirect costs' of SC students. DAC members where tuition is free may multiply costs per student by the number of SC students, recording this as a grant to SCs. In contrast to scholarships no actual payments are made, nor is the developmental value of the received education assessed. If students stay in the North, actually saving the 'donor' the costs of raising them to university level this is nevertheless ODA. ODA is recorded even if registrations are only made to get a residence permit but no lectures are attended. This method is not applied to foreign students from other industrialized countries – substantial grants (though by definition not ODA) thus go unrecorded. In Austria, the main user of this statistical technique, these imputed sums have frequently been higher than her total bilateral technical co-operation. Austria and Australia recorded double digit percentages of their total ODA under this heading.

Funding War and Repression

'In the declining years of the US involvement in South East Asia, Secretary of State Kissinger managed to provide material support to Vietnam by stepping up food aid donations to that country, in spite of the opposition of Congress to committing further resources to the war effort. Title I donations were sold on the open market in Vietnam and the proceeds were used for military procurement ... the South East Asian military debacle was funded by food aid' (Cathie 1982, p. 22). The ODA-financed road C.A.12 to one of dictator Somoza's *fincas* was part of his reward for allowing the Bay of Pigs invasion to start from Nicaragua (Pierre-Charles 1972, p. 397). Erler (1985, p. 9) reports German aid to Indonesian police while the regime was committing genocide in East Timor, and a road giving soldiers quicker access to the trouble region of Beluchistan, financed by Japanese ODA (ibid., p. 21) – Germany had refused to finance it after the Pakistani government had explicitly (and in writing) mentioned the strategic importance of this road.

The Destruction of the Environment

Destruction of the environment is often paid for by aid or development finance. To clear the forest more quickly 'agent orange' (known from the Vietnam war) was used when the Tucurui dam was built, an IBRD-financed project flooding 540 000 acres of tropical forest. George (1988, p. 157) reports that the defoliant allegedly killed some 40 people. Several drums with poison seem to have been left to rot under the water.

Funding Human Rights Violations

Big dam projects usually imply the 'involuntary resettlement' of hundreds of thousands of people. Not infrequently people are chased off their land by security forces – occasionally even death squads – to make room for development mega-projects. Compensation is quite often insufficient, if people are compensated at all.

The Indonesian *transmigrasi* programme destroys tropical forests, 'relocates' people to other islands with false promises and uses security forces when necessary. It has been financed most generously by the IBRD, the Asian Development Bank, the US, Germany and the Netherlands in spite of its ecological damage and human rights violations (George 1988, p. 158).

Further Examples

The EC sent vermin-ridden maize to Somalia, which was refused by the intended recipient. A short time later the same maize was brought to Mozambique, where it was refused and qualified as unfit for human consumption by authorities.

In his highly polemical book Hancock (1989) documents cases such as medicaments to cure chilblains and electrically heated blankets brought to Somalia along with slimming soups and diet drinks for the starving; a US NGO sending food as emergency relief to Cambodia, which San Francisco's zoo had refused to feed to its animals; a gift of high-heeled pumps to African women who have to carry water over miles every day; or thousands of rolls of toilet paper brought to Africa for a US-AID employee and then back to his US home after his assignment.

Statistics

US AID does not allow its food aid to be weighed when imported, inspite of the fact that the agency has been victim to fraud by its own agents. The amount actually delivered cannot be checked.

2. Aid as one aspect of North-South relations

AID IN PERSPECTIVE

Public opinion polls on aid in donor countries are highly consistent in one respect: people asked to estimate aid in relation to their government's budget or to GNP always think their country is more generous than it actually is. Paul Streeten (1995) quotes US polls according to which respondents believed Washington devoted as much as 20 per cent of the federal budget to foreign assistance. The median answer of one typical and recent poll was 15 per cent, the mean 18 per cent. The correct answer would have been less than 1 per cent. Streeten also quotes median answers produced by the questions about how much would be too little and how much aid would be appropriate, which were 3 and 5 per cent respectively. Overestimates of aid, though not necessarily as extreme as in the US, have been recorded in other donor countries as well.

This deep-rooted but wrong public perception of the amount of aid given proves that aid flows must be put into perspective. Aid is only one of several aspects of North-South relations. Its economic impact can only be understood properly if seen in relation to other important factors affecting development. Stressing the need for coherent policy approaches to development co-operation, the OECD (1992, p. 31) states: 'The importance of OECD country macroeconomic, trade, financial and aid policies in shaping the global environment for developing countries and development has long been recognized.' Unfortunately donors do not practise what they recognize.

Putting aid into perspective, this Chapter compares ODA with other international resource flows, such as trade or debt service payments, as well as with potential gains to SCs denied to them by the way the global economy is arranged. Examples in the latter category are losses suffered by Southern exporters because of protectionist barriers imposed by the Multi-Fibre Arrangement or income losses caused by terms of trade deterioration. Finally the effects of macroeconomic policies of one or more major OECD countries on the South can be of greatest importance, as the debt crisis proves.

Analysing ODA as one component of global economic relations qualifies its importance, illustrating how easily advances achieved by successful aid activities can be destroyed or nullified by decisions taken in other fields, frequently by the same donor(s). Technically this regrettable fact is referred to as policy incoherence. Its effects can be illustrated quite vividly with empirical cases such as subsidized EU beef exports to West Africa undermining EU aid to support local beef production (see Chapter 7), by food aid given on terms that render local production uneconomic, or by EEC sugar exports practically annihilating world sugar prices as well as all projects within the sugar sector, such as sugar refineries financed by aid. The UNDP (1992, p. 67) puts the annual income loss of sugar cane growers due to trade barriers at $7 billion.

To give a concrete figure for the total impact of present, incoherent policies is on the other hand hardly possible. The OECD (1992, p. 43) correctly points out that 'Assessing the costs of various kinds of policy incoherence is extremely difficult'. It underpins this statement by citing the well-known problems of assumptions and structures of models used, of linking causes to quantifiable effects, the capturing of dynamic effects, and unavailable or unreliable data. The OECD also cautions that the costs of incoherence will differ from country to country. Thus SCs with large stocks of debt at variable interest rates become vulnerable to changes in global interest rates. In plain and less diplomatic English, this formulation simply means that these debtors suffered enormously when the Reagan administration decided to combine a restrictive monetary policy reducing international liquidity with high fiscal deficits. The resulting dramatic increase in interest rates produced negative effects much higher than US ODA.

The impact of higher interest rates is well illustrated by the estimations of the IMF's Padma Gotur (1983). Of the total increase in current account deficits of non-oil SCs, which was $66 billion for the period 1978–81, $18 billion were caused by oil trade, while $24 billion resulted from net interest payments and $21 billion were traced to terms of trade changes. Net US ODA to SCs and multilateral agencies, by contrast, amounted to $23.3 billion during the four years 1978–81 (OECD 1982, p. 199), or to $5.8 billion per year. In spite of the 'second oil crisis' during this period the impact of interest rates was 1.33 times the impact of oil. According to the IBRD (WDT 1993) interest payments by 'all developing countries' amounted to $53.3 billion and an increase in the average interest rate of one percentage point cost debtors roughly $6.6 billion in 1980. Between 1970 and 1980 the average interest rate of new commitments rose from 5.0 to 9.3 per cent (ibid., p. 173).

While attempts to estimate all costs of policy incoherence on the South and to express them as a multiple of aid are beyond the scope of this book, comparisons putting quantitative and qualitative dimensions straight are mandatory to allow a fair and rational evaluation of what aid can be expected to achieve. In short, the aim of this Chapter is simply to put aid into proper

Table 2.1 Aid and other resource flows

	1985	1986	1987
ODA to SCs[(a)]	32.9	38.5	43.6
DAC ODA to SCs and MIs[(b)]	28.8	n.a.	n.a.
ODF[(c)]	44.1	50.1	56.4
Private Flows	30.1	26.0	31.9
of which:			
NGO-grants	2.9	3.3	4.0
NGOs (net)[(d)]	2.9	n.a.	n.a.
TDS[(e)]	137.5	136.5	151.3
Amortization[(f)]	65.0	70.0	83.7
Interest on:			
Long term debts	54.7	51.2	51.3
Short term debts	17.1	15.3	16.3
Total interest	71.8	66.5	67.6
Interest and dividends[(g)]	83.0	75.9	77.8
ODA as % of:			
Total interest	45.8	57.9	64.5
Interest and dividends	39.6	50.7	56.0
Real ODA[(h)]	61.5	57.9	57.0

Notes:

p provisional

(a) net resource flows to SCs

(b) net flow of financial resources from DAC members to SCs and Multilateral Institutions

(c) Official Development Finance (ODA plus other official flows too hard to qualify as ODA)

(d) net is used by OECD (1995, pp. A3f) in the sense of NGOs' own resources, while the line above (ibid., pp. A1f) comprises their own plus government resources channelled through NGOs according to information provided by Mr Bevan B. Stein, head of the OECD's Reporting Systems Division, whose help is gratefully acknowledged.

(e) Total Debt Service

(f) amortization of long term debt

(g) interest and dividends paid by SCs, gross

(h) total ODA receipts at 1992 prices and exchange rates

n.a. not available

Source: OECD 1995

1988	1989	1990	1991	1992	1993P
(All figures in current US$ bn)					
47.7	48.8	53.1	58.3	59.5	55.2
n.a.	n.a.	53.0	56.7	60.9	56.0
61.2	61.0	70.1	69.1	70.4	68.5
40.8	46.2	53.4	52.4	81.1	93.9
4.2	4.0	5.1	5.4	5.9	6.3
n.a.	n.a.	5.1	5.4	6.0	5.6
161.0	164.8	159.0	149.2	156.4	156.0
80.1	84.4	84.1	81.8	92.5	94.0
61.0	57.9	53.8	50.1	50.9	50.0
19.9	22.5	21.1	17.4	13.2	12.0
80.9	80.4	74.9	67.5	64.1	62.0
91.7	93.4	89.2	81.8	78.7	n.a.
59.0	60.7	70.9	86.4	92.8	89.0
52.0	52.2	59.5	71.3	75.6	n.a.
57.8	59.8	58.4	61.9	59.5	57.3

perspective. This is particularly important at a time of 'aid fatigue' when the overall results of decades of aid are heavily, and often unfairly, criticized. This criticism, as well as aid fatigue, has become more popular within the donor community since budget restraints have been increasingly felt. Undue criticisms of what development results are likely to be achieved by the limited amount of aid must therefore be checked by quantitative facts. Doing so, one must once again remember that not everything declared as ODA by the donor community is necessarily conducive to development. As shown in Chapter 1 real help is much smaller than the figures the DAC declares as aid.

Finally, relating aid to trade flows helps understanding of the 'aid or trade' debate on whether development could be better promoted by trade or by aid. This catch-phrase highlights the fungibility between these two sources of foreign exchange. On the other hand it has the drawback of formulating these two options in a way likely to make them appear as contradictions, which they are not at all. As early as the 1950s the dual gap theory saw both a domestic gap due to the insufficiency of savings to finance necessary investments and an external gap due to scarcity of foreign exchange. The latter was generated by the necessity to import most investment goods and posed a problem different from insufficient domestic savings as SC currencies were mostly not accepted internationally. It had to be overcome by external finance. As the marginal productivity of capital had to be higher in capital-scarce SCs, private capital was initially expected to flow eagerly across the North-South border. Empirically though it soon became clear that private capital was reluctant to invest in long term development due to high risks, relatively low profits accruing to individual investors and more attractive options in the North. Inspired by the Marshall Plan official aid was widely seen as the main instrument to fill the gap created by trade imbalances. Alternatively this gap could be closed by borrowing in international capital markets. To some extent trade, international loans, foreign direct investment and aid are therefore substitutes.

The value of flows recognized as ODA by the DAC according to the criteria described in the last Chapter, as well as private flows and debt service in the recent past, are shown in Table 2.1. Quantitatively private flows overtook ODA in 1990. Two years later they became larger than official development finance (ODF): 'For the first time in over a decade, private flows to developing countries exceeded ODF flows' (OECD 1994, p. 66). However a relatively small number of SCs (among them China, India and Indonesia) 'attracted almost all of the recent expansion of private flows. Net private flows to the poorest countries and to Sub-Saharan Africa in 1992 were negative' (ibid.).

The difference between the two first lines in the Table results from the statistical conventions adopted by the DAC. The first line (ODA to SCs) is measured according to the DAC's resource receipts framework, where 'ODA comprises disbursements of concessional development finance from both bilateral and multilateral sources to developing countries' (OECD 1994, p. 63). The second line measures bilateral disbursements plus the provision by donor governments to multilateral institutions. This is called the 'aid performance framework' (ibid.) focusing on what donors allocate to both groups. The difference between the two measures arises because concessional funding to multilaterals is recorded when these funds are deposited with multilateral institutions. This does not necessarily match multilateral disbursements to SCs in any given year, 'although there is obviously a correspondence over the long term' (ibid.)

With regard to NGOs the latest *Report* (OECD 1995) coined the expression 'Net grants by NGOs' without any explanation, although the usual OECD concept of 'net transfers' is not applicable to grants since they have no amortizations or interest payments. The explanation reproduced in footnote (d) however does not account for the fact that government contributions to NGOs (OECD 1995, pp. A3f) differ distinctly from the difference between the vectors NGO grants and NGOs (net). This difference is zero in 1990 and 1991 for example (possibly due to rounding), while official contributions to NGOs of around $1 billion are shown in the Annex Table 2 (OECD 1995, p. A4) for both years. In 1992 'net grants' were higher than 'NGO grants', which is the total of 'net grants' and official contributions, although official sources contributed $885 million to NGOs! Figures provided for 1993 also do not add up. As this example of NGOs shows, OECD data are unfortunately not beyond question. But right or wrong, they are the only data available to the public.

ODA IN RELATION TO DEBTS

Expressing ODA as a percentage of either interest payments or of interest and dividends, shows that the South paid much more to service interest obligations and for the services of private capital (expressed as dividends transferred back to the North) than it received as aid. Interest payments in Table 2.1 are dramatically lower than interest contractually due. Like the IBRD in its *World Debt Tables* they reflect interest actually paid. This 'cash base' is also used to calculate traditional debt indicators such as the Debt-Service Ratio or the Interest-Service Ratio. Due to the incapability of debtors to service their debts as stipulated, interest contractually due started to differ dramatically from interest actually paid during the second half of the 1980s. In 1990, arrears on long-term debt ($52.7 billion) and capitalized interest ($5.9 billion) for 'all developing countries' were greater than total ODA and some 76 per cent of interest paid (IBRD, WDT 1993). In 1992 this ratio deteriorated to 82 per cent. For the two debt-ridden regions, Latin America and Sub-Saharan Africa, this ratio is much worse, which puts ODA even more into perspective. Raffer (1994a) showed that interest arrears were perceptibly higher than interest payments in Latin America in 1990 and 1991. If one includes capitalized interest this has been the case during the 1990s except for 1993, for which projections by the IBRD (WDT 1993) expected that interest arrears would be roughly equal to interest paid. IBRD projections though are always very optimistic; Latin America paid only about half the debt service due during the 1990s and countries such as Brazil and Argentina honoured between one quarter and one-third of their contractual debt service obligations.

The situation is even worse in Sub-Saharan Africa. Interest arrears have been higher than interest paid in the 1980s, and have been up to double the amounts paid in the 1990s according to the IBRD's *World Debt Tables 1993–94*. Thus the ODA/interest ratios of Table 2.1 show a rather rosy picture. If interest due were used instead, the share of aid would be noticeably smaller.

As the debt crisis went on, aid and 'development finance' have often been used to bail out either commercial banks or – during the more recent past – multilateral institutions, such as the IBRD or the IMF. In a first phase after 1982, international financial institutions (IFIs) replaced private loans in debtor countries, thereby bailing out private banks and worsening their own exposure. At this time IFIs worked on exactly the same assumption commercial banks had used before 1982, namely that debtor countries could not go bankrupt and would therefore always service their debts. Keen to provide help for 'their' commercial banks Northern majority shareholders, granting an unjustified preferential IFI-status as creditors that have to be served first to Bank and Fund, encouraged this shift towards higher shares of IFI debts.

Not surprisingly this led to a situation where IFIs had to start lending for the sole purpose that debtors could honour debts to IFIs themselves on schedule. To keep up appearances third parties were involved repeatedly. The IMF and the IBRD particularly have developed quite elaborate systems of bail-outs. These were made necessary to maintain the claim that IFI debts cannot be re-scheduled and have to be cleared before new money from IFIs can be disbursed. This recalls the situation of private banks in the early days of the debt debacle. Mounting problems with debt service and arrears, and even calls upon Northern governments for help, are clear signs of alarm. The IBRD (WDT 1988, p. xxxvii) asked bilateral donors for money to help finance repayments of IBRD loans by countries now in the IDA only category. The total amount of debt outstanding was a mere $3 billion and its service could be covered neither by IDA nor by the revenues from these IBRD-financed activities.

Chandra Hardy (1994) describes such cases of financial manoeuvring in some detail. In June 1990 for example Guyana cleared its arrears to the IMF using a bridging loan from a commercial bank and SDR 131 million received from the Fund was used to repay the bridging loan. In 1993 Peru cleared its arrears to the IMF using funds from the US Treasury and Japan EXIM, as well as its own funds. The IMF then made a loan to Peru which was used to clear arrears with the IBRD, whose disbursements were than used to repay the US and Japan. Like quite a few other highly indebted countries Peru has a Support Group, a group of donors providing fuel for this financial merry-go-round.

Obviously aid disbursed to make a country liquid enough to repay a loan from another donor has no development effects in the country itself. Nor is it supposed to have because no projects are financed by it. The necessity to do so is also a clear indication that old inflows have not been put to economic use. As donors and particularly IFIs control the use of funds very tightly, this also calls their efficiency into doubt. Money given by a government for such bail-outs is naturally counted as ODA if the terms are soft enough.

During the first half of the 1990s until the Mexican debt crisis of 1995, new sources of capital gained importance relative to aid, namely private capital from non-banks such as institutional investors and private individuals in the form of bonds (as in the 1930s, before the pre-World War II debt crisis) and foreign direct investment. This increase in private flows directed to relatively few SCs was immediately declared to mark the end of the debt crisis. It must be seen in the context of changes in international capital markets in the 1990s.

First, commercial banks did not consider this optimism spread by multilaterals such as the IBRD sufficiently justified for them to lend again on a large scale to 'recovered' problem debtors. They handled securities for clients to earn fees but did not consider recovery secure enough to use substantial sums of their own money. According to the IBRD (WDT 1993, p. 5) Latin America's 'flows to private banks have actually been negative because of voluntary repayments'. Foreign direct investment (FDI) inflows were to a considerable extent due to privatization, that is the selling of public companies, and therefore singular, irreproducible events. Once those state enterprises finding takers are sold, inflows cease and repatriation of profits soon becomes the preponderant balance of payments effect.

Second, the improvement in developing country access to international capital markets 'has been supported by regulatory changes, particularly in the Japanese bond market. Quality guidelines for Samurai bond issues ... were relaxed further in 1992 and the minimum credit rating ... was lowered from A to BBB' (IBRD, WDT 1993, pp. 21f). Changes in regulation regarding equities making private placement generally more attractive occurred in the US too (IMF, WEO 1993). These regulatory changes, and a trend toward explicitly rating developing country borrowers at least partially triggered by them, allowed institutional investors to place money there.

The volatility of portfolio investments was repeatedly emphasized by IFIs. Calls for a new IMF facility to help countries facing problems due to a sudden withdrawal of capital could already be heard before the Mexican crash. This is all the more important as foreign exchange provided by these substantial inflows was used to service debts. One might suppose that arrears would even be higher without them. To the extent that new foreign exchange has been used for payments to banks or IFIs, it is no longer available to cover sudden withdrawals. Some of the risk of being 'stuck' with a debtor nation was shifted away from private banks and from multilaterals, having increased their exposure considerably during the 1980s. This is an analogy to the larger process of risk-shifting during the 1980s, when inflows by public institutions allowed commercial banks to receive higher (re)payments than otherwise possible. It can be interpreted as a gradual return to the situation until the 1930s, when Latin debt was held by private creditors and banks saw themselves mainly as fee-earning intermediaries. As Southern debts played the role of junk bonds until the 1930s, the opinion of the IMF that Third World bonds in the 1990s are the new 'junk bonds' (IMF 1992, p. 31) combines well with this interpretation. This shift to (or bail-out by) new creditors occurred with official support and possibly because of IFI optimism claiming that, except in Africa, the debt problem had been overcome. The Mexican crisis of 1995 finally showed that this shift had been 'successful'. It was no longer commercial banks or IFIs that had to be bailed out but these new investors. The debt burden, though, remains a problem for indebted SCs, and 'donors' will go on using aid to keep themselves, other donors and private investors financially afloat.

THE IMPORTANCE OF TRADE

The sheer size of trade makes it an important source of financial resources for development. Merchandise exports of the South (including China and the East Asian export economies but excluding Hong Kong's re-exports) amounted to $917 billion in 1993 and imports to $981 billion (GATT 1994). The deficit in merchandise trade is incidentally some 16 per cent higher than ODA. But SCs are also net importers of services for which the GATT does not provide similar data. Regarding services the UNDP (1992, p. 67) estimates that SCs could probably gain some $20 billion if they had the necessary access and finance to compete on an equal footing. These figures show the importance of the conditions and terms of trade. A 6 per cent increase in merchandise trade earnings would be equivalent to total ODA for all SCs. Comparing overall magnitudes it must not be forgotten though that trade incomes are quite unequally distributed. At present poor countries benefit least from trade. According to orthodox theory, trade is supposed to be a fountain of wealth for everybody. The widespread slogan expressing this view some 30 years ago was 'trade not aid'. When the influential Republican Senator Robert Taft was asked what he thought of this slogan he reportedly replied: 'I agree with the second part of it.' It should be noted that as a protectionist he was not really in favour of enlarged market access either.

Conservative economists, such as Milton Friedman (1970), oppose the idea of aid, recommending trade and the market mechanism as alternatives. According to neoclassical textbooks homogeneous factors of production must command the same price in a perfectly competitive market. Factors of production are paid equally according to their contributions to production but irrespective of location, gender or race. Technically this demands that Double Factoral Terms of Trade (DFToT) equal one. In that case exchange would be equal (Raffer 1987). Economists initially expected Southern Net Barter Terms of

Trade (NBToT) to improve because of industrial economies of scale, faster technical progress in the North, and the law of diminishing returns applying to the raw material exporting South. Regarding price relations, economies of scale and technical progress have the same effect: both reduce costs and must lead to lower prices in a functioning market. As Spraos (1983, pp. 21f) pointed out, this was 'the dominant a priori view' of NBToT. It necessarily results from the neoclassical model which was not challenged until 1949. Hence one could conveniently assume that actual trade was in fact as beneficial as its academic model. Professor Jevons was indeed so worried about price increases for raw materials so steep that a modest professor's income would be insufficient to heat his home that he stored as much coal in his house to provide for his bleak future as he possibly could. If Professor Jevons had been right, the market might actually have solved the problem of development as assumed.

Actual markets however do not live up to theoretical models. The Prebisch-Singer Thesis (PST) rocked the boat of professional complacency by exposing an apparent contradiction between theoretical expectations and practical outcome. Secularly deteriorating Southern NBToT documented by the seminal work of Prebisch (1949) and Singer (1950) destroy the whole established logic based on a beneficial world market (Raffer 1986). Unfortunately the PST was reduced to a less dangerous statistical debate on freight rates and the reliability of data, while its main point particularly stressed by Prebisch – that the world market does not allow the periphery to benefit appropriately from technical progress – quickly vanished out of sight.

While the discussion of whether a negative trend can be proved statistically is both interesting and important, one must not forget that secularly falling NBToT of the South are a sufficient, not a necessary condition for the loss of productivity gains, or what may be called the core of the PST (Raffer, 1986). If international markets and trade behaved according to academic predictions and models, NBToT would have had to improve for SCs. As productivity has grown faster in the North, global income relations (DFToT) can only remain constant *if* NBToT move against the North, distributing the fruits of technical progress equally (Prebisch 1949, p. 360). In this case it really would not matter in which product a country specializes. If trade is expected to narrow wage differences, as the factor price equalization theorem suggests, NBToT would have to increase even more in favour of the South. At constant NBToT however, DFToT deteriorate and global disparities in factor incomes increase. Trade disadvantages the periphery. Export earnings are lower than they should be according to neoclassical theory and resources needed to finance development are lost. This is the core of the PST so perfectly obfuscated by the discussion which followed. A declining trend of the periphery's NBToT merely reinforces the fall of DFToT (Raffer 1986; 1994b). There is however no statistical basis at all for improving NBToT of the South. In other words, the existing global market puts SCs at a disadvantage. This disadvantage can be overcome, as the Asian 'tigers' prove. But this is difficult and demands a combination of good policies and good luck.

In spite of damaging empirical blows to orthodox trade theory and the example of interventions in successful East Asian countries, liberalization is still recommended to and forced on SCs nowadays. Frequently ODA and development finance are used as a means to open SC economies to the world market despite the donor community's awareness of the shortcomings of really existing – as opposed to textbook type – markets. In contrast to textbook markets SCs are often charged higher prices than Northern clients, as Yeats's (1990) findings of customary overcharging of African countries proved.

Discussing the interrelations between trade and aid as part of the problem of policy coherence the OECD states quite clearly:

> Developing countries face higher tariffs and a larger range of non-tariff barriers than developed countries reflecting the fact that, in areas of their greatest comparative advantage, *industrial countries face difficulties in implementing structural adjustment programmes* (textiles, clothing, steel, etc.). *The cost of these measures has been estimated to exceed the value of aid flows*, but such measures do not take account of the most important aspect of these restrictions, which is that they retard entry into export-oriented industries which are most accessible to developing countries – namely commodity processing, light manufactures, and textiles and clothing.
>
> While developed countries have, in principle, encouraged developing countries to diversify into these kinds of exports and, indeed, the dynamic export-oriented developing countries have benefited dramatically from access provisions applying in developed-country markets, trade policies in the developed countries often obstruct diversification. For many commodities, tariffs escalate on processing activities. When developing country exporters, including those in the very low-income category such as Bangladesh, begin to have success, new barriers can suddenly be imposed, for example new quotas in the textiles sector, or anti-dumping actions and other selective trade-restricting provisions.
>
> OECD 1992, p. 37 (emphases added)

Non-Tariff Trade Barriers have become a significant form of protection and are more frequently used against SCs than against Northern competitors. The OECD (1992, p. 45) quotes findings by the IBRD based on 1989 data that there existed 171 'voluntary export restraints' against the South compared with 117 against developed countries, and 321 anti-dumping and countervailing actions against SC exports compared with 238 measures against developed countries. Nevertheless the North, and IFIs controlled by it, force SCs to pursue export-promoting policies. In the present protectionist environment this is about as useful as forcing someone to run head-on into a stone wall.

The OECD (ibid.) quotes numerous estimates of the effects of trade protectionism on the South. Naturally the figures obtained are not necessarily compatible with each other. Nevertheless it is of interest to illustrate magnitudes with the estimates quoted by the OECD as well as by others. The cost of exports foregone in 1980 is quoted as $55 billion (in 1990 dollars). An IBRD estimate (based on the Bank's SMART projection model) put the revenue gains of a 50 per cent reduction in protection on SC-imports by the EC, Japan, and the US at $50 billion (1988 prices), most of it in labour-intensive manufactures, such as clothing, footwear and furniture. An OECD study concluded that:

> a complete removal or alternatively, a 30 per cent reduction of OECD country border measures ... would lead to annual income gains of about $221 and $90 billion, respectively, for developing countries and formerly centrally-planned economies. (ibid.)

The UNDP (1994, p. 66) puts the costs of protectionism to the South for textiles and clothing at $50 billion. It provides illustrative examples for agrarian trade. In some African countries where it costs $74 to produce 100 kilos of maize, the local market price fell to $21 due to subsidized Northern exports. The UNDP (1994, p. 67) quotes possible gains from complete liberalization of trade in agrarian commodities of $22 billion for SCs and formerly centrally planned economies.

In 1992 the UNDP (1992, pp. 66f) compared aid with monetarized disadvantages inflicted on SCs by unequal partnership in the present global economy. Adding together the negative effects of higher real interest rates paid by SCs, negative capital transfers, unequal competition in services, and the effects of restricted market access from agrarian products to technology the Report produced a figure of $500 billion in 1990. This was roughly 10 times the amount of ODA. Even if one disregards market restrictions in the labour market (restrictions on immigration) and negative capital transfers, the remaining $200 billion are about four times the amount of ODA. These figures clearly support the UNDP's point about a widening gap in global opportunities.

The Multi-Fibre Arrangement (MFA) may serve as a prime example to illustrate the double standard prevalent in the global economy, not least because it shows so clearly how market opportunities are destroyed precisely where SCs have competitive advantages. It was introduced some 20 years ago, but protectionism in this sector dates back to 1935. In this year the US negotiated the first 'voluntary' export quota system on textiles with Japan, although US textile producers were protected by tariffs of 40 to 60 per cent. In 1961 the Short Term Cotton Textile Arrangement was negotiated under GATT auspices at the request of the US. It was replaced by the Long Term Arrangement Regarding International Trade in Cotton Textiles in October

1962, which ruled sectoral trade until 1974 when the first Multi-Fibre Arrangement, MFA I, replaced it. This was considered necessary because the use of synthetic fibres not covered so far had increased tremendously and some SCs had gained progressively larger market shares. The other main reason was that substantially increased productivity in the textile industry had led to a decrease of sectoral employment in the North (IBRD, 1987, p. 136). Thus labour-saving effects of technical progress in the North were simply shifted onto SCs. This was corroborated by many studies some time ago, for instance by Schatz and Wolter (1982) for West Germany, who found that job losses due to productivity changes in the case of textiles and clothing were between two and three times higher than jobs lost because of changes in imports. If one compares net import effects (job losses due to changes in imports minus job creation by export changes) productivity changes accounted for 44 times higher losses than foreign trade in the textile sector. For the whole economy, job losses due to imports were more than outweighed by increased exports during the period 1970–78, while productivity increases cost four times as many jobs as all imports (for other studies see Raffer 1987, pp. 225ff). Nevertheless Northern economies needed protection to adjust to SC exports.

Although the MFA is a clear contradiction of the very aim and essence of GATT – liberalizing trade in manufactures – the Textile Surveillance Body was established by GATT to supervise the implementation of this system of trade restrictions and to arbitrate disputes – or the breach of its own basic principle – thus siding with the North and openly condoning the MFA.

At the beginning of the Uruguay Round a suggestion arose to legalize rather than phase out the MFA in the new framework. As late as 1988 the US refused to discuss the MFA in the Uruguay Round. In January 1989, to give an example, both the EEC and the US stonewalled in Geneva against the idea of phasing out restrictions under the Uruguay Round, seeing this as only one (but not the only) option for integrating this trade into GATT. In comparison one may thus call the Agreement on Textiles and Clothing, which stipulated a phasing out of the MFA after ten more years, a 'success' of the South, although it remains to be seen whether the MFA will actually be discontinued after the next decade. There is no convincing evidence that it must happen this time, although Article 9 states that there shall be no extension of this Agreement, which is the prime example of the asymmetry of the Uruguay Round. It shows how easily industrialized countries are able and how readily they are willing to infringe on the very idea of liberalizing trade.

Even if restrictions in this field end as stipulated, this would mean that the North will have enjoyed 'necessary' protection in one small part of their economies for up to seven decades, while SCs are required to open their economies much more radically and much more quickly to 'free' trade. The continuation of the MFA means in plain English that the North cannot adjust to 'free' trade as quickly as they want and, with the help of the IMF and the IBRD, make SCs adjust theirs. The fact that the US has not been able to adjust one relatively small sector of its economy since 1935 must be recalled if one evaluates the special provisions for SCs, such as 'longer' implementation periods. The Agreement on Agriculture for example allows six or nine years for industrialized countries (Art. 1), and up to ten years of flexible adaptation for SCs (Art. 15).

According to the continued MFA, now officially anointed with GATT conformity, 'not less than 16 per cent' of 1990 imports shall be liberalized on the date of the WTO Agreement's entry into force (Art. 2.6). After three years at least 17 per cent (of 1990 imports) are to be integrated into GATT 1994, after another four years a further 18 per cent, and the remaining 49 per cent after ten years.

Safeguard clauses were also agreed to shield industrialized economies from undue shocks by 'serious damage, or actual threat thereof' (Art. 6.2). Although a lot of variables ranging from profits and employment to investments and productivity are enumerated in paragraph 3, no clear definition of serious damage or threat thereof is provided. Imminent – as opposed to actual – sharp and substantial increases in imports are a sufficient justification for countermeasures. Again no clear definition of how this counterfactual situation must be assessed is provided. In practice the question of actual or imminent damage will depend on bargaining power. The wording strongly recalls US laws, in particular §624, 7 USCA giving the President authority to limit any imports of agrarian products if there is 'reason to belief' that they might interfere with any agricultural programme. Clear proofs are not necessary. Similar discretion is given to the Secretary of Agriculture, for instance in matters of §612c or §608c. If this similarity is not mere happenstance but an intended copying of US practice, SCs can expect the worst. Mere 'parroting' of §608c is considered sufficient to justify import restrictions according to US courts (Raffer 1990, p. 864).

On the other hand, re-imports of products exported by domestic enterprises to have them further processed in other countries are explicitly allowed more favourable treatment (Art. 6.6(d)) when 'transitional safeguards' are applied. Apparently competitors exporting final products are to be kept at bay without restricting possibilities to cut costs. Investment and employment are only endangered by competition, not by relocation of labour-intensive processes.

The outcome of the Uruguay Round may worsen the position of the South further in many respects as the North was mostly able to shape the Final Act according to its views and against developmental interests (Raffer 1995b). Admittedly SCs were able to defend some interests, notably the principle of preferential treatment or the phasing out of the MFA, as well as to introduce small changes into the texts. The Agreement on Preshipment Inspection is one example where SCs have been able to defend both their legitimate interests as well as the essential market principle of the buyer's right to information on quantities and qualities bought, which the North considered unnecessary for Southern buyers (Raffer 1995b).

On the whole there is reason for concern that the new mechanisms will be used in the interest of the North, further compounding the disadvantages of SCs in the global economy. The total effects on SCs are summarized by the IBRD (1993, p. 33) in its study on East Asia. Noting increasing pressure on SCs to refrain from interventions that violate international trading rules, it concludes that '... export subsidies and directed credits linked to exports ... are incompatible with a changing world trade environment'. This means that empirically successful options for development are now ruled out for latecomers by the new GATT 1994. This is all right for the Bank, which feels anyway that the elaborate intervention systems of Japan, South Korea and Taiwan should not be copied by others.

Furthermore the World Trade Organization (WTO) Agreement's Art. III.5 demands that the WTO should co-operate, as appropriate, with the BWIs to achieve greater coherence in global economic policy making. Although co-operation with the IMF was already in Art. XV of GATT 1947, this fuelled fears of increased pressure on SCs by cross-institutional conditionality, whereby IBRD loans or IMF drawings may be made conditional on a good report from the WTO vouching that the country has followed its rules adequately. Such an evolution would weaken SC members considerably. SCs already governed by the IMF and the IBRD in all but name would lose whatever bargaining power they might still have.

Regarding agriculture, rather generous norms allowing interesting combinations of exemptions, special safeguard provisions and remaining legal trade barriers keep benefits for the South below the expected – or hoped for – results for food exporters. Restrictions of export subsidies though will have negative effects on food importers. Fewer subsidies of agrarian exports mean higher prices for importers, in practice mostly SCs. Net food importers in the South facing increased import bills at a time of scarce convertible currency will be severely affected. Art. 16 of the Agreement on Agriculture therefore demands measures in favour of net-importing SCs and LLDCs as provided for within the Decision on Measures Concerning the Possible Negative Effects of the Reform Programme on Least-Developed and Net Food-Importing Developing Countries. This Decision recognizes 'negative effects in terms of the availability of adequate supplies of basic foodstuffs from external sources on reasonable terms and conditions, including short term difficulties in financing normal levels of commercial imports of basic foodstuffs'. The main solution indicated is to draw money from IFIs 'in the context of adjustment programmes', thus increasing the dependence of SCs on the IMF and the

IBRD. Furthermore differential treatment regarding export credits and consideration by the North to improve agricultural productivity and infrastructure by ODA were agreed.

It must be questioned whether donors are really going to reduce their own export outlets in net-importing SCs by subsidizing competing agricultural production there. Art. 10.4 of the Agreement on Agriculture drawn up to avoid food aid being used to circumvent export subsidy commitments, indicates a clear concern for retaining export markets. The permission to subsidize the destruction of food ('definitive permanent disposal' of livestock) pursuant to para. 9(b) of Annex 2 also indicates a clear interest in managing the market. SCs would thus be well advised to use exemptions, such as for the purpose of food security or the provision of foodstuffs at subsidized prices (the latter is considered to be in conformity with para.4 of Annex 2 by the text), as fully as they can. The general problem apart of how such programmes can be implemented with 'no, or at most minimal, trade distorting effects or effects on production' (Annex 2, para. 1), debt-ridden SCs are unlikely to be able to finance such schemes on a level sufficient to safeguard food security. In the case of net food importers 'aid' is thus earmarked to counterbalance some of the harm inflicted by trade.

The harmful impact on net food importers would be further compounded by a reduction of the huge agricultural surplus stocks which have been overhanging the market and depressing international food prices (Singer and Shaw, 1995).

All these interventions distorting markets in favour of the North have been made although the OECD (1992, p. 46) found the effects of increased exports of manufactures from all SCs 'if they had experienced the same rapid growth rate of exports as did the Republic of Korea from 1980 to 1988' to be quite small, if not negligible. Under this strong assumption SCs 'would have supplied 3.7 per cent of manufactured goods in all industrial country markets by 1988, instead of the 3.1 per cent they achieved'.

This estimate has to be seen in connection with the so-called 'Trade Pledge'. This is the Trade Declaration adopted by OECD governments in 1974 'dealing with the need to refrain from protectionist action' (OECD 1985, p. 78). The sincerity of this pledge has already been documented above by very telling examples.

Finally OECD exporters have combined to limit price competition via better financing terms. The OECD Arrangement on Guidelines for Officially Supported Export Credits stipulates minimum interest rates for exports to the South (UNCTAD 1994, p. 37). These minima are differentiated by country groups and currencies. Analogous action by SCs to keep export prices high would be loudly condemned by the OECD, the IMF and the IBRD as market intervention.

THE IMPORTANCE OF AID: NORTH-SOUTH ASYMMETRIES

Summing up, one has to say that the South faces donors that inflict much more harm on it than they provide help, particularly so if one considers that part of aid that is really meant to help and does so successfully. Although the

Table 2.2 The importance of aid to recipients: bilateral ODA received by selected countries in 1992

	% of GNP	$ per head
Mozambique	115.6	92
Sâo Tome & Principe	108.3	433
Guinea Bissau	59.0	106
Equatorial Guinea	51.4	170
Tanzania	48.2	48
Cap Verde	41.5	311
Samoa	39.5	379
Guyana	27.5	117
Lesotho	13.3	77
Egypt	10.6	64
Jordan	8.4	88
Dominica	8.0	196
Fiji	4.4	85
Botswana	3.4	86
Tunisia	3.2	48
Costa Rica	2.3	43
Bahrain	1.9	133
Gabon	1.5	56
China	0.7	3
Colombia	0.6	7
Mexico	0.1	4
Brazil	0.1	2
SSA*	10.4	35
LLDCs**	13.6	30
All SCs	1.3	11

Notes:
* SSA Sub-Saharan Africa
** LLDCs Least Developed Countries

Source: UNDP 1994, pp. 166f

impression persists in the public at large that aid is a major diversion of resources, it is of rather limited relative importance to the North. An Austrian NGO compared total aid (as defined by the DAC) in 1993 to the costs of the Gulf War in 1992 (roughly $61 billion) and to world-wide expenditures for keeping infant buttocks dry, which means around $50 billion spent on nappies, baby powder and so on. The UNDP (1994, p. 71) points out:

> if all foreign aid were stopped tomorrow this would enable the industrial countries to increase their domestic social safety nets from an average of 15.0% of GNP to only 15.3 % of GNP – hardly the handsomest bargain in history.

At the same time some SCs, notably but not exclusively in Africa, depend on aid inflows to keep the remnants of political and economic systems from breaking down totally. Not infrequently even recurrent government expenditures are financed by ODA. Table 2.2 illustrates the importance of aid to some SCs as well as their dependence on donors. The percentages need no further comment.

Put into perspective, aid is far less impressive than people are often inclined to believe. The quantitative dimension of other factors such as trade, commodity prices and debt service obligations is precisely why the effectiveness of aid as a means to really foster development must be improved. It is all the more important that aid compensates for these other unfavourable factors both in quantity and quality.

3. Multilateralism in the aid and development business

THE RISE OF MULTILATERALISM

Bilateral aid came increasingly under attack during the 1960s. It was argued that donor countries used it to their own economic advantage or to support their foreign policy rather than to foster development. A quick look at regional distributions of ODA flows immediately showed a close match between main receivers and areas of political interests. Another criticism was that bilateral ODA was subject to changes and interruptions from budget to budget. The malpractice by donor countries of tying procurement to their exports or their carriers was particularly strongly criticized as increasing the cost of aid. Bhagwati (1970) for example documented extreme cases of differences in freight rates of up to 113 per cent due to tied aid. Chenery (1989, p. 141) quoted estimates that tying reduces the value of bilateral aid by '25 percent or more as compared to the system of competitive bidding' of multilateral institutions. Bilateral aid came under obloquy and such severe attack that Balogh (1970) felt urged to defend its merits.

Since many shortcomings of bilateral aid are encouraged by the lack of transparency and control quite usual for dealings between two governments, multilateral aid was seen as *the* alternative. Information available to other members of multilateral institutions and the need to justify decisions considered unwarranted, at least to other donors, would reduce the possibilities of tying. Tendering processes would bring prices down to the world market level.

The Pearson (1969) Commission, officially called Commission for International Development and appointed by the IBRD, recommended that the share of aid channelled through multilateral institutions should be increased substantially in order to secure more equitable use of available funds. Quite naturally multilateral institutions, such as the IBRD, were not unhappy about this recommendation. As Chenery (1989, p. 141) pointed out, the multilateral share increased from 10 per cent of OECD aid in the 1960s to around 30 per cent in 1985, a share held in 1993 as well (OECD 1995).

More recently multilateral flows, particularly in the case of the IBRD, have come under severe criticism. One main argument is that these institutions are influenced unduly by the North or even by one country. To illustrate this in the case of the IBRD, a title in *The Economist* (22–28 April 1978) proclaimed: 'It's the World Bank – Not the American One, So Keep American Politics out of Its Affairs'. As will be shown in more detail later (Chapter 12), lack of transparency and unbelievably serious shortcomings by some multilateral institutions have spurred strong criticism, particularly from the NGO community. Again the IBRD was the most important target. It has been repeatedly accused of undertaking too many environmentally, socially and economically detrimental projects at the expense of the poorest.

High hopes of dissociating aid from foreign policy and export interests have not been vindicated. In May 1995 the IBRD advertised in two major Washington newspapers that its loans 'give you more bang for your buck' (*Time*, 29 May 1995). Although made in defence against congressional plans to cut resources this description is guarded. The Bank could have quoted US Treasury Secretary Nicholas Brady's statement: 'For every dollar provided to these [multilateral] banks, the U.S. economy gets back $9 in U.S. procurements' (Islam 1991b, p. 205). But this would certainly have antagonized other shareholders.

THE MULTILATERAL SYSTEM – AN OVERVIEW

It is neither intended nor possible to present or discuss the host of multilateral institutions. This Chapter will focus on the most important ones.

The multilateral aid system can be divided into a fully global system (the UN system), a regional aid system including the regional development banks in Latin America, Asia and Africa, and multilateral aid programmes like those of the EU directed by the Commission in Brussels, which are in addition to the national 'bilateral' aid programmes of individual EU member countries.

The global UN system is divided in turn into the 'Bretton Woods system' (the IMF and the IBRD, or the 'Bretton Woods Twins') and the UN system (the UN, its regional commissions and a large number of affiliated 'specialized agencies' dealing with agriculture, industry, labour, health, education, trade, environment, children, population and so on). The 'Bretton Woods system' does not formally exist as, legally, the IMF and the IBRD are 'specialized agencies' of the UN, no different from the FAO (Food and Agriculture Organization) or ILO (International Labour Organization). In practice however their different voting system (a 'dollar-a-vote' as against a 'country-a-vote') has placed the Bretton Woods twins under the firm control of the industrial donor countries and thus has secured them preferential allocation of resources and political support from the rich countries. As a result the focus of aid activities has shifted from the UN system to the Bretton Woods system, much beyond what was originally intended when the global system was created 50 years ago.

A good example is the field of technical assistance. Under the 'Kennedy Compromise' of around 1960, soft financial aid was allocated to the IBRD (it received IDA) while technical assistance and food aid were allocated to the UN (UNDP and WFP). The UNDP was supposed to be the chief funding and co-ordinating agency for technical assistance throughout the UN system. Yet today the IBRD gives as much or more technical assistance than the UNDP, and the IMF is rapidly expanding its technical assistance operations without having to rely on funding from the UNDP. In an effort to restore the role of the UNDP, attention is now focused on enhancing the role of the UNDP resident representatives to that of UN co-ordinators or even UN ambassadors. Similarly there is a parallel effort to place the technical assistance activities of UN agencies into a country-programming framework, devised and negotiated by the UNDP. All such proposals may improve the efficiency and coherence of UN technical assistance and enhance the role of the UNDP, but they do not solve the problem of the relationship with the Bretton Woods system. To give the UNDP or UN representatives the enhanced role aimed at, the suggestion may be made that the UN co-ordinator should take part in the discussion of stabilization and Structural Adjustment programmes, as should perhaps representatives of specialized agencies. Some of these programmes have a crucial impact on say agriculture and health, and presumably the field officers of the FAO and WHO (World Health Organization) have more concrete country knowledge and competence than Washington-based macroeconomists. (Similarly on the governments' side, one would wish for these negotiations not to be limited to ministries of finance and central bank officials but to include representatives of the ministries of agriculture, health and so on – but that is a matter for governments rather than the UN system.)

In pursuit of this greater co-ordination of technical assistance and operational programmes by the UN at the country level, it has been proposed that all these programmes (UNDP, WFP, UNICEF, UNHCR and so on) should be merged into a single institution. However this proposal ought to be resisted. It could make matters worse by depriving UN operations even of some of the support which they now enjoy. Organizations like WFP, UNICEF and others have established a clear identity of their own; their concrete purposes attract both political and financial support and they have backing in public opinion which in the long run may influence governments of contributing countries. It would be counter-productive to throw all this away by a merger into one large omnibus institution without the identity and distinctive appeal of the present agencies.

The EU finances multilateral aid out of its own budget, via the off-budget European Development Fund and, to a small extent, the European Investment Bank. The latter two institutions finance aid to the so-called ACP group under Lomé (see Chapter 7).

Furthermore there exist other multilateral institutions, most notably those established by OPEC or Arab countries, such as the OPEC Special Fund, the Arab Bank for Economic Development in Africa (BADEA), the Islamic Development Bank and the Islamic Development Fund.

A chapter on multilaterals would not be complete though without mentioning institutions wanted by the South but either not realized at all or only technically in operation. These are of interest because they document attempts by SCs to create new institutions with differing power/voting structures and less under Northern control. In the 1970s the South demanded a Common Fund to stabilize commodity prices. Its so-called Second Window was meant to finance projects such as research and development and diversification away from raw material production. After a long period of bargaining the Common Fund was agreed on just before the UNCTAD meeting in Manila in 1979. Voting shares were allocated to groups: 42 per cent to the North (Group B in UN terminology), 47 per cent to the Group of 77 (the South), 8 per cent to Group D (communist countries) and 3 per cent to China. Regarding financing, developed economies (East and West) agreed to contribute a much higher percentage than their share in voting rights. Although agreed on at the end of the 1970s, the treaty did not come into force until 19 June 1989 – it took roughly a decade until enough countries had ratified it to bring the Fund into existence. However inadequate resources have prevented it from playing any role.

Another demand presented in 1980 by SCs at UNIDO III in New Delhi was the Global Fund which envisaged the sum of $300 billion being made available for development projects until the year 2000. Predictably this demand did not even get earnest consideration.

This Chapter is going to focus on the IBRD and development banks. Obeying the OECD's concern for coherence the IMF is discussed in this book as well where appropriate, because of the effects of its policies on development prospects. First however the International Fund for Agricultural Development (IFAD) will be presented briefly, because of its specific and relatively democratic approach of de-linking voting and financing quite strongly.

IFAD: AN ATTEMPT TO INTRODUCE A LITTLE MORE DEMOCRACY

Established in December 1977 with the strong political and financial support of OPEC to finance projects in favour of the rural poor, IFAD was a successful attempt to make multilateral structures more democratic. Active participation by the projects' beneficiaries has been sought. Votes are equally split among three groups – the North, OPEC countries and other SCs. The procedure of allocating votes within each group can be decided independently by each group's members. This de-links the connection between payments and voting further. In 1994 IFAD's membership comprised 22 OECD countries, 12 OPEC countries and 116 SCs. In spite of having one-third of votes each, it was agreed that Category I (industrialized) and Category II (OPEC) countries have to finance 60 and 40 per cent of the Fund's resources respectively. Other members may contribute on a voluntary basis. This far-reaching separation of votes and contributions did not make it particularly popular with industrialized countries used to having comfortable voting majorities.

IFAD focused on rural development with the objective of mobilizing additional resources from wealthy countries (including oil-rich ones) to assist small farmers and agricultural labourers. Article 2 stipulates the fundamental goal of IFAD as helping the poorest SCs fight hunger and chronic malnutrition (Maurizio 1983, p. 109). Loans are highly concessional (for example at 1 per cent with 50 years maturity and ten years grace) and the involvement and active participation of the poorest rural strata, as well as the use of local consultants and institutions (for example for monitoring) are considered essential. Technical assistance may be granted free of charge to the poorest countries.

Initial contributions were $1.05 billion, of which Category I paid $595 million, OPEC $435.5 million. Category III countries provided $19.3 million (Maurizio 1983). Already the first replenishment led to quarrels when OECD countries announced intentions to cut their contributions, but a compromise was reached (ibid.). Finally the drying up of OPEC liquidity in the 1980s has made OPEC countries reluctant or unable to finance as generously as before. Each replenishment has faced problems since the drop in oil prices. Negotiations have become more and more difficult. The traditional quotas of 60:40 for Categories I and II respectively broke down at the third replenishment, although the amount was in nominal terms little more than half the sum raised in 1977. This outcome could only be secured because industrialized countries offered to treble any voluntary contributions by Category III countries. Negotiations for the fourth replenishment of $600 million broke down, although the 'special rôle of IFAD in rural poverty alleviation is increasingly recognised' (OECD 1988, p. 104). The essential point was thus not quality but the gain of control by the North.

OECD countries demanded the restructuring of IFAD so as to distribute votes according to contributions. A special committee was established in 1994 to look into the possibilities of structural changes and to present its conclusions in 1995. There is no doubt that IFAD, a child of the South's drive for a New International Economic Order in the 1970s, will finally be brought in line with the realities of the 1990s. At a time when the power of industrialized countries has reached its apex since decolonialization, a multilateral institution where the North has only one-third of the votes instead of absolute control is simply not wanted. One may assume that IFAD, once industrialized countries hold a controlling majority of votes, is likely to obtain funds much more easily.

THE BRETTON WOODS TWINS

By contrast multilateral institutions firmly under Northern control have not experienced similar resource problems. The most important example is the IBRD, which calls itself informally the 'World Bank'.

The IBRD conglomerate, informally called the 'World Bank Group', consists of three main institutions, the IBRD, the International Development Association (IDA) and the International Finance Corporation (IFC). Furthermore MIGA (Multilateral Investment Guarantee Agency) and the ICSID (International Centre for the Settlement of Investment Disputes), two organizations concerned with international investments not with development finance, are affiliated.

The IBRD has tried to increase its influence by offering itself as a coordinator for bi- and multilateral aid, as well as by branching out into new spheres. Thus it was able to secure an important role in administering the Global Environmental Facility (GEF). Established in 1991 the GEF is administered jointly by the UNDP (responsible for technical assistance and cooperates in identifying and assessing projects), UNEP (secretariat for the Scientific and Technical Advisory Panel and contributes environmental expertise) and the IBRD. The IBRD administers the Facility, is responsible for investments and is the custodian of the Global Environment Trust Fund, GEF's most important source of finance.

Furthermore the IBRD has served as the secretariat of CGIAR, the Consultative Group on International Agricultural Research, an institution financing agricultural research. In 1994 the IBRD tried to take control of CGIAR and its germplasm collection, one of the largest collections of socially and economically critical biomaterial, in exchange for debt forgiveness and increased funding. This was opposed by NGOs arguing that CGIAR and the germplasm collection in particular should be managed by an intergovernmental body governed by the one-nation-one-vote principle. Finally an agreement was reached making FAO, an organization where this principle applies, the custodian of CGIAR's germplasm collection.

THE IBRD

The IBRD was founded in Bretton Woods in 1944, together with the IMF. The OECD (1985, p. 140) describes the initial tasks of the Bretton Woods twins: 'The IBRD was there to guarantee European borrowing in international (North American) markets; the IMF was there to smooth the flow of repayments'. In the meantime both institutions have shifted their activities to the South. Like the IMF or other development banks, the IBRD is a joint stock company. However all its shareholders are governments. IBRD membership was made conditional on IMF membership. Loans are only given to members (or have to be guaranteed by them). The largest source of IBRD loans are capital markets, where the IBRD itself borrows (for example by issuing bonds). Paid-in capital and accumulated profits are further, though less important, sources to finance loans.

Like other development banks the IBRD is not accountable to any UN body, nor can the UN influence its policies. Proposals to co-ordinate the IBRD's activities more closely with the UN and mechanisms to bring the Bank (and the IMF) closer to the UN were made recently. In 1994 the UN Secretary General proposed a 15 member executive committee of ECOSOC (Economic and Social Council) with the mandate to make policy recommendations to the UN specialized agencies, including the IMF and IBRD, in order to achieve better co-ordination. The Bank however wants to go on operating independently from the rest of the UN system, refusing any control by ECOSOC or other UN fora. One of the main arguments used by the IBRD and its staff is the claim that the Bank – in contrast to the political institution UN – is non-political and not influenced by political considerations.

This argument is not new at all. The Bank has always stressed that its lending decisions are exclusively based on economic considerations and not influenced by the political predilections of potential borrowers. Expropriations without 'fair compensation' or at least serious attempts to reach agreement with the former owners is the only exception admitted early on by the IBRD (1976, p. 13). This happens to coincide with the US attitude expressed in the Hickenlooper and Gonzalez Amendments. The latter required US executive directors at the IDA and regional banks to vote against any loans to countries that had nationalized or seized the property of US citizens, taken steps to repudiate or nullify contracts or agreements, or discriminated against US firms (van der Laar 1980, p. 78). The former, legislated after strong lobbying by the transnational ITT, a firm notorious in the 1970s for its involvement in bringing down Chile's democratically elected Allende government, contained similar regulations.

In IBRD publications of the 1970s it is argued that a full assessment of the viability of a loan necessitates political judgments (IBRD 1976, p. 13), and that loans may be conditional upon economic reforms or policy changes (ibid., p. 20). Since the 1980s the IBRD has openly connected its lending with measures diminishing state activities, favouring private enterprise and implementing its 'free market' ideology. All these conditions doubtlessly interfere in a country's political decisions and it may be argued whether they are purely economic in character. Since the mid-1980s the IBRD has become more openly political, quite visibly heading for greater political conditionality.

Critics of the IBRD point at a long history of 'strategic non-lending', arguing that facts document a considerable political bias. The Bank for example did not lend to Brazil under Goulart, Algeria until 1973, Egypt under Nasser, Chile under Allende, Indonesia under Sukarno, Ghana under Nkrumah, Argentina under the Peronist government in the 1970s, Jamaica under Manley or Grenada under Bishop. This list is by no means exhaustive. Invariably the refusal was based on 'technical reasons'. Hayter (1987) illustrates this with the example of Algeria where the rates of return of an irrigation project were lowered because the IBRD insisted on including the capital costs of a dam previously built by the French. Tetzlaff (1980) defends the IBRD by arguing that it had been willing to lend to Allende's Chile, but could not do so because of strong US pressure. On the other hand the Bank was induced by the US to organize a consortium of donors to provide aid to Saigon shortly before the fall of the city (Hayter 1987; Ayres 1984, p. 57). However no money was actually disbursed.

It is of course logically possible that all projects considered during the periods of non-lending mentioned above were economically unsound, and that a flood of economically sound projects appeared suddenly, for example right after the coup of General Videla in Argentina. The IBRD had already been able to find such projects in that country under the military dictatorship before the Peronists. The situation in Chile before Allende and after the coup by Pinochet was exactly the same. Pure logic does not exclude the possibility that the Bank might always have been guided by strictly economic criteria, untouched by political considerations. Practically however the probability of strictly economic decisions is – to be extremely polite – very low. Human rights records of right-wing dictatorships have certainly never blocked projects.

Nor did they in the case of Ceaucescu's Romania, one of the most abusive communist dictatorships, but an Eastern bloc country with a relatively independent foreign policy, frequently antagonizing the Soviet Union. Under the heading 'Ceaucescu's Bank', Rich (1994, pp. 100ff) describes how the country became a large and privileged IBRD borrower: 'In 1972, while the Bank was cutting off all loans to Allende's Chile, it geared up to lend to its newest member, Romania, at McNamara's personal urging. Indeed, the Bank made several unprecedented exceptions for the Ceaucescu regime.' According to Rich no information on key economic indicators was made available to the IBRD's first mission. Romania's creditworthiness could not be determined according to customary criteria. While Chile for example had been forced to settle outstanding pre-World War II foreign debts before getting its first loan in the late 1940s, Romania did not have to do so until 1975. This exceptional leniency was again very much in tune with US politics.

Making the concept of basic needs and redistribution with growth acceptable is doubtlessly a great merit of the IBRD during McNamara's era, irrespective of whether the Bank actually reached the poor. It is of interest though that, as van der Laar (1980, p. 78) observes, the IBRD closely followed the changed focus on 'poor majorities' of US bilateral aid policy. In introducing 'country targets' and 'regional targets' McNamara also introduced the 'pressure to lend', the concern of IBRD employees to channel money out quickly to meet these targets. This has had enormous negative consequences for the quality of operations and thus for the IBRD's borrowers.

Voting rights at the Bank depend on capital subscriptions, but an equal allocation of 250 votes to each member to which one vote per share is added softens the strict principle of connecting votes and subscriptions. Capital increases since 1944 have drastically diminished the importance of this equalizing element.

As Figure 3.1 shows, the US, Japan and the EU enjoy a comfortable majority of 55.57 per cent. Eight industrialized countries (the G7 plus the Netherlands) command 50.2 per cent. The influence of big and populous SCs can be easily illustrated by comparing voting rights. India had 3.46 per cent of all votes on 30 June 1992, exactly the same percentage as Italy. The PR of China had 2.71 per cent, Brazil 1.94 per cent, while the Netherlands controlled 2.75 per cent and Belgium 2.08 per cent. During the 1970s OPEC countries tried to increase their votes in exchange for larger financial contributions but these attempts were blocked by the North. The fact that even rich countries from the South were not allowed to buy influence might have been one factor explaining OPEC's support for IFAD.

Certain important decisions, though, require a qualified majority, initially 75% and currently 85%. This majority has been changed along with the reductions in the US share from 35.07% in 1947 to 15.12% in 1990 so that the US has been able to preserve its veto power even when it fell below the 17.37% it held on 30 June 1992.

A small remark on the political changes between 1990 and 1992 seems appropriate. After a period of relative neglect the US has apparently found

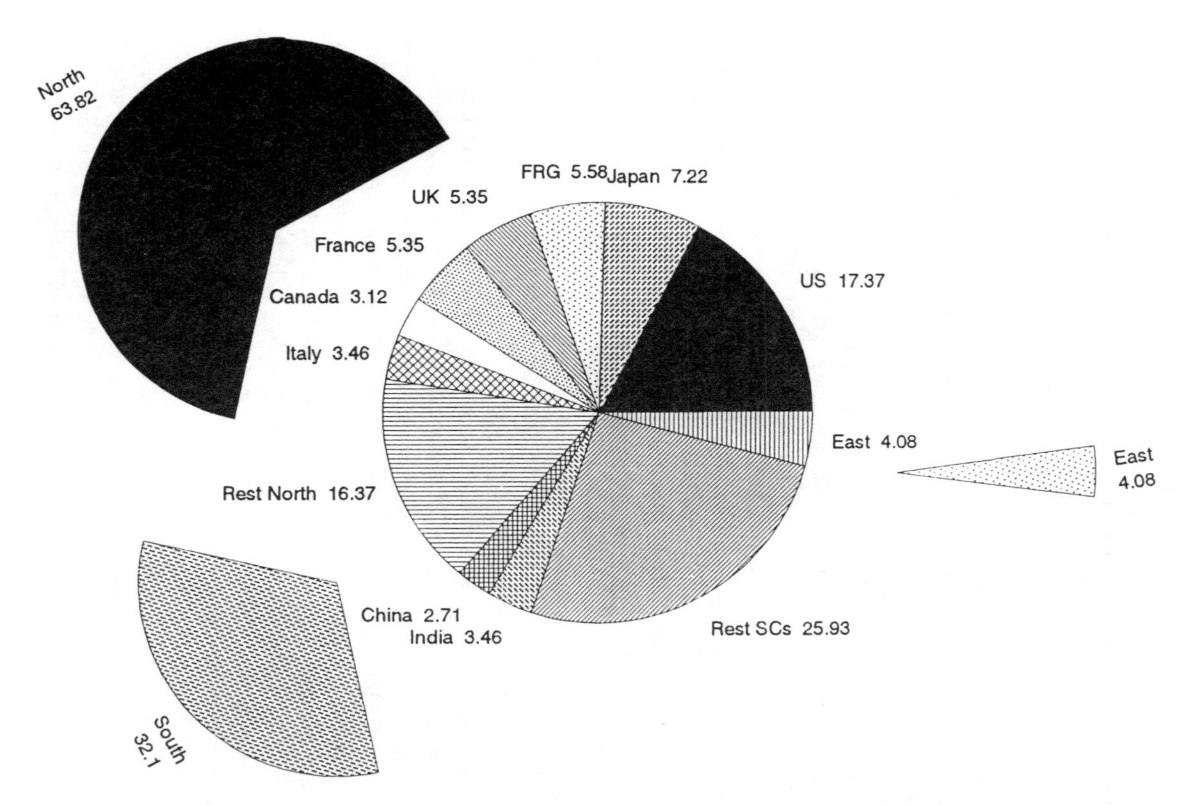

Figure 3.1 *IBRD: voting power (percentages as of 30 June 1992)* *Source:* IBRD, Annual Report 1992

renewed interest in the Bank, an orientation that might again change under the new Republican Congress. Although some Economies in Transition, most notably Russia, joined the Bank, the US increased its own voting power quite perceptibly by 2.25 percentage points, reducing dramatically the importance of the next three biggest shareholders. Japan (8.74 per cent on 30 June 1990), the FRG (6.47 per cent) and the UK (6.47 per cent) lost 1.52, 1.17 and 1.12 percentage points respectively. France could increase its share slightly, Canada and Italy quite strongly. The distance between the US and other big members has increased enormously. The relation between the shares of Japan and the US fell from 1.73 in 1990 to 2.41.

Within the South, China (3.27 per cent in 1990) and India (2.97 per cent) have, so to say, 'swapped' ranks. The voting power of all SCs fell to 32.1 per cent. This is an interesting sign of increased Northern power. Nevertheless considering actual power structures in the IBRD this is hardly of practical importance.

The Board of Governors consists of one representative per member state. With few exceptions (membership, use of sometimes considerable profits, changes in capital stock) all decisions are delegated to the Board of Executive Directors. The five largest shareholders, the US, the UK, Japan, France and the FRG, nominate one director each. Other members are split into 15 groups. The members of each group elect one director. Voting is weighted – each director's vote is the sum of the voting power of the group members. As the director must cast all votes as one bloc, the view of dissenting group members is not only lost – their 'No' is turned into a 'Yes' as the director casts all votes in favour of 'Yes'. This arrangement is not only highly undemocratic but it would also be considered highly unorthodox in any private joint stock company. It is somewhat softened by the practice of consensus rather than decisions by conflicting votes.

Technically the president, who is also the head of IDA and the International Finance Corporation (IFC), is elected by the executive directors. Practically, he (only men have been considered qualified so far) has always been appointed by the US president, mostly from the banking community. The IMF on the other hand has always been headed by a European, due to 'an informal understanding among governments that the Bank president will be an American, and the Managing Director of the International Monetary Fund, a European' (IBRD 1976, p. 6). As only the president proposes IBRD loans, this office is of the greatest importance.

Until 1979 the IBRD almost exclusively financed specific projects, for example dams, roads, industrial plants and production of cash crops. Since then it has moved strongly into programme lending, financing adjustment programmes for sectors or whole countries, which presently account for roughly one-fifth to one quarter of its activities and will be discussed later.

Programme lending is connected to the change of economic structures and is better known under the names Sectoral or Structural Adjustment. The Bank monitors and supervises its operations closely as it has occasionally stated with pride, for example when arguing that its 'detailed supervision of projects' ensures that the money cannot be used for other purposes. Portions of loans are disbursed when required directly to suppliers or to refund 'identified payments already made' by the borrower (IBRD 1976, p. 18). The Bank checks the specifications of goods supplied, supervises the tender and award process for contracts, and sends supervision missions to check periodically on the project's progress. 'These missions ensure that problems are identified and dealt with, and that funds are not misused' (ibid.). According to the IBRD's own internal controllers '*borrower preferences are not always seen as important in supervision management, although the outcome often has a critical impact on the borrower*', as its Operations Evaluation Department (OED 1989, p. 26; emphasis added) states with utmost clarity.

In spite of close supervision and decision making on projects and economic policies (extremely pronounced in the case of Structural Adjustment), the IBRD has never considered accepting its part of the risks. This shift of accountability away from the Bank and onto its clients has become particularly pronounced during the last decade. Confronted with strong criticism of its Structural Adjustment lending, the IBRD has become increasingly eager to claim that all their operations are actually 'owned' by their borrowers. Clear statements on decision making such as those quoted above are therefore increasingly difficult to find, but even recent publications decry a 'lack of ownership' by client governments. This would be logically impossible if operations were actually ideas of SC governments only 'supported' by the Bank.

Decision making is thus separated from (co-)responsibility. Not only the IBRD but also other multilateral institutions insist on full repayment of all loans even if failures caused by their staffs contributed or led to unsuccessful results, as will be documented in greater detail in Chapter 12. This problem is not unique to the IBRD but common to all multilateral institutions. Grave failures by donors may of course also occur with bilateral projects. But their impact is likely to be less detrimental since many bilateral projects are financed by grants and bilateral creditors have – in sharp contrast to development banks – repeatedly granted debt reductions for development loans.

Development banks argue that they have to insist adamantly on full repayment in order not to impair their own standings as borrowers, which would in turn increase their costs of borrowing and ultimately the interest rates they have to charge their own clients. If this argument were true, no commercial bank would have a good standing as a borrower because no commercial bank ever gets all its loans repaid. Therefore it does not seem to be a valid excuse for protecting multilaterals from the market mechanism of combining decisions with risks. Not surprisingly the present situation of riskless decisions and profitable mistakes has led to sloppy preparation and implementation of projects, inappropriate expertise and optimism regarding expected results as the IBRD's Operations Evaluation Department (OED 1989) states in the case of the Bank. The establishment of this internal control unit, whose findings are routinely disregarded, (occasionally for decades), owes much to US pressure for more accountability (van der Laar 1980, p. 78). Only 49 per cent of the projects evaluated by the OED (1989) were considered 'likely to sustain their benefits' (ibid. p. 9). Suffice one more quote here before referring to Chapter 12 for a closer look at this problem: 'Most operations staff were, however, neither experienced in nor trained for procurement work, nor professionally stimulated by procurement problems or enforcing Bank procurement policy' (OED 1989, p. 25).

Alleged positive effects of IBRD projects have always been described in vague terms, for example 'benefits of 210 of these projects are expected to accrue predominantly to the rural poor' (Christoffersen 1978, p. 20), or even 'They aim at affecting [?] directly between 15 and 20 million rural families or some 90 to 120 million individuals' (ibid.). Reviewing IBRD publications Tetzlaff (1980, pp. 438ff) calls such figures a bluff, because the exact meaning of benefiting or affecting is nowhere explained.

Rich (1994, p. 198) reports an apparently more recent meaning of 'affected': 'people living in project areas are either "beneficiaries" or, if their livelihoods and culture will be harmed or destroyed, "project-affected population".' But as the IMF/IBRD meeting of October 1991 in Bangkok shows, one might also be 'affected' by the Bank and the Fund without any project. Rich (ibid., pp. 1ff) describes how slums were razed and people forced to relocate to 'leaky army tents' in order to spare delegates discussing poverty the sight of poor people. Compensation was modest, or as Rich puts it, per family less than the costs of one single night of one delegate in a hotel room.

Strong criticism and considerable pressure by NGOs, most notably in the US, as well as by parliamentarians, have forced the IBRD to defend their operations publicly. In the case of the hotly debated Sardar Sarovar project (Narmada dam) in India this even led to an investigation into the project which involved involuntary resettlement of people. Public pressure became so strong that the IBRD's president, Barber Conable, established the first commission under the chairmanship of Bradford Morse to assess the Bank's involvement, against objections by the Bank's India country department. The Morse Report was devastating and finally the Bank was forced to stop financing the project.

Further pressure, even from some of its own executive directors, has recently made the IBRD establish an in-house Inspection Panel to investigate whether decisions by the Bank or its soft loan window IDA failed to conform to the Bank's operating rules and procedures. Originally two proposals were made, both relating to an internal 'independent' (which means independent of the inspected unit, but not independent of the IBRD) inspection unit for ongoing projects. One proposal advocated by the Bank's executive directors Aris, Fischer, Flano, and Herfkens (also called the February 10 Proposal within the Bank) was a permanent unit able to inspect a limited amount of projects subject to the agreement of a quorum of executive directors. The second idea, the Inspection Panel with a more restricted mandate, was preferred within the IBRD. There is of course no reason why the IBRD's president or board should not create such a unit as an internal measure of control, although one might be tempted to ask whether its fate might eventually be similar to the OED's. However this internal arrangement does not guarantee accountability by the Bank in its external relations. The Panel can only submit recommendations to the executive directors and the president for their consideration. Panel members are officials of the Bank 'subject to the requirements of the Bank's Articles of Agreement concerning their exclusive loyalty to the Bank'(IBRD/IDA 1993, para. 10). In spite of these problematic shortcomings and restrictions the Panel is a unique feature that should be copied by other IFIs. Although much remains to be done to achieve access to impartial and external arbitration making the IBRD really accountable and one party instead of party, judge and jury, it is a step in the right direction. Giving greater publicity to problematic projects is at least a modest improvement.

In October 1994 four Nepalese citizens acting through the Arun Concerned Group filed the first request for investigation of the proposed Arun III hydroelectric project, which IDA has offered to help fund. One complaint was that the Bank violated the requirements for determining adequate compensation for involuntarily resettled people (for details see Bradlow, 1995). This is a particularly important issue. First, multilateral financiers have often been accused of turning a blind eye to human rights violations in connection with their own projects. Second, the Bank has always been very determined to protect property rights of transnational firms, thus the question of whether expropriation occurred with fair compensation of former owners should be extremely important. Present evidence appears to support the view that the Bank, like many other development financiers, has entertained double standards depending on who the expropriated were and whether expropriation occurred for and within a project or not.

Initial official reactions to this first case were not encouraging. The Bank management has made an extra-procedural but unsuccessful attempt to influence the Board's decision on the request for investigation. Already 'Some Executive Directors also appear to be reconsidering the wisdom of their decision to establish the Panel' (Bradlow 1995, p. 4). As a result of the very first case, the Bank is looking for procedural requirements to restrict access to the Panel in the future. Since the Bank alone defines the rules this is rather disquieting for the victims of development finance.

Nevertheless the Bank finally cancelled the Arun III loan in August 1995. Defending its decision the Bank cited cost overruns and questioned the ability of the Nepalese government to co-ordinate the project and to raise electricity prices enough to pay for it (*The Economist*, 26 August 1995). As none of these problems were unexpected or new, public pressure by NGOs seems to have been the determining factor.

IDA

The International Development Association (IDA) was established in 1960 as an alternative to UN controlled soft financing, proposed under the name (S)UNFED (see Chapter 4), and under strict control of the rich donors. In spite of proposals to establish a more democratic voting structure, also supported by some industrialized countries (essentially the Netherlands and the Nordic countries), voting rights in IDA followed the IBRD model. The Bank, initially opposed to the principle of soft financing, saw things differently once it became clear that this would be carried out by an institution administered by the IBRD. Again van der Laar (1980, p. 57) sees US interests as a major cause for the establishment of IDA as US surplus agricultural commodities sold under Public Law 480 for domestic currencies of recipients (a practice called 'quasi-grants' by the OECD) had resulted in embarrassingly high and practically useless holdings of inconvertible currencies. In 1958 Senator Monroney therefore proposed the establishment of IDA as an affiliate of the IBRD, recommending that the US should pay in these surpluses as their contribution.

IDA is run by IBRD staff and reimburses the Bank for administrative expenses by a management fee. Two classes of members were established: 'Part I' countries or high income members paying their entire subscriptions in convertible currencies, and 'Part II' countries, allowed to pay 90 per cent in their own currencies, which may not be used without the respective member's consent. The terms of IDA credits (as they are called internally by the IBRD to distinguish them from IBRD loans) are extremely soft. Initially they carried no interest but an annual service charge of 0.75%, had ten years grace and 50 years maturity. At present maturities are between 35 and 40 years. In contrast to IBRD loans they clearly qualify as ODA and are limited to the poorest countries.

IDA receives transfers from the IBRD paid out of its profits, and uses its own income as a source of credits. Any fund operating on terms similar to

IDA's would not be able to operate on a revolving basis but would need replenishments. The Ninth Replenishment of IDA took place in 1990. Presently the eleventh replenishment is on the agenda. The arduous negotiations for IDA-2 may serve to illustrate that tied aid is not excluded by multilateralism. The US favoured procurement tying arrangements for IDA, which met strong opposition from other countries. A compromise was reached allowing the US to contribute only that portion of its share matched by identifiable IDA procurement in the US until 1 July 1971 at the earliest (van der Laar 1980, p. 63).

THE IFC

The IFC was founded in 1956 to encourage private investment in SCs. Its loans are on market terms and it takes part in such private investments. Like the International Centre for the Settlement of Investment Disputes (ICSID) which is subordinated to the president of the IBRD, or the Multilateral Investment Guarantee Agency (MIGA), which is linked to the IBRD, it is not an ODA institution. Recent 'free market' ideology has made the IFC more popular with important Northern governments.

THE IMF: THE SECOND TWIN

The IMF is not officially regarded as a development institution, although all its facilities are used by SCs and it has influenced the development prospects of SCs fundamentally, particularly so since it started 'adjustment measures' shortly after 1973. Loans by the IMF Trust Fund – financed by selling gold in the second half of the 1970s – or the resources of the (Enhanced) Structural Adjustment Facility (SAF and ESAF) are given on financial terms soft enough to have a grant element above 25 per cent. These Structural Adjustment resources are administered jointly with the IBRD. Therefore criticism against SAF or ESAF is logically addressing both institutions. The Development Committee, formed by the IMF and the IBRD in 1974, has a mandate to foster development.

Proposals to link the creation of Special Drawing Rights (SDRs) to development by allocating SDRs in a way more favourable to the South than the present quota system have repeatedly been made, but have never been able to gain the necessary support. One important counter-argument was the potential inflationary effect of money creation on the global economy. This idea, the so-called 'Link', would have transformed the IMF much more, both de facto and de jure, into a development finance institution.

REGIONAL DEVELOPMENT BANKS

Modelled after their flagship, the IBRD, regional development banks were established in Africa (African Development Bank), Asia (Asian Development Bank), and America (Inter-American Development Bank (IDB) and the Caribbean Development Bank). Membership is not restricted to states from the region and many industrialized countries have joined these regional banks. Similarly to IDA, funds for concessional credits exist such as the African and Asian Development Funds or the IDB's Fund for Special Operations. Since 1986 the IDB also has a counterpart to the IFC in the International Investment Corporation (IIC).

The Washington-based IDB is the oldest regional bank, founded in 1959 by the US and 19 Latin American countries, immediately after Castro came to power in Cuba. This might be one reason why regional developing members had been given the majority of votes, which they still hold. Under the agreement establishing the IDB each member is allocated 135 votes plus one vote per share of ordinary capital. There are two highly specific constraints on the distribution of votes:

- the voting power of regional developing members must not be reduced below 53.3 per cent
- the share of votes of the US and of Canada must be at least 34.5 and 4.0 per cent respectively.

Concerning the Fund for Special Operations, voting power is determined in the same way. On 31 December 1993 regional developing member countries controlled 53.8 per cent, the US 34.61 per cent and Canada 4.39 per cent of the IDB's votes. Non-regional members held 7.16 per cent. Most DAC countries are non-regional members, but Croatia, Slovenia and Israel, countries classified as developing by the DAC, are also in this group. In contrast to the IBRD, the OECD countries control a modest 46.06 per cent.

Apparently this majority of borrowers did not result in a bad performance as US Assistant Treasury Secretary David Mulford, when attacking the IDB, had to concede that it had 'an effective record as a project lender' (IPS News Agency, 17 March 1988). As in the case of IFAD, power and voting structures rather than the quality of projects must thus have been the problem. The Reagan Administration withheld funds, exerting pressure on the IDB to change its voting structure, make it adopt IBRD-type programme (Structural Adjustment) lending, favour the private sector in its lending policy, and obtain an effective US veto power within the IDB – in short, to create a regional IBRD. By 1990 the IDB had earmarked about 25% of funds for programme lending and had undertaken massive changes within its originally about 70 per cent

Latin American staff, according to US wishes. However the US did not get veto power.

At present non-African members, led by the US, France, Germany, Britain and Japan, plan a capital increase of 50 per cent at the African Development Bank (AfDB) once a new ownership structure is in place and conditions regarding the bank's management, such as stronger management controls, are met. According to the *Financial Times* (31 August 1995), 'The donors want to increase their combined shareholding from 35 per cent to 50 per cent'. The fight for control was no doubt a major factor in the downgrading of the AfDB's rating by Standard & Poor's on 30 August 1995. The bank's senior debt rating was downgraded from the coveted triple-A to double-A plus, making the AfDB the only multilateral development bank to lose a triple-A rating as a debtor. Although it retained a triple-A rating from Moody's, the other main rating agency, this was a blow to the AfDB. It may be assumed that after the capital increase and after a change in voting rights according to the wishes of Northern members, the triple-A rating will be restored. Standard & Poor's expressly cited the 'increasing politicisation' (*Financial Times*, 31 August 1995) of the AfDB as the reason for the downgrading. African countries are apparently less able to retain present voting structures than the Latin American members of the IDB. This is no doubt also a result of grave management failures at the AfDB.

4. Aid during the Cold War

Until the demise of the Eastern bloc, aid policies were dominated by the perception of a bi-polar world or the Cold War. Naturally colonial history and economic and political ties surviving independence were another important root of aid whose influence can still be seen, for instance in the geographical orientation of aid flows. The importance of East-West relations can be best illustrated with the OECD's (1992, p. 5) identification of the end of the Cold War as an impediment to increased concessional flows because of:

> growing uncertainty as to the context and rationale for development assistance in the post-Cold War world. The search for this new rationale is most notable in countries like the United States, but to a considerable degree a re-examination is under way in most DAC Member countries.

Development aid was inseparably connected to the policies of the bi-polar world. It has often been used as a means of foreign policy to influence recipients, to stabilize 'friendly' governments (not seldom dictatorships with dismal human rights records, but *vis-à-vis* the 'right kind' of people) and to keep countries within the 'Free World'. Important changes in development policy can be explained by political events. IDA and the IDB (including its special voting structure) owe their existence to Castro's orientation towards Moscow. The IBRD's behaviour towards Chile and Romania is explained by Cold War political perceptions. The regional distribution of aid allowed the discernment of the major political theatres at any given time.

To understand both the evolution and the future of aid it is therefore necessary to briefly discuss the history of aid during the Cold War.

THE ORIGINS OF THE POST-WAR SYSTEM OF DEVELOPMENT CO-OPERATION

During World War II the idea of a new global order developed, able to abolish the problems of short-sighted national policies typical of the 1930s in favour of globally orchestrated strategies along Keynesian lines. In 1942 Keynes and his associates prepared memoranda on an International Clearing Union, on Commodity Buffer Stocks and Plans for Relief and Reconstruction. John

Maynard Keynes conceived the idea of a supranational currency administered by a World Central Bank, which would employ equilibrating mechanisms forcing both surplus and deficit countries to adjust. The International Trade Organization (ITO), incorporating commodity price stabilization, was intended to preclude depressing effects from trade. An international fund was intended to finance the recovery of Europe.

Compared with the Keynesian vision, the new order established after the war was both distorted and incomplete. It was distorted in so far as the original intention of pressure on balance of payments surplus countries rather than deficit countries, or at least symmetrical pressure on both, proved to be unworkable. It was incomplete as the ITO did not come into being (Singer 1989, p. 6). An international currency, which no single country could issue, was not acceptable to the US. Nevertheless the final outcome – a far cry from Keynes's ideas as it was – had enormous effects on development co-operation. The Bretton Woods twins came into being. Ironically Keynes's bank became the Fund and his envisioned fund became the Bank. The IMF's objective was to stabilize exchange rates *vis-à-vis* the dollar, considered equivalent to gold at that time, far removed from its present activities. Originally the Bank was intended to serve mainly as a financing institution for the reconstruction of Europe, as the OECD admitted quite frankly. The word development was inserted into the title after reconstruction as a result of the presence of SCs at Bretton Woods, demanding their share of resources.

In spite of its initial focus on Western Europe and its name, the Bank was soon crowded out by the Marshall Plan. Furthermore a large US loan to the UK, negotiated by Keynes towards the end of his life, bypassed the IBRD which had to turn increasingly to the business of development, while the recovery of Western Europe was financed by others.

The Marshall Plan, officially known as the European Reconstruction Programme (ERP), has its origin and takes its name from a speech made by General George Marshall at Harvard in 1947. The initiative's original intention also included the USSR but was soon strongly influenced by the new situation of East-West rivalry. It intended to reconstruct Western European economies as well as to contain communist influence. After approval by Congress in 1948 the US spent 2–3 per cent (excluding military aid) of its GNP under this initiative during the six years 1948–53, almost entirely on a grant basis. This represents four times the famous UN target for ODA and more than ten times the present level of aid given by the US in relation to GNP. The Marshall Plan played a crucial role in setting a pattern for aid to SCs later on. Many guidelines and institutional arrangements for the subsequent aid programmes were developed under the Marshall Plan. One example is the institution of counterpart funds, now a common feature associated with aid including food aid.

The characteristic of the Marshall Plan was that it had a clear intention of promoting regional co-operation among recipients. On the recipient side there was to be a joint assessment of needs and joint requests to the US. Another and unique difference is that recipients were allowed to monitor each other, something still unthinkable in the North-South context, in spite of the undoubtable success of the Marshall Plan and its procedures.

In 1948 the recipients of Marshall Plan aid signed the convention establishing the Organization for European Economic Co-operation (OEEC), which was reconstituted as the OECD at the beginning of the 1960s. The OEEC served as a monitoring agency for Marshall aid recipients. Europeans were encouraged by the US to monitor one another's performance and 'the heavy hand of the US government was kept out of it' (Streeten 1994a, p. 126). Each Western European government submitted a plan which was inspected, vetted and monitored by other European recipient governments in the OEEC. Streeten does not fail to point out that 'Control by peers rather than superior supervisors is also a principle advocated in business management'.

Apart from the OEEC formed at the outset, the Marshall Plan also led to the formation of the EPU (European Payments Union) in 1950 and of other regional institutions. Thus the Marshall Plan paved the way for the present EU. In this respect the subsequent aid programmes to SCs were different in that they were largely on a country-by-country basis.

Besides being an organization of self-monitoring aid recipients, the OEEC was also the cradle of the present donors' club. In 1961 the OEEC published 'the first comprehensive survey of *The Flow of Financial Resources to Countries in Course of Economic Development, 1956–59*' (OECD 1985, p. 69), the predecessor of the *Chairman's Reports* now published annually under the main title *Development Co-operation*. Shortly before being transformed into the OECD, the OEEC also initiated the Development Assistance Group (DAG), the forerunner of the present DAC.

The Marshall Plan is an example of tied aid since at least three-quarters of the goods financed came from the US, much of it in the form of commodity aid. Most of the commodity aid was in the form of food aid: food, animal feed and fertilizers accounted for 49 per cent of all procurements in the early phases of the Marshall Plan, declining in the later phases but still representing 30 per cent overall. The practices in food aid administration which were then created have in large measure continued until the present day. At the same time there was not much need for formal tying since the US, then representing over 50 per cent of the world's GSP, was the only effective source of supplies for many of the Marshall Plan requirements.

The Marshall Plan is generally acclaimed to have been a great success and in that respect is often favourably contrasted with present aid to SCs. Much of the difference is no doubt due to the sheer volume of Marshall Aid and to the political support of the aid programme in the donor country. But another part of the difference would be that this was essentially a reconstruction and rehabilitation programme and the recipients were countries where the human infrastructure was already in place. It is a general experience that reconstruction and rehabilitation investment is more productive than investment for new development in low-income countries. In this respect Marshall Aid should best be compared with US aid to Korea and Taiwan, which went on simultaneously and which also turned out to be very successful.

The pioneer role of the Marshall Plan in creating a body of operating principles and procedures for subsequent aid, was best expressed in the statement by Paul Hoffman, the first administrator of the US aid agency created to administer the Marshall Plan (ECA – European Co-operation Agency): 'We have learned in Europe what to do in Asia.' Paul Hoffman subsequently became the first Administrator of the UNDP, indicating a continuity from the Marshall Plan to multilateral aid.

Thus the Marshall Plan had strong effects on North-South relations. Its success made people perceive it as a promising model for development policy on a global scale. It was suggested that the UN should administer this ambitious enterprise. Theoretically the idea of large transfers of resources to the South could be based on generally accepted reasoning. Since capital tends to have higher returns where it is scarce, investments in the South would not only alleviate poverty but also be economically more productive. The Keynesian consensus that the availability of capital determined growth, which in turn was needed to improve the lot of the poor, was generally accepted.

The IBRD however successfully defended its privileged position as the only multilateral lender to the South against the UN. When a (Special) UN Fund for Economic Development (S)UNFED was to be set up to administer large-scale soft aid, inspired by the Marshall Plan, the 'long opposition of the World Bank not only to involving the UN in financial aid but even to the principle of soft aid, also served to prevent this idea materializing' (Singer 1989, p. 8). This fund remained what the first acronym proposed suggested: UNFED. (It might be added that the second acronym SUNFED was no more encouraging.)

The idea of multilateral aid gained ground again during the Kennedy era for political reasons (Castro's coming into power), though in a very different form. Naturally there was no question of a UN-controlled (S)UNFED any longer but, like the Bretton Woods Institutions (BWIs), the new institution was to be established under firm Northern control, also in marked contrast to the IDB. The IBRD dropped its reservations against soft aid when it became clear that it would be administered by the Bank, not the UN. Thus IDA was established as the Bank's soft loan window. Western donors were 'not ... willing to channel it [aid] through the UN where the developing countries had a major say, but through the World Bank which they controlled' (Singer 1989, p. 8; also Singer and Roy 1993). This judgement is fully supported by the OECD (1985, p. 141) itself: 'The developed countries preferred this to the alternative proposal, a special fund ensconced in the United Nations, because the structure of the World Bank ensured weighted voting in their favour.' It is after all the North's Bank, not the World Bank.

The idea of a New Marshall Plan for the South was taken up again in 1958 by Bruno Kreisky (Haselbach 1981), who also advocated it quite vocally in the 1970s and 1980s as Austria's Federal Chancellor (Kreisky 1980; 1981). It gained some support but not enough to become more than a concept (Kramer-Fischer 1981), although it focussed on resource flows and did not recommend any emulation of the participatory procedure of the original Marshall Plan.

AID AND POLITICS: THE WEST

Mixing politics and aid was by no means confined to the US. The FRG for instance granted aid only to countries accepting the Hallstein Doctrine, whereby a recipient was not allowed to recognize the German Democratic Republic. The Berlin Clause – accepting the West German view of the status of divided Berlin – was a criterion for bilateral German aid as well as multilateral EEC aid well into the 1980s.

The regional distribution of aid mirrored major political concerns. According to the Clay Report presented to the US President in 1963, '72 per cent of total (military and economic) assistance appropriations' were concentrated on 'allies and other countries on the Sino-Soviet border'. After criticizing this too big dispersion of aid to an 'excessive number of countries' the report concluded that 'economic assistance to some non-allied countries was beyond that necessary for our interests' (Ohlin 1966, p. 21). In view of the present debate on Africa's fate it might be of interest to note that this report recommended limiting US aid to the continent to a minimum. The committee spoke in favour of multilateral aid, especially recommending the newly established IDA. Considering US interests, this is no surprise.

Wolf (1960, p. 280) concluded in his survey on US aid policy *vis-à-vis* South Asia that '... in terms of this test, humanitarian objectives are not, nor do they appear likely to be, prominent among the continuing objectives of US foreign aid'. While humanitarian reasons appear to have been the main driving force behind proposals by academics and NGOs, their importance in donors' *realpolitik* was minute at best. Not surprisingly the *dependencia* school saw aid as another instrument of domination.

The economic success of East Asian 'tiger' or 'dragon' economies has one important root in the Cold War too. The communist threat made South Korea and Taiwan two major recipients of foreign aid. Between 1952 and 1961 the 'Mutual Security Act' was the legal basis of US aid, leading to major aid programmes for South Korea and Taiwan (OECD 1985, p. 67). According to Kwack (1986, p. 71) foreign aid financed 'more than 68 per cent of total imports and about 60 per cent of total investment' of South Korea in 1953 and 1954. South Korea's heavy dependence on external resources can also be illustrated by the fact that nearly 80 per cent of gross domestic fixed capital formation was financed from without when the country started the first five-year plan in 1962 (Kohama 1995, p. 215). Kohama also emphasizes the importance of aid in other countries.

From the end of the Korean War until the beginning of the 1960s aid, mostly from the US, amounted on average to 8 per cent of South Korea's GNP each year (Serfas 1987, p. 204). Nevertheless the IBRD's (1993) *East Asian Miracle* study – to use the words of a Bank economist – 'devotes little attention to the role of external assistance in East Asia'(Page 1995, p. 221).

Exceptionally generous ODA flows are by no means a sufficient condition for successful development and the evolution of these two countries cannot and should not be reduced to this monocausal explanation. However generous aid was certainly one major starting advantage, as was the relatively favourable treatment of these two bulwarks against communism by the US in the field of trade.

At the beginning of the 1960s Latin America too experienced a wave of generosity: 'The period 1960–1963, immediately after the Cuban revolution, coincided with the epoch of the greatest official generosity of the United States, producing the highest amount of credits and grants' (Pierre-Charles 1972, p. 392). The Inter-American Development Bank (IDB) was founded with a majority of votes for regional members and the project of a soft loan institution, aborted some years before in its early stages, was taken up again. As in Asia, the threat of communism proved to be particularly conducive to development co-operation.

AID AND POLITICS: THE EAST

The West was soon joined in its practices to use aid as a means of foreign policy by the communist countries, notably the Soviet Union, by far the biggest donor of the Eastern Bloc. North Korea for instance received substantial military and economic aid during the Korean War as well as during the reconstruction period. In 1954 aid from communist countries amounted to 'one-third of North Korean national revenues' (Brezinski 1986, p. 93), but dropped considerably later on. Soviet aid was immediately available to nations facing problems with the West, for instance in the case of the Aswan

Dam in Egypt, some projects in Afghanistan and India, or Guinea where Soviet aid arrived promptly after the French had announced their withdrawal. India is a country which managed to profit substantially from this competition for some time. Annual US promises of aid sky-rocketed from $4.5 million in 1951 to $87 million in 1954 (Goldman 1967, p. 197). Like the West, communist countries concentrated their flows on political allies and 'friendly' countries. As there were far fewer SCs orienting themselves towards the East – or Group D in UN terminology – Eastern aid was even more concentrated than ODA from the West. Cuba under Castro became the main beneficiary of Soviet funds; North Korea, Mongolia, and later on Vietnam and Afghanistan were other important aid recipients. Mongolia, Cuba and Vietnam also became members of the Council of Mutual Economic Assistance (CMEA, also called COMECON in the West), the integration movement of communist countries. The financial burden of these developing members on Eastern economies was apparently so great that the East turned down Mozambique's application for full membership in 1980. This was a strong indication of the economic constraints of communist economies. It led to a re-orientation of Mozambique and Angola to the West, and ultimately to their becoming signatories of the Lomé Treaties.

Estimates of aid by the Eastern Bloc were a difficult and cumbersome business due to the unwillingness of communist countries to disclose meaningful or verifiable data in the way the DAC does for most Western donors. The situation was very similar to trade data, which were also never of a quality comparable to Western sources. In contrast to their reluctance to provide proper statistical proof, the Eastern Bloc was always eager to stress the particularly positive effects of its trade and aid relations with the South, particularly so during the 1970s when the South demanded a NIEO (New International Economic Order). By contrast, data on communist aid published by the DAC were always more readily available.

The problem of measuring communist aid, which was largely aid by the Soviet Union, is not merely of historical interest. It is an excellent example of the way in which aid statistics can be used for political purposes. This was done without much success by the East but with considerably more success by the West. Naturally the West could not have done so if the East had provided sufficient and credible information. Eastern aid during the Cold War is an excellent example of the caveats which should sometimes be applied to data published by international organizations. To serve as a case study on data reliability communist aid is therefore presented in more detail.

STATISTICS ON COMMUNIST AID: ANNIHILATION BY NUMBERS

Communist official information tried to convey the impression of generosity, as in the Soviet statement of July 1982 in the ECOSOC claiming an average of 1.0 per cent of GNP given as aid during 1976–1980, rising from 0.9 per cent in 1976 to 1.3 per cent in 1980. Such statements did not produce the desired impression. Apart from verification problems they did not allow 'meaningful comparisons' with other donors according to UNCTAD (1983, p. 67), nor was it clear whether they were 'consistent with internationally agreed upon norms established by the General Assembly in the International Development Strategy' (ibid.). Drawing attention to flaws such as apparent mix-ups of dollars and roubles (inflating the figures by 40 per cent on average according to Kaiser), or of Net Material Product (NMP – the communist method of national accounting) and GSP, Kaiser (1986, p. 48) less diplomatically calls such practices 'no surprise but characteristic for Soviet propaganda'.

While this is not an unexpected result Walter Kaiser (1986) also proved by a thorough and very detailed analysis of DAC publications on Soviet ODA that DAC figures on Eastern, most notably Soviet, aid cannot be correct either. Due to the evident lack of Eastern data as well as their unreliability the author relied on Western sources, mostly the DAC itself, but also on sources from the US (including the CIA) and on the IBRD. Analysing the DAC publications meticulously he concluded that the data were manipulated to provide a basis for attacks on the East in general and the Soviet Union in particular.

Two main areas of manipulation are singled out: the thorny problem of estimating GSP-data from NMPs and the much simpler question of price subsidies granted to SCs, most notably Cuba. The latter means that the Soviet Union bought Cuban sugar and nickel above world market prices, selling crude oil at a substantial discount.

Generally the DAC presented extremely high GSP estimates, up to 72 per cent higher than those by the CIA, and higher than those published by the IBRD until 1980, the last year covered by the Bank. In contrast to the figures published by the CIA, which show similar trends as NMP values, Kaiser finds no explicable connection between DAC estimates and NMPs. The 1980 *Report* (OECD 1980, p. 171) claims that the calculation method of the IBRD had been used and additional information provided by the Bank, drawing attention to the sensitivity of figures to the choice of exchange rates. The 1984 *Report* (OECD 1984, p. 121, footnote 5; Kaiser 1986, p. 34) states that the DAC had used 'GNP figures published by the World Bank' until 1980.

DAC extrapolations for 1981 and later years were said to have been made on the basis of national incomes or NMP growth rates (OECD 1984, p. 121).

However while Soviet NMP grew by 3.4 per cent in 1981 and 4.2 per cent in 1982, Kaiser showed that its GSP growth rate implied by the DAC figures was nearly 15 per cent in each year (14.94 and 14.98 respectively) – a stark contrast to the 2.7 percent estimated by the CIA (Kaiser 1986). With the benefit of hindsight one might say that had the Soviet Union actually grown according to DAC perceptions this economic miracle would certainly have avoided the demise of the Soviet bloc.

Conveniently the West had two conversion figures for Soviet GSP. GSP per caput figures obtained by the CIA conversion method and published in the studies prepared by the CIA at the request of the Joint Economic Committee (1982, see the JEC chairman's acknowledgement in the preface), were low. These were used to argue that the Soviet Union's economy was far weaker than Western economies due to its inefficient management. The much higher GSP per caput figures of DAC conversions on the other hand were only used to obtain smaller ODA percentages of GSP. Both a low and a high Soviet GSP per head could thus be quoted by the West, depending on whether the issue was the competition of economic systems or aid. Politically it was a quite successful attempt both to 'keep one's cake and eat it at the same time, but in different places' (Raffer 1989, p. 105).

Price subsidies, which were quite substantial in the case of Cuba, were initially included as ODA. Economically there is no reason not to do so, especially as Cuba was officially allowed to sell any unused Soviet oil for hard currency (OECD 1985, p. 117). Technically they conform to the DAC definition quoted at the beginning of the Chapter 1, and the DAC explicitly recognized these sums as ODA until 1973: 'Aid from communist countries to Cuba has mainly taken the form of balance of payments support and sugar subsidies' (OECD 1973, p. 410). The inclusion is called debatable in a footnote because 'the world market price was higher than the price paid by the U.S.S.R.' in the early 1970s. Mathematically there is no subsidy in such cases anyway. After 1974 price subsidies to Cuba were excluded without mentioning this change explicitly until the 1980 DAC *Report* stated their exclusion for the first time. In the case of Vietnam such subsidies were only excluded at a later date (OECD 1981, p. 169) without any justification of this different treatment in comparison with Cuba. Incidentally, if trade had occurred at world market prices, and a sum identical to the difference between them and the subsidized prices had been given to Cuba every year as a grant, the debatable point that such subsidies, given by the East but rather uncommon in the West, were not considered by the DAC as ODA on principle could not have been used.

Kaiser draws attention to many further inconsistencies regarding Eastern aid, such as figures of ODA to non-communist countries, exclusion of countries and/or flows without any reason given, or quite different GSP values for the same year used in different *Reports*. Finally the OECD (1985, p. 118) disclosed that debt forgiveness, routinely accepted as aid in the case of DAC members (nowadays even for non-ODA debts), and balance of payments support (accepted in 1973) were not taken into account.

A remark by the OECD on Eastern aid deserves quoting as an example of double standards:

> On the other hand the CMEA countries are repaying themselves by selling equipment at higher than world market prices, by reselling raw materials imported from the developing countries at higher prices on the world market, or through fishing rights obtained from many African countries. OECD (1985, p. 118)

The West as well has sold at higher prices, not least because of 'tying' of aid previously discussed in Chapter 1. Reselling at prices above those received by SCs occurs every minute on Western commodity exchanges. The EU has secured fishing rights in Africa in exchange for aid. Food aid – apart from being a form of tied aid – is conventionally valued at the donor country's domestic prices, which are almost invariably much higher than world market prices.

Naturally these techniques of calculation drastically changed Soviet aid expressed as GNP percentages, starting incidentally at a time when the GNP percentages of US aid fell perceptibly and the Soviet Union came uncomfortably close according to DAC figures. The exclusion of price subsidies to Cuba reduced Soviet aid in 1970 from $1.1 billion (OECD 1972, p. 69) to $870 million (OECD 1974, p. 135) as Kaiser points out. This was 0.27 per cent of GSP, well below the US figure of 0.31, while the initial amount would have resulted in 0.34, well above US ODA. Considering the notion of philanthropy and generosity associated with the term 'aid', this would have been embarrassing both because of the Cold War and because of the forceful criticism of the Old Economic Order and the West by a newly self-confident Third World at that time.

Figures on Soviet ODA were thus transformed from an embarrassment for the US into a propaganda asset, the USSR from a more or less average donor in quantitative terms into a tight-fisted miser. Immediately the West began using these figures for its own political purposes. During the following years Soviet ODA dropped to practically nothing, to a minimum of 0.03 per cent of GNP in 1977 and 1978. Eventually Soviet aid in current dollars even fell below Chinese ODA (Kaiser 1986, p. 39).

The first upward revision after many downward revisions occurred in the 1980 *Report*, followed by substantial revisions for the years 1981 and 1984 (Kaiser 1986). As figures published at the end of the 1970s had become incredibly low – not least in comparison with data published by the US government – Kaiser concludes that these revisions were triggered by a fear of eventually losing credibility. Growth rates of 15 per cent as the figures implied for 1981 and 1982 cannot be credibly extrapolated forever either.

In 1985 the DAC mentioned briefly that figures on GNP percentages of aid 'differ substantially from one source to the other, depending on the methodology used … GNP estimates used in this Report are somewhat lower than those used previously by the Secretariat' (OECD 1985, p. 118). Both methodologies used and changes are not explained, but the changes can be illustrated by comparing the figures for the same year published in different *Reports*. In terms of GSP percentages, Soviet ODA in 1977 ranges from 0.03 (*Report* 1977) to 0.15 (*Report* 1984). For 1971 it fell from 0.25 reported in 1972 and 1973 to 0.1 in 1977, 'recovered' to 0.2 (in 1981) and fell again to 0.16 in the 1984 *Report* (Kaiser 1986).

Kaiser identifies three phases of DAC reporting:

1. Between 1961 and 1974 the DAC tried to estimate Soviet aid as correctly as possible, which was no easy task.
2. From 1974 to 1980 Soviet aid was deliberately reduced to provide a basis for criticizing the Soviets. This worked quite successfully, not least because of the refusal of the East to provide proper data themselves.
3. The upward revisions of the 1980s due to the fear of losing credibility.

In the 1980s the refusal of Mozambique's CMEA membership made it clear that the Soviets were unable and unwilling to finance any further nations on a substantial scale. The early post-war competitive situation was over, leaving the West as the only realistic source of finance for SCs. The impetus of Southern demands for a NIEO began to lose momentum. Complaints against the global economic order discriminating against the South and dominated by OECD countries, as in the 1970s, were heard less frequently. Trying to benefit politically from the call for a NIEO, communist countries had always been quite vocal in accusing the West of exploitation by trade and in supporting the South, although available information shows that their own trade followed Western patterns quite closely (Raffer 1989). In the North-South confrontation of the 1970s, when the East was eager to score politically by siding with the South, reports of very low GSP percentages of Eastern ODA were a welcome means of defence, losing its usefulness when calls for a NIEO subsided.

After the breakdown of the Centrally Planned Economies, these countries have ceased to provide aid, turning from donors into competitors for OECD funds. Parts of the former Soviet Union, such as Azerbaijan, Uzbekistan or Kyrgyzstan, were put on the DAC list of 'developing countries'. Afraid that this recognition might lead to a widespread diversion of ODA away from them, SCs have so far been successful in blocking attempts to classify all of Eastern Europe and Russia as 'developing' according to the DAC list. Aid to 'Countries and Territories in Transition' is therefore still listed separately. The activities of former communist countries in the South seem to be mainly restricted to collecting repayments of old ODA loans. Cuba, which financed a model public health system as well as educational facilities which were outstanding by SC standards, was particularly strongly affected by the discontinuation of aid as the country was never able to finance these expenses itself.

0.7 PER CENT – THE MAGIC TARGET

The frequent use of aid as a means of political influence must not disguise the fact that total ODA as a percentage of donor GSP declined perceptibly during the Cold War. Apparently politicians became aware that even generous aid could not always prevent undesirable evolutions. ODA fell sharply from 0.52 per cent of DAC GSP in 1960 (0.54 in 1961) to 0.31 in 1970. It increased somewhat later, oscillating around 0.35. In 1993 it was 0.30 (OECD 1995), dropping from 0.33 in 1992. This fall might be one effect of the end of the bipolar world. The decline of the 1960s was mainly due to the US whose ODA was 0.57 per cent of GNP in 1962 and 0.33 in 1969.

By contrast some smaller countries, such as Sweden, Norway, Denmark and the Netherlands, increased their aid substantially after 1960 (mostly from rather low bases), all of them surpassing 1 per cent at least once. During the 1970s these countries also formed the core of the group of 'Like-Minded Countries', Northern states more open and supportive to ideas from the South than other members of Group B. In their case at least their political statements have been accompanied by quantitative, financial commitments. The Norwegian and the Swedish Parliaments for example adopted plans to increase aid substantially (to 0.7 and 1 per cent respectively) as early as 1968 (OECD 1985, p. 73).

The most famous ODA target is 0.7 per cent of GNP, accepted by most but implemented by few DAC donors. It was an important feature of the Second Development Decade as well as the feature with which Jan Tinbergen is most often associated. Its origin is, according to Tinbergen (1990, p. 169) 'somewhat obscure'. Be that as it may, the UN General Assembly adopted this subtarget and it was eventually accepted by all DAC members except Switzerland and the US. France's adoption of this target for independent SCs led to two separate figures of ODA shown for France by the DAC. Including its own DOM/TOM (French overseas departments and territories) France had usually been above 0.7 per cent.

This obscurity of the origin of the 0.7 per cent target could result from the fact that it emerged from informal discussions between the UN Committee of Development Planning, headed by Tinbergen, and the UN Secretariat (Singer 1994). In one sense the 0.7 per cent target is the direct progeny of the target contained in the proposals for the First Development Decade, that is the 1 per cent target for all financial flows mentioned above. The two targets were often confused in the subsequent debate. The first target had already been influenced by Tinbergen – he published his calculations of the 'savings gap' at about the same time in *Shaping the World Economy* (Tinbergen 1962). His approach was based on a Harrod-Domar type calculation, assuming a target rate of growth of 2 per cent per caput and a capital/output ratio of 3:1. If the target for financial flows for the First Development Decade had been reformulated in terms of ODA rather than total flows, it would in fact have come close to 0.7 per cent. Around 1961–62 aid did constitute about 70 per cent of total financial flows. Thus the Tinbergen target for the Second Development Decade in fact represented a high degree of continuity from the target of the First Decade in which his calculations had already played a major part. Such continuity is not surprising, not only because of Jan Tinbergen's association with both exercises but also because during the First Decade of the 1960s things had gone pretty well according to plans and there seemed no need for quantitative changes.

In his ripe old age Jan Tinbergen (1990a) carried out some further sophisticated work on the aid target. He proposed three new criteria all of which resulted in considerably higher amounts. Characteristically he was not afraid of being branded a Utopian for proposing higher targets when the lower targets were not reached or even approached. As he wrote in his contribution to the *Human Development Report 1994* (UNDP 1994, p. 88): 'The idealists of today often turn out to be the realists of tomorrow.'

Riddell (1987, p. 270) described Tinbergen's attempt in the 1960s and 1970s to link aid levels to Third World needs as 'heroic if highly questionable'. Today we know that the 0.7 per cent target did not exercise the degree of moral and political compulsion Tinbergen expected from it, perhaps overgeneralizing from his own moral position and that of the Netherlands. Although the target has been repeatedly accepted and confirmed by nearly all DAC countries and presents in theory a legal obligation, total DAC aid has never reached it and we have been moving away from it rather than towards it. The DAC average of actual ODA dropped to 0.30 percent in 1993 after hovering around 0.35 per cent of GSP for quite some time. There are some honourable exceptions however, including the Nordic countries and the Netherlands. Whether the target had any impact at all is difficult to say. Would aid flows have been even lower without it? This is one of the pieces of counterfactual history where answers are impossible to prove or disprove.

PART TWO

Specific Sources and Forms of Aid

5. Food aid: A conceptual and statistical quagmire

At first sight food aid statistics appear to be a neat little segment of aid statistics. They are based on a distinction between financial aid and food aid where food aid represents aid tied both to the supply of food and other forms of tying which can apply to food aid as well as financial aid, in particular tying by source of donor. Food aid is not the only form of aid tied by commodity, but other forms of commodity aid are insignificant today. Additionally, food aid is distinguished from food trade or commercial transactions by an element of concessionality. This has been arbitrarily defined as a grant element of at least 25 per cent of the commercial price.

Some immediate problems arise from this last distinction between food trade and food aid. The commercial price of food in international trade is itself a policy-determined quantity. It is not a textbook free market price with a significant reference function but, as Peter Uvin (1994) describes it, a 'residual' and 'largely devoid of significance'.

The policies of subsidizing national agricultures in the main industrial countries result in surpluses and surplus capacities. It is these surpluses which both enable and induce the countries producing these surpluses to tie their aid to food. But these same surpluses and surplus capacities also depress the commercial price of food in international trade. Hence the 25 per cent concessionality limit which defines food aid is not 25 per cent off a true free market price, but 25 per cent off a world price which is already itself at a discount from what commercial prices would be in a free market. In other words, if the 25 per cent concessionality were measured from a true free market price in international food trade, many more transactions would be defined as food aid.

Moreover more than half of total food 'trade' is covered by various forms of bilateral agreements, providing discounts from the 'commercial' international price (itself reduced by overhanging surpluses and domestic production subsidies) in many direct and indirect ways difficult or impossible to quantify – export credits, linkage with other trade concessions, linkage with financial aid and so on. Under the Uruguay agreement such subsidized exports are to be reduced by 36 per cent over six years – but it is doubtful whether this 36 per cent will catch all the hidden and indirect subsidies involved in this game. With 'commercial' imports of SCs running at seven times 'food aid', it would only need an overall subsidy factor of 14 per cent to double statistical food aid once again. The 14 per cent figure, while no more than a guess, may well be within the realm of the possible – perhaps even an understatement. The effective price of wheat has been estimated to be 30–40 per cent below the official Chicago price, with similar discrepancies for coarse grains and rice.

We have thus a 'double whammy'. Real food aid may have to be doubled to allow for international prices being lower than true free market prices, and then doubled again to allow for direct and indirect discounts from this already lowered international price. While difficult to quantify statistically, this does illustrate the precariousness and conservatism of the traditional 11–12 million tons figure.

This point has acquired current realistic importance by the agreement on partial liberalization of agricultural policies recently reached in the GATT/Uruguay Round. On the basis of various economic models based on more-or-less plausible assumptions, it has been possible to make quantitative estimates of the rise in prices in international food trade consequent upon agricultural liberalization. The best-known of these models is the Rural/Urban-North/South (RUNS) model developed by the OECD Development Centre and the IBRD. This model would suggest that even the relatively mild degree of partial liberalization under the Uruguay Round agreement (20 per cent reduction in subsidies to national food producers and 36 per cent reduction in subsidized exports spread over six years) would result in a rise in world wheat prices of 5.9 per cent, with rises of 3.6 per cent in coarse grains, 7.2 per cent in dairy products and 4.1 per cent in vegetable oils. If we take an average of 5.5 per cent for these four main items of food aid (giving them appropriate weights according to their importance in food aid) we would find that the 5.5 per cent discount from the higher commercial price without the partial GATT liberalization is roughly equal in value to the income transfer to the food importers under the current statistical definition of food aid (which also comes to 5–7 per cent of world food trade).

In other words, if we include the 5.5 per cent discount from the higher commercial price in our definition of food aid, food aid would be approximately double the present figure. This would raise the current tonnage of food aid from around 12 million tons per annum to around 24 million tons. This higher figure makes talk of 'the decline of food aid' (Clay 1994) somewhat questionable. It also brings food aid within the range of the status quo assessments of food aid needs by the US Department of Agriculture and the FAO. It also brings the share of food aid in total development assistance from around 8 per cent to about 15 per cent, giving it a distinctly more important profile.

With more radical assumptions, moving from the partial GATT liberalization to full liberalization and defining any discount from a fully liberalized commercial international free market price for food as food aid, we might well find the true volume of current food aid thus measured further increased – quadrupled rather than doubled – to something in the nature of 40 to 50 millions tons equivalent. Under the RUNS model for example the price of wheat would increase by 30.2 per cent instead of 5.9 per cent, the price of coarse grains by 19.0 per cent instead of 3.6, for dairy products by 52.6 per cent instead of 7.2 and for vegetable oils by 17.7 per cent instead of 4.1 (see Goldin, Knudsen and van der Mensbrugghe 1993, p. 91, Table 3.1).

This would bring food aid to the level of the United States Department of Agriculture (USDA) estimate of food aid needs including nutritional requirements. The important qualification to such comparisons must be that the food aid implicit in the artificial lowering of international food prices and trade discounts – the food aid that dare not speak its name – is not in any way targeted on food needs, food security or nutritional requirements. It is broadly and blindly given across the board. If this hidden food aid could be brought into the open and properly targeted on needs, the world would have taken an important step in dealing with the hunger problem.

Another implication of including this 'grey area' in food aid is that much food aid is in fact, although involuntarily, given not by the countries which appear statistically as donors, but by food exporters among developing countries, such as Argentina, Thailand or Zimbabwe which do not appear as donors at all (except insofar as they figure as sources of procurement in triangular transactions).

In fact such developing country food exporters are doubly hit by the present situation. In the first place, they suffer from the downward pressure on international food prices due to overhanging surpluses and surplus capacities of countries protecting and subsidizing their agriculture. In the second place, they see their normal markets pre-empted by food aid (including 'grey area' food aid, subsidized exports, export credits and so on) which they cannot afford to give. Theoretically this second burden should not exist: their sales should be protected by the provision for 'Usual Marketing Requirements' (UMRs), monitored by the FAO Committee for Surplus Disposal. However in fact it is generally accepted that at least a part of programme food aid replaces commercial imports – that indeed is one of the strong arguments in favour of programme food aid. Since it replaces commercial imports, it amounts to the provision of balance of payments support and foreign exchange and thus has all the advantages of greater flexibility of financial aid and built-in monetization. Moreover, insofar as commercial imports are displaced, programme food aid does not add to total food supplies and hence, unless sold at subsidized prices, cannot have disincentive effects on local food production. On the other hand, by the same token, it does not in itself deal with hunger and nutrition problems. There is however a secondary exception to all this: if the foreign exchange set free by the food aid is at least partially used to import additional food, then we might have both the risk of disincentive effects but also potential nutritional benefits.

The prospective rise in international food prices as a result of agricultural liberalization will also affect the UMRs. The commercial market requirements – or rather commercial market possibilities – of the poorer food-importing countries will be fewer at the higher prospective post-liberalization prices, given their limitation of foreign exchange earnings and the drain of debt service. There is thus a case for reconsidering and reducing the UMRs. Perhaps it would be best to abandon the whole UMR exercise which is in any case conceptually doubtful and by general agreement largely ineffective.

So far we have identified two types of 'grey' food aid which are not included in the statistical definition. These are the 'light grey' area of subsidized exports, export credits, and other forms of concessionality which remain below the 25 per cent concessionality limit but apply to a very high proportion of total food exports by food aid donors. In addition, we have identified 'dark grey' food aid in the concealed subsidy to food importers resulting from the lower prices in international food trade due to the pressure of overhanging surpluses and surplus capacities. But beyond these two categories of 'grey' food aid there looms yet another statistically unrecorded set of transactions which amount to food aid in economic effect. (Once we cross the Rubicon into the 'grey area' there are no obvious landmarks telling us where to stop.) Some at least of the financial aid, especially financial programme aid including Structural Adjustment lending, finances balance of payments deficits, enabling countries to acquire additional imports. Insofar as some of these additional imports are food imports we could say that this segment of financial aid is in fact aid for food finance or food aid. As a first approximation, we may assume that financial aid which in effect finances additional food imports should be classified as food aid in the same proportion as food imports to overall imports of recipient countries. Since for the low income and lower-middle income countries (other than China and India) food imports represent 14 per cent of total imports, we may roughly assume that of the over $50 billion of annual ODA some $7 billion represents finance for food imports or, in the broader sense, food aid. The inclusion of this latter sum would almost treble food aid by comparison with its present highly limited definition.

A special difficulty arises with the IMF Food Financing Facility (FFF) which was added to the Compensatory Financing Facility in 1981. Although it has not been much used and under the stringent IMF rules may not be much used in the future (and also only doubtfully treated as 'aid'), it was specifically intended to enable food-insecure low income countries to maintain cereal imports in the face of supply failures or unexpected drops in export earnings. With this mandate, it is difficult to avoid the conclusion that, at least conceptually, transactions under the FFF should be treated as food aid – presumably part of emergency food aid. This is particularly the case since the IMF has recently developed sources of funds on highly concessional terms (as low as 0.5% in the case of ESAF).

So far we have identified areas in which the present statistical definition of food aid appears too limited and broader definitions may well be suggested. There is however also a countervailing element where the present definition of food aid could be said to be excessively wide. Some food aid represents financial aid in that it sets free foreign exchange. This relates to that part of programme food aid which in fact replaces commercial imports. As already pointed out, this type of food aid is equivalent to financial aid in the form of free foreign exchange. In any functional definition of food aid, distinguishing it from financial aid, it may well be that the border line should be drawn to bring the import-replacing element in programme food aid into the category of financial aid. This is easy to suggest as a conceptual procedure but statistically it will be very difficult to determine which part of programme food aid replaces commercial imports and which part is additional. Under the UMR rule, in principle all food aid should be additional as already pointed out. But this is a principle rather than a fact. There is no doubt that there is some substitution, but its magnitude is a matter of counterfactual evidence which is notoriously difficult. Saran and Konandreas (1991) put substitution as high as 60–70 per cent although this may be on the high side.

How much would a country have imported commercially if no programme food aid had been available to it? The same question could also be asked with respect to emergency food aid, although in this case it would be much less likely that commercial imports could have been afforded. In the circumstances the size of this sector of statistical food aid, which in fact amounts to financial aid, must remain more a matter of speculation than of practical adjustment – more in the nature of a statistical footnote.

A second area in which the present food aid statistics may be overstated relates to the value figures rather than tonnage. Food aid is usually valued by donors at the budget cost to themselves, but this is inflated by the subsidies and high domestic prices involved in their own agricultural policies. According to Saran and Konandreas, the actual value of the food donated at international prices is only about one half of the budgeted value (ibid.). On the other hand it must be remembered that international prices are themselves artificially lowered by the same agricultural policies so the true value would be somewhere between the international price and the budget cost price – nothing could better illustrate the quagmire of concepts and statistics.

A third cause of possible overvaluation of food aid in present statistics relates to triangular transactions and local procurement. Some of the food aid donors without any surplus food (yet committed under the Food Aid Convention to participate in 'food aid') give cash instead to buy food in other countries or locally in the recipient country. These triangular transactions are an increasing element in total food aid and, by many criteria, a particularly desirable element. However it is by no means always clear how they should appear in food aid statistics. If the UK buys surplus white maize from Zimbabwe to transport as food aid to Zambia, it seems clear that Zambia is a recipient of food aid. But the case could well be presented as a combination of UK-financed expansion of South-South trade between Zimbabwe and Zambia, with the actual food coming from Zimbabwe rather than the UK. The UK presents this as a case of dual aid, or killing two birds with one stone: the transaction is claimed to be financial aid to Zimbabwe by providing foreign exchange for their maize surplus, yet it also provides food aid to Zambia. Since the Zimbabwean type of white maize is preferred in the region but considered inferior on the world market, Zimbabwe could only sell below the price paid by the UK, if at all. Yet it would clearly be double-counting for the same transaction to be counted both as financial aid to Zimbabwe and food aid to Zambia. Which is it to be? To count it as food aid would in effect understate financial aid, and to count it as aid to Zambia only would understate the aid figures for Zimbabwe. To count it as financial aid would run the opposite risk. The road of the food aid statistician is clearly full of dangerous landmines.

This last example illustrates clearly that the real quagmire is conceptual rather than statistical. When we deal with subsidized and financially promoted trade, what part of it is trade and what part aid? What is the grant element which distinguishes trade from aid – is it 10 per cent, 25 per cent, 50 per cent? Why should 25 per cent (the DAC-agreed benchmark) act as a magic number? Where is the borderline between financial aid and food aid? On which side of the borderline fall monetized food aid, triangular transactions or balance of payments support either through financial or programme food aid? How should the hidden subsidies to food importers arising from the agricultural policies pursued by the US and EEC be treated? Where is the benchmark for full commercial prices as against actual prices in international food trade? The more we broaden our definition of food aid and ask some of the foregoing questions, the more it becomes clear that food aid must be understood as an element in world food policy and world food security.

Such a shift towards a broader conception of food aid will be all the more necessary since the historical link with surplus disposal and the resulting popularity of food aid, especially in the farming communities of the industrial countries, are now likely to be weakened as a result of agricultural policy liberalization. Partly as a result of this link, and partly because of the direct association of food aid with poverty alleviation and humanitarian relief, food aid has consistently enjoyed greater political support than financial aid. While financial aid is stagnating at below 0.35 per cent of donor GNPs – less than half the accepted UN target – food aid, even on the narrow definition, has amounted to around 2 per cent of total food production in the major donor countries (US, EC and Canada) and has consistently exceeded the UN target under the Food Aid Convention. Peter Uvin (1994) points to the remarkable similarity of this percentage in the US, EU and Canada as evidence of wider and more general forces determining the willingness of major donors to give food aid.

The Food Aid Convention also represents a multi-annual commitment of a kind never achieved in the case of financial aid. On the surplus side, food aid is now threatened both by a reduction of surpluses and also by higher food prices which will mean less volume of food aid for given budgetary appropriations. Yet at the same time, on the demand side, the need for food aid will increase as a result of higher costs of commercial food imports. According to the Final Act of the GATT Uruguay Round Agreement, the balance between the reduced willingness to supply and increased need should be found in the maintenance of food aid in the post-liberalization era – presumably in volume terms.

The cutting of the historical link between surpluses and food aid may be a blessing in disguise. Surplus disposal and the resulting popularity of food aid for this reason were always a flawed motivation for food aid. We have heard a lot about possible disincentive effects of food aid on policy makers as well as producers in recipient countries. We have heard less about the disincentives on policy makers in the industrial countries, that is the incentive to continue with harmful agricultural policies on the grounds that some of the resulting surpluses could be disposed of by food aid. Similarly if the hidden food aid which dared not speak its name is now forced to come out into the open, it can be more purposefully targeted on developmental and humanitarian objectives. This will not only help to clear up the present conceptual and statistical quagmire, but more importantly it will promote the fight for development and against poverty.

6. Advantages and disadvantages of food aid

Food aid is only 10 per cent in value of total aid flows but it has generated a good deal more than 10 per cent of the total aid discussion, both for and against. There are a number of reasons for this:

1. For some important aid donors including the US, and even more so for EU aid, food aid represents much more than 10 per cent of total aid flows.
2. Food aid has much more political support than financial aid in donor countries where the farmers' lobby is strong and agricultural subsidies and protectionism are rampant – again the US and EU are outstanding examples.
3. Food aid has shown a tendency to increase in recent years (although it has not yet come back to the high levels of US food aid under the Marshall Plan and also under PL480 in the late 1950s and the 1960s particularly to the Indian sub-continent).
4. Food aid is more concentrated than financial aid on the poorer countries, particularly on Africa and Bangladesh.
5. Emergency food aid to support famine victims or refugees has a popular appeal and is easily dramatized by the media (although in fact in normal years emergency food aid is only a small fraction of the total and even at the height of the Ethiopian famine, the bulk of food aid was developmental rather than emergency).

This list could be added to but should be sufficient to explain the intensity of the food aid debate.

Emergency food aid has been largely exempt from the controversies raging around other types of food aid. To feed the hungry, improve the nutrition of small children, keep refugees alive and so on is more or less accepted as a non-controversial moral duty, especially in view of the existence of huge food surpluses. This does not exclude controversy concerning the effectiveness of emergency food aid: the critics rightly point out, and the defendants of food aid admit, that all too often emergency food aid arrives too late when it does more harm than good, that it fails to be properly and efficiently distributed to the neediest regions and groups, that it may consist of the wrong commodities and that, in emergencies, assistance with transport, medical supplies and financial aid may be as or more important, than food aid. The emergency food aid given by the EU has been especially subject to criticism in these respects. However the principle of emergency food aid is universally accepted, although where emergency aid helps to ease the situation for repressive governments the moral case becomes more debatable.

This universal support for the principle, at least, of emergency food aid may show a way of resolving some of the objections put forward by the critics of food aid. There are narrower and broader concepts of 'emergency'. A broad concept of emergency would include the timely prevention of future emergencies, the creation of reserve stocks of food in strategic locations, improvements in local food production practices, environmental improvement such as afforestation and so on, as well as rehabilitation and resettlement after the acute emergency is over. If supporters and critics could agree on this broader definition of emergency, a good deal of what is now described as developmental food aid could be brought under the umbrella of uncontroversial emergency aid.

We have already mentioned the political support for food aid from the farmers in donor countries. This link between the surplus mountains of food which are building up as a result of senseless agricultural policies, and the willingness to give food aid, forms one of the planks of the critics who describe food aid as surplus disposal – a way of dumping surpluses rather than genuine aid. It cannot be denied that the historical origin of food aid to SCs in the US was the desire to get rid of unwanted surpluses: the original US programme set up in 1954 under Public Law 480 was called a 'surplus disposal programme' – perhaps a more honest name than subsequent titles such as 'Food for Peace'. However a selfish interest of the donors in wishing to get rid of surpluses is not inconsistent with developmental and humanitarian motives. In financial aid the motives of donors are equally mixed: the desire to build up export markets, to benefit local producers by aid tying, to utilize idle surplus capacity or reduce unemployment – all these are just as much mixed in with a desire to promote development or reduce poverty in financial aid as in food aid. Moreover some of the criticism of food aid seems to be misdirected in the sense that what the critics really mean to criticize (rightly) are the agricultural policies, such as the Common Agricultural Policy of the EU, which lead to the surpluses and, in turn, to food aid. However it does not seem plausible that food aid is a significant causative factor in these agricultural policies. If it were, food aid would be very much larger than it is; in fact it is relatively insignificant in comparison with the enormous food surpluses.

A frequent criticism of food aid is that it is an inferior form of aid compared with financial aid. It is true that normally, other things being equal, it would be better from the recipients' point of view to have freely usable money and to buy food, if that is the top priority, in the open market. However as we have already said, food aid has a special political and economic appeal to a number of donors and it seems almost certain that at least a considerable part of total food aid is not an inferior substitute for financial aid but is additional. In the nature of things, this is an area in which it is difficult to be certain. If food aid were abolished tomorrow, would financial aid increase, and if so by how much? Nobody can tell. In any case, we cannot be all that certain about the alleged inferiority of food aid. On the one hand, financial aid also is often tied to specific commodities or to specific donor sources of supply; to that extent it is also worth less to the recipient than free financial aid. On the other hand much of food aid, possibly as much as two-thirds, is in the nature of programme food aid or balance of payments support which to some extent at least replaces commercial imports. In so far as this is the case, food aid releases foreign exchange which can be freely and unconditionally used by the recipient country – to that extent it may be better than tied financial aid subject to severe conditionality. The line between food aid and financial aid is far less clear than the debate about the inferiority or otherwise of food aid would suggest: much of what is called financial aid really helps to finance food imports and to that extent is food aid, while much of food aid releases foreign exchange and to that extent is financial aid.

Perhaps the most serious and frequent criticism of food aid is that it induces the recipient governments to use it as an easy alternative to the much more difficult task of increasing domestic food production and thus leads to 'food dependency'. There is no doubt that many SCs in the past have shown an urban bias in neglecting investment in agriculture and food production. But it is far from clear whether food aid has played any significant part in this. The forces making for urban bias are deeply rooted in the greater political leverage of the urban population and in the attractions of industrialization as the perceived highroad to economic development. Neither history nor empirical analysis suggests any close correlation between the receipt of food aid and neglect of domestic agriculture. The biggest recipients of food aid were Western Europe (in the days of the Marshall Plan), India (under PL480 during 1955–70), South Korea, Israel, Greece and so on. Yet in all these countries domestic food production has increased quite vigorously. In India for example food aid at the very least has not prevented the Green Revolution in the Punjab; on the contrary it could be argued that the additional resources provided by food aid and the revenue derived by the Indian government from the sale of food aid have helped to finance the investments in irrigation, transport, extension services and research which were the necessary infrastructure for the Green Revolution. Food security is an essential element in national sovereignty and one does not easily see newly independent SCs, keen on establishing their national sovereignty, making themselves readily dependent on the uncertain flow of food aid.

However the critics have done a useful service in suggesting that food aid will only be helpful in the context of an economic strategy by the recipient country which mobilizes all possible resources for the promotion of domestic food production. Such a link of food aid with a 'policy dialogue' or 'food strategy' is becoming increasingly frequent, as is also the link of food aid with Structural Adjustment lending and stabilization schemes which normally also insist on proper incentives for domestic food producers. Here as elsewhere it can be said that the critics of food aid may have been wrong in arguing that food aid is intrinsically bad, but they may have been right in pointing out dangers; in that way they may have pointed the way towards improvement in food aid procedures. There is now an emerging consensus that food aid given in the context of bad policies and bad management practised by the recipient will do more harm than good, while food aid given in a good context has the potential to be a useful and powerful development tool.

In food aid literature, another criticism has played an even bigger role. This is to the effect that the arrival of additional food supplies in the markets of the recipient country will drive down prices and thus discourage domestic food production, even if the recipient government is not tempted by the availability of food aid to shift its priorities away from agriculture. This criticism depends of course on the assumption that the food supplied as food aid represents additional supply. To the extent that food takes the place of commercial imports, there would be no additional supply and no reason why prices should be lower (although some of the critics have tried to have it both ways, criticizing food aid both for replacing commercial imports and for driving down prices). The food aid would also not depress local food prices if it were handed out (either free or at subsidized prices) to people who for lack of income had no present effective demand for food. Third, food aid, especially food aid given as programme aid and balance of payments support, should enable the recipient country to follow more expansionary domestic policies which would result in additional demand for local food and thus offset (or more than offset) any depressing price effect of increased supply. Food and foreign exchange constraints being two of the major obstacles to expansion, food aid given as balance of payments support and setting free foreign exchange has the advantage of relaxing both these constraints at the same time. As an alternative, it is always open to the government to utilize the revenue obtained from the sale of food aid either for additional price incentives to local food producers – perhaps operating a dual price system – or subsidizing essential inputs to local food producers such as fertilizers and agricultural tools, or to finance rural infrastructure projects essential for domestic producers such as transport and irrigation, or to use food aid directly for work projects which maintain rural employment and hence demand for local food.

There are thus many possibilities of avoiding depressing price effects of food aid in recipient countries. The previously mentioned linkage between food aid and an agreed food strategy is another way. But perhaps the most important answer to the critics of food aid on the grounds of price disincentives is to question whether food markets in SCs actually operate on the free market paradigm where prices are determined by the interplay of supply and demand. This has been one of the most hotly debated issues surrounding not only food aid but the whole question of agricultural development in SCs. Most of the knowledgeable investigators have come to the conclusion that prices ruling in SC food markets are more typically administered and regulated prices rather than free market prices, with a dominant role played by marketing boards and similar parastatal organizations. Price is at most one of many factors determining the response of local food producers, and perhaps not the most important single element. Here the debate on the advantages and disadvantages of food aid has tended to merge with the broader debate on the role of prices and markets in SCs.

Another criticism of food aid may be briefly considered. This accuses food aid of promoting an undesirable shift in consumption patterns away from traditional local staple foods and towards the commodities supplied as food aid, specifically wheat, wheat flour and dairy products. The importance of this line of criticism depends on a consideration of the driving forces behind the undoubted shift in consumption patterns in SCs towards wheat and dairy products. Nobody questions that the main driving force is urbanization; food aid would at best be a subsidiary factor, subsidiary also to commercial imports. Moreover as we shall point out later, there are methods available for using food aid to promote demand for local food staples. On the other hand, we must concede to the critics in that once again they have rendered a useful service in drawing attention to the dangers involved in shifting consumption patterns. As a result, there is an increasing tendency in food aid now to look at triangular transactions, where the food for food aid is obtained from neighbouring countries having export surpluses available, for instance maize from Zimbabwe or rice from Thailand. As far as dairy products are concerned, which play such a big part in EU food aid, there are good grounds for accepting the critics' case and for advocating a shift away from dairy products to cereals. The pros and cons of the most important dairy food aid project, Operation Flood in India, are among the most hotly debated issues; the project has ardent advocates as well as ardent critics.

What of the future? Food aid is a fact of life and will certainly not disappear in any foreseeable future. In fact food aid represents an international commitment of the donor countries, at least to the amount of 7.6 million tons of cereals on a multi-annual basis, a situation which has never been achieved in the case of financial aid. Moreover food aid in the last few years has shown signs of increase exceeding the UN target of 10 million tons; this again is in sharp contrast to the situation in financial aid where there is a shortfall of over 50 per cent on the UN target of 0.7 per cent of GNP. There is a general expectation that food aid is likely to increase – partly as a result of the new initiatives to be discussed – and both the FAO and the US Department of Agriculture have estimated the amount of food aid which can be effectively absorbed at 18–20 million tons of cereals, much higher than the present flow of around 11 million tons (although considerably less than the volume of food aid some 25 years ago). Certainly the food surpluses from which food aid is being fed are larger than ever.

If food aid is certain to continue and likely to increase rather than diminish, what can we say of its future shape? One possible, and desirable, development is to use food aid to solve some of the intractable problems of the debt burden and balance of payments difficulties of SCs. The present methods of adjustment and conditionality under IMF/IBRD auspices are now generally criticized as being too harsh and having undesirable social consequences. Some of the critics go even further and maintain that the present methods are also counterproductive in undermining rather than promoting future economic growth. The most articulate criticism has come from UNICEF in its advocacy of 'adjustment with a human face'. It is also recognized that in return for the painful adjustments expected from SCs they must be given a greater quid pro quo in terms of additional resources. It is therefore not surprising that the uses of food aid in Structural Adjustment lending have caught the attention of those concerned, including even the IMF and IBRD. Food aid would have the special advantage of representing both additional resources to ease adjustment and also of being capable of providing particular relief for vulnerable groups, such as children, landless rural people, unemployed and other direct victims of 'tough' adjustment policies. It is to be hoped that such possibilities will be actively explored and not allowed to fall victim to any bureaucratic division between food aid and financial agencies (or within the UN system between World Food Programme/UNICEF versus IBRD/IMF).

A second desirable and likely development is the increasing concentration of food aid on Sub-Saharan Africa. The net import needs of Sub-Saharan Africa have rapidly increased and all the projections are for further increases in the future: per caput food production has actually fallen and its revival will be a long-term business which for some time to come will require additional aid including food aid. At the same time Africa also carries the heaviest debt burden and is most affected by the weaknesses in primary commodity prices.

While attention is focused on the big debts in Latin America, the debt service ratio (which measures the percentage of export earnings swallowed up by debt service) is actually even higher in Sub-Saharan Africa.

Thirdly, and related to a concentration on Africa, one may foresee a developing consensus on a broader definition of emergency. As already discussed, emergency aid represents the uncontroversial aspect of food aid. If we could extend our concept of emergency to include prevention at one end and rehabilitation at the other, it should be possible to provide a basis for substantial additions to present flows. The insight, which we owe largely to Amartya Sen (1981) from his work on famines, that famine is often caused not so much by real shortage of food but rather by a breakdown of incomes or other 'entitlements' providing access to food, should further support such protective and non-controversial extensions of food aid. For example rural public work schemes supported by food aid or by the proceeds of counterfunds from food aid, would be well designed to maintain rural incomes; they could be planned so as to cover specifically the 'hungry months' before the harvest and could be stepped up at times of crop failures.

A fourth line of development for expanded and improved uses of food aid in the future is through wider use of the potential of monetization. This trend is also clearly visible and offers considerable scope. We have already pointed out that by means of monetization in one form or other, food aid can be sold in urban areas while the revenue is used for rural investment, strengthening the demand for local food. Monetization is also very helpful in financing the non-food costs of food aid supported programmes such as emergency food aid, food-for-work schemes and feeding programmes for children. All these projects require financial as well as food resources but some of the food aid agencies, such as the World Food Programme, suffer from chronic shortages of cash and from restrictions on permitted monetization to raise cash from food aid. If this bottleneck on food aid could be lifted it would have great advantages. A related desirable development would be better linkages and combinations of financial and food aid, including better co-operation among the agencies concerned.

A fifth improvement would be the greater use of triangular transactions of the type already described. There are still a number of SCs with exportable surpluses. These countries are presently hard hit by the Common Agricultural Policy of the EU and similar policies in the US and Japan, and by the resulting low international food prices. Short of a revision of our own agricultural policies, it would be highly desirable for such surpluses to be bought at remunerative prices for use in deficit areas, perhaps combined with the establishment of regional buffer stocks in which such internationally financed regional surpluses could be held under international control. Such an imaginative approach could be supplemented by methods to encourage transfer of surplus food from surplus regions to deficit regions within individual SCs; this would require investment in transport as well as the encouragement of financing of local reserve stocks.

These are just some of the lines of possible future developments in the field of food aid. In conclusion however we must return to a basic concession to the critics of food aid: as long as food aid is badly administered by the donors and/or the recipients no real benefit can be expected. One basic pre-condition is the creation of a good framework on the part of donors, ideally including a revision of our agricultural policies; food aid must be given for the right reasons to the right countries in the right way. Similar improvements are necessary on the recipients' side: food aid must be increasingly devoted to its two essential purposes which are to reduce poverty and to help develop domestic food production.

7. Lomé: from contractuality to conditionality

THE HISTORY OF LOMÉ: A MIRROR OF NORTH-SOUTH RELATIONS

The EEC's approach to development co-operation with the group of ACP states (countries in Africa, the Caribbean and the Pacific) is unique in several respects. Co-operation under Lomé deserves a more detailed discussion because of its special features, most notably the STABEX and SYSMIN schemes, the changes from Lomé I to Lomé IV and its foreseeable demise, which mirror the changes in the political environment of North-South relations very clearly.

While not accommodating the South's demands for a New International Economic Order in the 1970s, the first treaty, Lomé I, was very progressive, taking into account many demands of the South. Therefore even critics who considered Lomé I not a good arrangement must concur that it was the best a group of SCs ever got from any group of donors. It combined aid and trade aspects. The pronounced emphasis on equality between Northern and Southern partners resulted in an unprecedentedly strong SC position under Lomé. This is most clearly documented by the fact that compensatory payments for fluctuations in export earnings of some commodities (the STABEX scheme) were introduced as a contractual right of ACP countries, very much like insurance payments.

Lomé II already saw a slight shift towards greater influence by the European donor side, a tendency strongly accentuated during the 1980s, as Lomé III and IV document. The present mid-term examination of Lomé IV, which allows changes in the duties and obligations initially agreed on under Lomé IV, marks another big shift in favour of donors. The history of Lomé illustrates very well the deterioration of donor attitudes during the last two decades, the worsening position of the South and the loss of whatever power they might have had during the 1970s.

Paradoxically the roots of Lomé lie in the colonial past of some EEC member states, most notably France. When the EEC treaty was signed in Rome in 1957 several members of the new economic community were still colonial powers. Since they had no intention of severing economic links with their colonies the Treaty of Rome contained clauses (Art. 131 et seq.) to link these colonies with the Community and the first European Development Fund (EDF 1) was established. Naturally the colonized were not asked for their approval.

At the beginning of the 1960s, when many African countries became independent, the nature of this association had to be altered and an international agreement became necessary. The first Agreement of Yaoundé was signed between the Six (original EEC members) and 18 newly independent African states. It abolished tariffs and trade barriers for nine agrarian commodities and reduced them for other products except for those considered sensitive (that is whose production was of interest to EEC agricultural policy). Provisions for capital movements and locations of firms were included and financial aid by EDF 2 and the European Investment Bank was agreed on. In return European exports had to be granted preferential treatment – or 'reverse preferences' – by the Yaoundé countries.

Other developing countries complained about massive trade diversions due to Yaoundé. This led to the Arusha Agreement with Kenya, Tanzania and Uganda, which was less generous than Yaoundé I but the first breakaway from the strong concentration on francophone Africa. Yaoundé II invited all African states with 'structurally similar' economies to join. Mauritius did.

Reverse preferences were heavily criticized by the US and the UK, worrying about their export markets. Britain ceased her attacks when she decided to become a member of the Community. Britain's accession, more precisely her relation to the Commonwealth, made new arrangements necessary. Negotiations were launched in July 1973 and their outcome was signed on 28 February 1975 in Lomé, the capital of Togo.

Under the UK Treaty of Accession, Asian Commonwealth countries were not offered association. There was only a declaration of intent to seek 'appropriate solutions' for problems that might arise in the field of trade. Although it is difficult to prove the real reasons behind this decision one may safely assume that France might have objected to the integration of all former British colonies into Lomé I. Integrating Asian countries into the associative system would have further diminished the concentration of aid on former French colonies– a concentration hardly to the detriment of the French economy. The US, never in favour of any European attempts to maintain colonial ties, saw Asia and Latin America as its main spheres of influence. The ACP group of Lomé I might have been a viable compromise within the enlarged Community of Nine as well as with Washington. The treaty still concentrated mainly, but less exclusively, on Sub-Saharan Africa (relatively few and small countries outside Africa signed) without abolishing the dominating influence of francophone states.

LOMÉ I: A GOOD ATTEMPT AT PARTNERSHIP

While the treaty comprises many provisions on development co-operation, STABEX is certainly its core and best known part, although the amounts allotted to this programme were only 11.6 per cent of total funds. Initially the scheme covered agrarian products such as groundnut products, cocoa products, coffee and coffee extracts, coconut and palm products, tea, fresh bananas, timber, sisal, cotton, hides and skins, but also iron ore and pyrites.

For the first time in history STABEX granted ACP countries a legal right to transfers for the purpose of stabilizing export earnings under Lomé I. A certain proportion of total funds was set aside for this purpose. Each ACP country was entitled to transfers if export revenues of STABEX products from exports to the Community fell by at least 7.5 per cent (6.5 per cent in the case of sisal) below the moving average of the preceding four years (fluctuation threshold) and the product concerned amounted to at least 7.5 per cent of export earnings (dependency threshold). For LLDCs, landlocked and island countries (LDLICs) these thresholds were 2.5 per cent. Most ACP countries fell into one of these three groups. Transfers were given as interest free loans to be repaid when export earnings recovered, except for LDLICs where they were grants. The percentage of grants was usually high, as much as 100 per cent in 1977. As in the case of insurance payments the country was free to decide how to use the money, the recipient's only and merely formal obligation being information concerning its use. STABEX was administered in a very co-operative way – demands for transfers were accepted after the deadline, or another reference system was applied in a case where drought had severely diminished export earnings during the four preceding years. Although small, the amount allocated to STABEX was sufficient under Lomé I. It no longer was during Lomé II.

Particularly after the political backswing of the 1980s it is important to stress the uniqueness of this entitlement to compensation. The decision to stabilize incomes rather than prices – which the Group of 77 had demanded in the debate on the Common Fund to stabilize commodity prices – reflected the North's position. Nevertheless no other donor has been prepared to grant similar concessions. Naturally STABEX was created to cover EEC-ACP trade, but exceptions (covering all exports) were possible. The EEC thus corrected the effects of its trade cycle on the ACP group by compensating for losses in earnings. Although it allowed exceptions, it declined to cover exports to all destinations generally. As an EEC official explained, entrepreneurs do not pay social security contributions for workers not on their payroll (Friedeberg 1975, p. 694). However Brussels proposed a global STABEX-like system, at least for SCs classified as LLDCs by the UN, inviting other industrialized countries to finance it jointly. No other industrialized country was willing to do so. The EEC finally introduced a similar system for those few LLDCs not signatories of Lomé, under the name of COMPEX. Its resources remained quite limited, as did its effects on beneficiaries. Nevertheless it was a unique attempt by a donor to establish a global export revenue insurance scheme for poor countries.

STABEX was criticized by both left and right. Champions of the 'free market' interpreted it as the first sign of dawning global interventionism, or decried the high concessionality of STABEX funds as a dangerous deviation from the market mechanism. On the other hand Arghiri Emmanuel (1976), widely known because of his model of unequal exchange, called STABEX an 'alibi of exploitation', attacking specifically the moving averages as a means to define reference levels of export earnings. He pointed out that this will reduce transfers progressively when the trend of export revenues is falling. This is quite true.The transfers were introduced to stabilize revenues but by no means to change existing trends. The reason was to preserve market conformity. All too familiar from their own agricultural policy with the problems of petrifying structures, Europeans insisted on smoothing out trends rather than guaranteeing a certain income level forever.

Nevertheless STABEX was also criticized for its disincentive to industrialization due to the fact that only (some) agrarian commodities plus iron ore enjoyed this kind of income insurance. This, it was argued, would encourage ACP countries to specialize unduly on STABEX products, which were either unprocessed or semi-processed raw materials. While transfers guaranteeing constant revenues – as suggested by Emmanuel – would have offered even larger disincentives to diversify, this critique is to some extent valid. It should also be added that STABEX covers tropical timber, obviously not a prime measure to encourage the preservation of forests and the environment. On the other hand export stabilization has to focus on those commodities actually exported and ACP countries have never exported industrial products on a worthwhile scale. It is difficult to stabilize export earnings of potential or barely existing exports.

STABEX as well as Lomé were criticized for their small impact. The funds allotted to Lomé have been quite small in comparison with total ODA by EEC members. STABEX was also criticized as being worse than the IMF's Compensatory Financing Facility (CFF). Even though the CFF was largely unconditional at the outset – it is so no longer having fallen in line with other IMF drawings – this is simply wrong. The CFF has never offered interest-free loans or grants, in sharp contrast to STABEX.

Special regulations for bananas, rum and most notably sugar were laid down. The Sugar Protocol guaranteed a minimum price for sugar linked to the price of beet sugar within the EEC for a quota of roughly 1.22 million metric tons per year. This means that ACP exporters participated automatically in intra-EEC policies preserving European peasants' incomes, another unique feature. The practice of reverse preferences, heavily opposed by the US, was discontinued.

Finally institutions were created within Lomé with ACP countries treated as equal partners, such as the Council of Ministers (the highest authority in all problems arising from Lomé I), the Committee of Ambassadors (more or less an executive board), and the Consultative Assembly (nowadays the Joint Assembly). In all these institutions donors and recipients have the same number of seats. Informally however the economic and political leverage of the Nine actually financing the convention was much stronger. This leverage was not used against ACP countries by the Europeans.

FROM LOMÉ I TO LOMÉ IV: INCREASING EUROPEAN INFLUENCE

While Lomé I had been greeted with many cheers, Lomé II was much less enthusiastically received because it did not bring the same fundamental changes as those between Yaoundé and Lomé. The big innovation of Lomé II was SYSMIN, the SYStem for MINerals. Officially labelled 'Aid for Projects and Programmes' it covered copper and cobalt, phosphates, bauxite and alumina, manganese, tin, iron ore and pyrites from new sites. Pits already in operation continued to be covered by the more favourable STABEX transfers still given without any conditionality under Lomé II.

This prima facie surprising split of iron ores between the two schemes can be explained by diverging interests. The ACP group wanted an extension of STABEX to minerals, since some countries (such as Jamaica and Zambia) are highly dependent on such exports. The Europeans, wanting to control mineral exports much more closely, found minerals much too important for a scheme like STABEX. Thus SYSMIN was created, a system without the automaticity of STABEX. Programmes and projects have to be approved by the Commission. Europeans thought iron ore belonged logically to other minerals rather than to the agrarian products covered by STABEX whilst the ACP group fought against this deterioration of conditions for iron – the resulting compromise was two kinds of iron ore and pyrites.

An ACP country could apply for funds if its production or export capacities or its export revenues (from exports to the Community) have diminished or can be expected to diminish substantially. This may be as a result of natural or man-made disasters, or economic disasters such as a collapse in prices of the main export commodities. If export revenues fell short of the moving average of the last four years by at least 10 per cent and the share of the mineral in exports was at least 15 per cent during that period (10 per cent for LDLICs), the country had to suggest projects and programmes. These were financed by 40 year loans at 1 per cent interest (0.75 per cent for LLDCs) with a ten year grace period. However the sum is fixed and approved by the EEC Commission (Art. 54 of Lomé II), not by an EEC-ACP institution. This gave the Europeans a massive leverage on some ACP economies. The principle of participation under Lomé I starts being transformed into the principle of control.

The EEC did not try to conceal the reason for this change. Klaus Meyer (1980, p. 10), then Director General for development, stated quite frankly in the official EEC-ACP journal with regard to SYSMIN, that it:

> takes account of the heavy dependence of certain ACP states on exports of mineral raw materials and also of the supply interests of the Community. In contrast to STABEX there is no question of automatic application ... This new chapter in the Convention is intended to enable specific Community action ... to halt the dangerous decline in mining investment, particularly in Africa.

STABEX experienced minor changes under Lomé II. Some ten more items were included, both thresholds were reduced and repayment conditions made more favourable. The exceptionally steep decline of commodity prices at the beginning of the 1980s however proved too much for the system. In 1980 only 53 per cent of legitimate ACP claims could be covered due to financial restrictions. In 1981 available funds covered less than one-quarter initially, but financial manoeuvring finally allowed the payment of around two-thirds of established claims. This is hardly surprising because STABEX resources were calculated according to the much less pronounced income reductions before the 1980s. To deal with such steep declines either the amount of money would have had to be increased substantially or claims would have to be reduced. These 'difficult years' for STABEX resulted in a new Article 155 in Lomé III containing more detailed rules than Lomé II on how to reduce transfers if the total of legitimate claims exceeded STABEX allocations.

The tendency away from de facto unconditional balance of payments financing, characteristic of the original STABEX, was strongly reinforced by Lomé III. Characterizing it by a catchword, one may speak of a SYSMINization of the whole convention. STABEX was changed so thoroughly that it might be justified to talk of two schemes, the old one with automaticity and the new STABEX of policy dialogue introduced by Lomé III. As expected iron ore has disappeared from STABEX to be subsumed exclusively under SYSMIN, as the EEC had wished.

Strict control of the use of transfers as well as of all Lomé funds was introduced by the third treaty. In the words of Edgard Pisani (1985), then Commissioner for Development and the man whose ideas largely formed Lomé III, its mechanisms were designed to 'make the Convention clearer, more solid and stricter in its execution'. It was also found that 'the means and the will had to be better harnessed towards the objective of development' (ibid.)

For the objective of 'rendering them more effective in development terms', as the official EEC-ACP publication *The Courier* (no. 89, Jan–Feb 1985, p. 21) formulates it, a rather elaborate, not to say cumbersome, planning and execution system was established. These procedures demanded by the Europeans were founded on Pisani's idea of a dialogue on development policy, which should allow the better integration of aid within the framework of national development policies. Objectives such as self-reliance, regional co-operation, food security and cultural development should be fostered by optimal co-ordination. Microprojects, small undertakings at the grassroot level, should spread the benefits beyond the reach of large-scale projects. Pisani also hoped that this dialogue would allow Brussels to understand better the real needs of their partners.

Within the ACP group there was a great deal of scepticism about the European idea of elaborate co-ordination. The term 'policy dialogue', also used initially, strongly recalled the 'dialogue' with the IMF. Finally however: who pays the piper calls the tune.

The operation of Lomé III can be described in a simplified and schematic way as follows:

1. The Commission allots financial resources to each ACP state and provides any other relevant information.
2. The ACP state produces a draft indicative programme, which contains such items as priority development objectives, focal sectors for which EEC aid is considered the most appropriate, the most appropriate measures and operations for attaining these objectives, specific national projects and programmes designed to achieve them.
3. This draft is discussed between Brussels and the ACP state. The result of this discussion is the indicative programme adopted by agreement. It is binding on both the EEC and the ACP state. Revisions are possible; one revision has to take place during Lomé III. Programmes and projects (with exceptions such as emergency aid) have to be based on the indicative programme. Appraisals have to be made in close co-operation between the EEC and the country and result in a financing proposal.
4. The EEC's decision shall be taken on the basis of the financing proposal. It is drawn up by the relevant departments of the Community and may be amended to take account of comments by the ACP state. However the Community can refuse to adopt proposals. In case of disagreement the country may request that the matter be referred to either an ACP-EEC Committee composed on the basis of parity but without decision-making

powers (Art. 193 Committee) or a hearing by the Community's decision-making bodies. Pursuant to Art. 220(7), following such a hearing the 'relevant body of the Community' decides definitely whether to adopt or reject a proposal. The ACP state 'may forward any facts which may appear necessary to supplement the information available ... before the decision is taken.'
5. A timetable of commitments must be agreed on.
6. The Commission appoints a Chief Authorizing Officer to 'commit, clear and authorize expenditure and keep the accounts of commitments and authorizations' (Lomé III, Art. 226). But (s)he also approves proposals for the placing of a contract subject to the powers exercised by the delegate. In other words, Brussels has allocated these tasks to two European bureaucrats. (S)he can make necessary adaptations of arrangements subject to the powers exercised by the National Authorizing Officer.
7. Each ACP state has to appoint a National Authorizing Officer to represent the country in all operations. (S)he has to co-operate closely with the Commission delegate.
8. The Commission delegate (or a deputy resident if the delegate is appointed to several countries) in the ACP country has ample powers of surveillance ranging from the approval of invitations to tender dossiers to the endorsing of 'contracts, riders thereto and estimates, as well as payment authorizations issued by the National Authorizing Officer' according to Art. 228. Naturally the delegate has to prepare the financing proposals. Decisions on financing proposals are taken by the Community.

In effect a mechanism for intervention down to details is created by the third convention. It is however still hampered to some extent by the necessity of agreement with the ACP country. Nevertheless the Community can withhold funds and the principle that the donor decides can be clearly perceived in spite of all rhetoric on partnership and equality. The double-tracked procedures introduced by the Europeans seem well in line with Pisani's idea of a constant dialogue. The existence of institutions based on the principle of parity but without real powers to make decisions may indeed be conducive to dialogue. But the arrangements of Lomé III are hardly conducive to efficient management, even though Art. 225 demands that the execution of technical and financial co-operation shall be carried out with a minimum of administrative formalities, using simplified procedures, so that implementation can be rapid and efficient.

The effects on STABEX can be clearly seen by comparing the second and third convention. Art. 47 of Lomé II stated that the ACP country decides how to use STABEX resources, its only and merely formal obligation being to inform the Commission of the use of funds. Technically the ACP country was required to indicate the planned (probable) use when demanding the money, and to inform the Commission how it had actually been used. If the ACP country wished to use STABEX funds in sectors other than those producing exports covered by the scheme in order to diversify its economy, no justification was required in Lomé II.

By contrast Art. 157 of Lomé III demands 'substantial information on the loss of earnings [beyond necessary statistics] and also the programmes and operations to which the ACP State has allocated or undertakes to allocate the funds'. Art. 170 explains the term 'substantial information' and specifies that it has to be provided before the transfer agreement is signed. A report on the use of funds has to be submitted within a year. If questions on the use of funds by the Commission are not answered in time to their satisfaction they have the right to suspend subsequent transfers. Financing diversification measures with STABEX transfers must now be justified to the Commission. In the language of the convention the country must communicate reasons for this allocation if funds are to be used in another sector than that where the revenue losses occurred. The initial automaticity, or the insurance function against the ups and downs of the world market, is replaced by a conditional application for aid supported by detailed data and justifying information, a most substantial change to the disadvantage of ACP countries.

Lomé IV consolidates and continues this SYSMINization with minor changes. As an example, the Commission now finalizes the financing proposal and forwards it to the Community's decision-making body. ACP countries shall be given an opportunity to comment on any amendment of substance, which the Commission intends to make. The Chief Authorizing Officer approves the tender dossier before invitations to tender are issued, subject to the powers exercised by the delegate. The list of tasks of the delegate has grown slightly. A national Paying Agent is introduced to handle payments made under the convention.

Regarding STABEX and SYSMIN there are small changes too. The list of products covered has grown. Transfers under both titles are exclusively grants, in the case of SYSMIN to the country but not to the final borrower. The calculation period of STABEX compensation is changed to the six preceding years less the two years with the highest and lowest figures. The dependency threshold was lowered to 5 per cent (1 per cent for LDLICs, 4 per cent for sisal). The fluctuation threshold is abolished and a so-called excess clause is introduced instead, which means that the transfer basis must be reduced by 4.5 per cent (1 per cent in the case of LLDCs) to calculate the transfer. If STABEX resources turn out to be higher than claims at the end of the financial protocol, these deductions can be proportionately repaid to the ACP country. The reduction is waived for small sums in the case of LDLICs. This contrasts again with previous conventions where no such deduction was made but 1 per cent (Lomé II) or 2 per cent (Lomé III) was added to the difference between reference level and actual earnings to account for statistical errors and omissions.

Art. 186 of Lomé IV restricts diversification to 'appropriate productive sectors in principle agricultural, or for the processing of agricultural products'. This new limitation of industrialization options is a late vindication of the criticism that STABEX hinders diversification, which was not valid initially.

A comparable restriction was newly introduced into SYSMIN. A 'very detailed' analysis of 'the situation of the Community market in the products concerned' as well as 'of the possible implications ... for the competing mining products of Member States' must be made prior to any Community decision pursuant to Art. 217(2). However, the possible implications of non-implementation on the ACP country must also be included.

Formal inclusion of support for Structural Adjustment was an important innovation of Lomé IV. Interestingly this is done with clear criticism of the Bretton Woods approach. Even the text of the convention contains criticism of the BWIs: adjustment should be economically viable and socially and politically bearable; programmes should be adapted to the different situation in each country and sensitive to its social conditions, culture and environment, improve the social and economic wellbeing of the population as a whole, reinforce long-term development efforts, achieve greater economic diversification, and be realistic, flexible, and adapted to a country's management capacity; negative social effects should be softened from the outset, and particular attention shall be paid to vulnerable groups; the ACP country should be primarily responsible for preparing programmes. In short, this part of the convention reads like a compendium of criticisms of the BWIs. The subtle final touch is that Community support is in the form of grants, not loans. An ACP country need not have a reform programme approved by multilateral institutions in order to qualify. Their seal of approval though automatically means eligibility for Lomé resources.

The vice-President of the European Commission, Manuel Marin (1990a; 1990b), repeated these criticisms in two contributions to the *Courier* issue containing the text of Lomé IV. He expressed his confidence that Lomé IV could contribute to 'an improved conception and implementation of structural adjustment', after stating that 'a number of structural adjustment programmes were not successful or experienced serious difficulties' (Marin 1990a, p. 9). He also stressed the originality of Lomé's 'individual approach', demanding that 'lessons must be drawn from certain mistakes made in the past' (ibid.). He also points out though that the Commission can now co-ordinate better with other donors (1990b, p. 13).

The European Parliament expressed even stronger criticism. The report of its Committee on Development and Cooperation on Structural Adjustment (1992 p. 8) notes 'the substantial overall failure of the "first generation" structural adjustment policies proposed by the IBRD and the IMF'. It called on the IMF to reconsider the very foundations of its Structural Adjustment policies in the light of their obvious inadequacy, and even demanded a new 'European approach' to Structural Adjustment different from the Bretton Woods variety.

The Directorate General VIII has indeed tried to influence BWI practice and to implement an alternative adjustment model in the case of Surinam, an endeavour which met stiff resistance by the BWIs. However the resources of DG VIII remained limited. After a change in the position of Director General such attempts to influence and change BWI programmes were discontinued. Presently Brussels supports the BWI model as strongly as the EU's member states do in Washington. The shift 'from contractuality to conditionality' (German and Randel 1994, p. 133) has occurred.

LOMÉ IV: ENDING THE SYSTEM OF PARTNERSHIP?

In contrast to the first three conventions Lomé IV was concluded for ten years, commencing on 1 March 1990 although its financial protocol was to be renegotiated after five years. Pursuant to Art. 366(3) this negotiation can be used to demand changes of the convention itself. This possibility of a mid-term review is used by the EU to revamp the Lomé system substantially.

The experience of rather limited results of Community aid – the Commission (1992) speaks of 'mediocre results' – has led to severe criticism of Lomé. It is true that Lomé has not been able to stop the marginalization of SSA or to increase trade ties between the EU and the ACP group, but its means have always been quite small. The first financial protocol of Lomé IV for instance amounts to 12 000 million ECU for five years, or 2400 million ECU per year. Compared with total ODA flows from DAC members of $56.7 billion in 1991 or $60.4 billion in 1992 (OECD 1994) this is not overwhelming. Fluctuating a little with the dollar/ECU exchange rate this was around 5 per cent of total DAC ODA or about 10 per cent of total ODA by EU members. The share of STABEX, an institution meeting particularly strong scepticism (Bossuyt et al. 1993), is 12.5 per cent of all Lomé funds, less than 1 per cent of total DAC ODA. Remembering that total ODA itself is only a small percentage of flows such as trade, expecting substantial impacts from either Lomé or STABEX is unwarranted. Comparing these resources with the funds flowing into Eastern Germany since re-unification and their results so far, renders such expectations absurd.

Putting Lomé into a more global perspective by comparing these sums with EEC ACP trade or the effects of protectionism in the North are very much justified. The impact of EU aid may be and actually is often reduced or cancelled by measures in other fields. In technical terms this is referred to as lack of 'coherence'. German and Randel (1994, p. 135) illustrate this point with the example of subsidized beef exports to West Africa. The EU has spent more than 400 million ECU in the last decade in order to reduce its beef surpluses. In doing so it has undermined EDF support for beef production in the region which was also financed by the taxpayer. Fairness demands to add that export practice was changed. When European NGOs started a campaign against subsidized beef exports in 1993 the Commission reacted. 'Under growing pressure by NGOs, media and Parliamentarians' (Commission 1994) the situation was assessed and export subsidies were cut several times. Art. 130(v) of the Maastricht Treaty demanding coherence between trade and development policies was expressly quoted as particularly important in the Commission's document.

No one could say that everything within Lomé is perfect at present. The strict allocation of funds to each country for instance makes the system inflexible. If a country practically dissolves due to civil war, the money might even be blocked since no one can present the necessary plans.

The so-called Post-Fiji study, an evaluation of EU ACP development co-operation by Price Waterhouse (1992), shows severe shortcomings and inefficiencies both within ACP countries and with the EU. Considering the elaborate framework introduced by Lomé III this was to be expected. But different views between donor and recipient may also lead to a deadlock which cannot be solved in the traditional manner by donor-decision, due to the still relatively participatory structures. Contrasting the two fundamental relationships of donor/agency power (illustrating the former *inter alia* with the IBRD) and partnership under Lomé the study summarizes with great clarity:

> We do not make any value judgements here as to the relative merits of the differing systems. They represent different approaches to the provision of aid and have developed accordingly. Centralised or donor dominated systems may be faster but risk imposing a solution that may not be the most suited to local circumstances. Conversely, a decentralised system in which significant weight is given to obtaining local agreement and consent carries with it the risk that progress will be slow. (Price Waterhouse 1992, para. 179)

The expert report formulates equally clearly that the nature of the partnership envisaged under Lomé is a fundamental difficulty. Its co-operative nature means that different views taken by the Commission and national administrations do not allow the Commission the freedom of action bilateral donors enjoy (ibid. paras 195 ff). Thus the principle of partnership creates problems absent in a command-obey relationship.

Although the Post-Fiji study was only meant to examine causes of delay, not as a full audit of the system, it was used by the European side to erode participatory structures further in their favour, while little emphasis, if any, has been put on tackling inefficiencies on the European side. These are by no means less serious than on the ACP side. Examples are differing interpretations of the formal procedures between Brussels and the delegation, problems of communication between them both in terms of comprehension (such as unclear or misunderstood questions) and of physical adequacy (such as slow transmission of documents) or insufficient knowledge of procedures in Brussels and at the delegations (not only in ACP countries).

The most important points demanded by Brussels (no similar list of proposals from the ACP side exists) were:

- an *essential elements clause* allowing the partial or total suspension of the convention in the event of serious violation of the principles of democracy, human rights or the rule of law;
- the sum earmarked for an ACP country under the national indicative programme should be paid out in two separate tranches. The second tranche should be conditional upon the country's performance as well as 'the situation in each ACP State' (*The Courier*, no. 144, March–April 1994, box on p. 6). As the *Courier* remarks 'There is some uncertainty over what this exactly means' (ibid.), but it goes in the direction of IMF conditionality. The changed attitude towards BWI activities makes this highly likely;
- the political dialogue should be reinforced;
- more competences, already at the preparation stage, for the Commission in the areas of financial and technical co-operation. Examples are sole responsibility for carrying out studies, or dealing directly with tenderers. This is believed to permit easier comparison of proposals and to enable the Commission to use its knowledge of markets to negotiate directly and untroubled by outside interference. Given EU export interests this is not unlikely to affect trade. More financial and other leverage for Brussels is sought.
- STABEX is to be used more fully for purposes related to BWI-type Structural Adjustment. In view of insufficient funds it is seen as a necessity to reduce compensation claims as much as possible; consultations on reductions are thought to have merely a token value.
- more powers for the Chief Authorizing Officer, and a reduction in the powers of the National Authorizing Officer
- the Joint Assembly must consist of elected members from their na-

tional legislatures. At present this is not an obligation and ACP countries are often represented by diplomats, who after serving in that capacity for a long time have often acquired useful inside and procedural knowledge. New people would naturally be less familiar with such important matters.

The fact that the Commission has already suspended aid to several ACP countries shows a resolve to intervene (German and Randel 1994, p. 133). Multi-annual guidelines adopted for aid to Asia and Latin America to facilitate planning and implementation may indicate that some mechanisms of Lomé IV – in contrast to its participatory components – are valued in Brussels.

To understand the seriousness of the EU's demand for democracy and for parliamentary institutions, we may quote the report on the way the item 'mid-term review' was dealt with under time pressure by the Joint Assembly at Strasbourg:

> As stated earlier, the proceedings at this stage were difficult to follow. No fewer than 91 amendments had been tabled to the interim resolution and these were only made available in French and English at a very late stage. Indeed, the session had to be suspended for an hour in order to allow members the opportunity to read the texts. When voting finally began, Mrs *Cassagnmagnago Cerretti*, the presiding [European] co-president, proceeded at breakneck speed. Each time, as the rules require, the rapporteur [a European] was asked for her view (for or against) and on each occasion her opinion appeared decisive, with the Assembly adopting amendments that she accepted and rejecting those that she opposed. Everything was going smoothly until amendment number 69 by Mr *Saby* which proposed the insertion of a new paragraph 50a. At this point it was discovered that there were two English texts of the resolution in circulation – and that the numbering of the paragraphs had diverged at paragraph 50. Thereafter it was difficult to believe that everyone present actually *knew* what they were voting for (or against) since, for many, the remaining amendments could no longer be matched to the paragraphs in the draft resolution. Despite this apparently fundamental flaw, drawn to the attention of the Chair by Mr Verhagen, Mrs Cassagnmagnago Cerretti pressed ahead with the voting and the resolution, as amended, was finally agreed by 59 votes to five with seven abstentions.
>
> The important question, of course, is what the Joint Assembly actually decided at the end of this confused session.
> (*The Courier*, no.144, March–April 1994, p. 7; emphases as original)

According to the EU these fine and democratic procedures obviously demand that only parliamentarians from representative assemblies participate. As a footnote it should be mentioned that the European Parliament, though consisting of elected members, lacks real legislative powers.

Thus the co-operation under Lomé has been transformed from a very progressive approach based on partnership to a traditional power relation.

The EU has become more and more a 'normal donor', though a donor equipped with more than the normal means of control. Historical evidence clearly shows that this evolution was not planned from the beginning. In contrast to Lomé IV, Lomé III appears to have still been guided by a desire for discussion, participation and equality.

In spite of substantial transformation according to European wishes the whole Lomé system is unlikely to survive. Shifts in the interests of EU member states such as 'the political and economic imperatives on the eastern and Mediterranean flanks of the EU' (UN 1995, p. 133) or the desire to develop closer ties with emerging Asian markets and with Latin America (particularly pushed by Spain), have made the EU lose its former interest in the ACP group.

The protracted and sharp wrangling on the second financial protocol of Lomé IV (EDF VIII) and its sobering result show a clear orientation away from Lomé. One may doubt in fact whether the present result would have been obtained without the existing contractual obligation to renegotiate. In mid-1995 the EU agreed at the Cannes Summit on ECU 13.3 billion (12.9 billion of which is new money), an increase of just 7.5 per cent. As this nominal increase would be more than wiped out in real terms by an annual inflation rate of 1.5 per cent over five years, this means a reduction in practice, although the EU increased its financial capacity by the accession of three new members. By contrast, aid to the former East and to the southern Mediterranean rim was significantly increased.

The fact that Lomé is not financed from the budget but directly by members may also have contributed. It is believed that this provided an opportunity to draw back from the consequences of the decision to increase external spending by up to 6 per cent annually in real terms for the rest of the decade, a decision taken at the Edinburgh Council meeting in December 1992. It was felt that savings in the off-budget EDF can 'offset' increases in budgetary aid. The UK objected to EDF increases for instance, arguing that about 40 per cent of the UK aid budget would then be under EU control (UN 1995, p. 133). This argument must be analysed more closely. Mathematically of course the non-EU share of a member with stagnant or declining bilateral aid spending decreases if EU aid grows. But the same is valid for any multilateral contribution. If the decision to reduce or stop bilateral aid is an autonomous decision by the country, it is almost absurd to speak of external control of that country's aid budget.

Last but not least there appears to exist little desire to preserve and reform the Lomé system, which still contains an element of partnership or, put less diplomatically, restraint on donor decisions. Lomé V is very unlikely to be signed.

8. Japan, the emerging aid giant

DAI ICHI – BECOMING NUMBER ONE

The main events of 1989, a political and historic watershed year, are summed up by Islam (1991a, p. 1) quite pointedly: 'as Washington celebrated the collapse of communism in Europe, Tokyo raced to become the unchallenged Santa Claus for the world's poor and needy.' After graduating from a major recipient of IBRD funds to its largest source of finance – in 1987 Japan was the largest contributor to multilateral agencies – the country finally became the world's largest source of ODA.

This evolution is remarkable in three respects. First, Japan 'transformed itself from an aid-recipient to an aid-giver in a very short span of time' (Ozawa 1989, p. 97). Its graduation from a country rehabilitating its 'economic infrastructure and factories with US financial assistance' (Kinoshita 1993, p. 120) to the main source of ODA is a unique experience. Yanagihara and Emig (1991, p. 40) identify the year 1964 as the threshold between recipient and donor status when Japan shifted to Article 8 status in the IMF, that is when it agreed not to use foreign exchange restrictions for balance of payments adjustments. Second, Japan is, as the Japanese Ministry of Foreign Affairs puts it, the 'first country with a non-European background to succeed in modernising, then becoming one of the leading ODA ... donor countries' (Healy 1991, p. 101). Third, the Japanese views on development and the role of aid differ significantly from donors with a European background. As the country is a successful late developer, its perception appears to be of particular interest to SCs, whose economic and political environment resembles Japanese conditions much more strongly than the historical experience of other OECD members. But in contrast to other donors the Japanese have not encouraged recipients to become culturally similar to them (Kinoshita 1993, p. 119). These special features, as well as the sheer volume of Japanese aid and the fact that relatively little is known of Japan's ODA internationally, justify a closer look at this donor.

For the sake of fairness it must be added that Japan's information policy is comparatively liberal. According to Nuscheler (1994) no other donor publishes so much nor such detailed information on its activities. He sees a sharp contrast to the US and Germany, concluding that 'if the German public were allowed to see in writing how many projects financed by the BMZ [Federal Ministry of Co-operation] go to Siemens, "criticism of aid" would be a great deal stronger'.

Japan's Overseas Economic Co-operation Fund (OECF), to quote just one example, publishes information on its activities in English, French and Spanish, as well as in Japanese. Its Annual Report (OECF 1994, pp. 158ff) contains a special table 'Principal Contractors under OECF Loans to Foreign Governments' for the last fiscal year, with occasionally over a dozen names for one project, indicating the countries where these firms come from and whether they are consulting firms. Such detailed information is by no means normal donor behaviour. On the other hand NGOs demanded an 'information access policy at least matching the World Bank's' in an open letter to the Prime Minister in September 1995.

In 1989 Japan became the world's biggest ODA source in absolute (dollar) terms – number one, or *dai ichi*, as this would be expressed in Japan – spending some 16.8 per cent more than the US for the first time (OECD 1992, p. A-35). This is a truly historic turning point. While traditionally trailing far behind in terms of ODA as percentages of GNP, the US had always been the most important source of ODA measured in dollars or as a share of the DAC total after World War II until that year. Being overtaken by Japan as the world's Number One might have been one reason why the US tried to get military debt cancellations recognized as ODA by the DAC.

By including debt forgiveness of non-ODA claims, which were quite important sums in the case of the US particularly with regard to military debts, the US defended its position as top donor of the 1990s in DAC statistics until forgiveness of military aid was finally excluded in 1993 (OECD 1995, p. 74) and Japan ranked first again. Without the inclusion of reductions in military debts Japan would have ranked first in 1992 and 1991 (Takayanagi 1993, p. 32) as well. Recently the strong yen was, no doubt, also an important factor boosting Japanese aid expressed in dollars.

Like the US, Japan has never reached the DAC average expressed in percentages of GNP, although it has always been much closer to it than the US. In 1993 for example Japan's ratio was 0.26 per cent, the DAC average 0.30 per cent and US ODA 0.15 per cent. Japan followed the decline in DAC aid though. In 1991, when the DAC average was 0.33 per cent, Japan's ODA amounted to 0.32 per cent (OECD 1995, p. A10). Compared with small donors such as Denmark, Sweden or Norway, all of which allocated more than 1 per cent of their GSPs as ODA in 1992, both big donors are rather tight-fisted.

INSTITUTIONS OF ECONOMIC CO-OPERATION

The responsibility for aid is widely dispersed, rendering the Japanese ODA system rather complex. Sixteen ministries and agencies are involved in economic co-operation (Goto 1992, p. 65; Healy 1991, p. 112). Four ministries however are the most important decision makers: the Ministry of Foreign Affairs, the Ministry of Finance, the Ministry of International Trade and Industry (MITI) and the Economic Planning Agency. Although theoretically serving as a co-ordinator, the Economic Planning Agency's role has been limited. Three main government institutions implement development co-operation: the Japan International Co-operation Agency (JICA), the Overseas Economic Co-operation Fund (OECF) and the Export-Import Bank (JEXIM).

Initially named Export Bank of Japan and catering exclusively to Japanese exports JEXIM was established in 1950 to facilitate 'through financial aid Japan's economic interchange, mainly in the field of foreign trade, with foreign countries' as the very first Article of the EXIM Bank Law stated (Ohlin 1966, p. 49). Fully government owned, it may be seen as the chief implementing agency for concessional yen loans in the early days and the oldest instrument of Japanese aid. Neither focused on the South nor on ODA, it had seldom supplied untied loans before 1986. Nowadays its export credits account for as little as some 15 per cent (Agata, 1994), while it also finances development projects and economic policies in SCs with untied loans, extends credits for Japanese foreign direct investments and import credits at preferred interest rates for imports of raw materials and manufactured products to Japan. Launched in 1983 as part of the government's policy to adjust balance of payments surpluses, import credits are not restricted to domestic firms, but are also available to foreigners exporting to Japan.

In 1961 the Overseas Economic Co-operation Fund (OECF) was established as a source of development loans. Its specific aim was to provide loans to SCs on softer terms than JEXIM. Wholly owned by the Japanese government the OECF borrows at low interest rates from the postal savings scheme and social security funds, and issues government guaranteed bonds. Since the fiscal year 1979 the Fund is legally permitted to borrow three times the amount of capital and reserves. In addition to SC governments it also lends to Japanese corporations engaged in the South or takes equity in them. Its softest terms are very close to IDA credits (Healy 1991, p. 128).

On 14 March 1995 the Japanese government decided to effect a merger of JEXIM and the OECF in four years, as well as to slim down JEXIM's credit operations by limiting them to exports to SCs. This decision was preceded by an escalating political battle over state financial institutions, taxes and public spending between the Liberal Democratic Party and the smallest coalition member, the New Harbinger Party. Both multilateral institutions and recipient countries urged the government not to break up JEXIM. During this debate, which was quite unusual by Japanese standards, JEXIM defended itself against accusations of inefficiency by pointing out that it 'lends $15bn a year, almost as much as the World Bank itself, but with a tenth – 550 people – of the Washington-based bank's staff' (*Financial Times*, 23 February 1995). Even considering the high ratio of co-financing with multilateral institutions (well over 50 per cent) which might help reduce administrative work, this is a rather impressive comparison not to JEXIM's disadvantage.

The Overseas Technical Co-operation Agency (OTCA) was founded in 1962 to administer parts of Japan's technical assistance. OTCA's technical assistance was initially recorded under the same heading as export promotion (Ohlin 1966, p. 49). In 1974 it was incorporated into JICA, which operates under the aegis of the Ministry of Foreign Affairs. As its two full-time executive directors are appointed from among the directors of JEXIM and from the OECF with the recommendations by the respective presidents, it is administratively linked to these other two institutions (Healy 1991, p. 126). It, too, is wholly owned by the government. Its funds are split into a grants and an investments budget from the Ministry of Foreign Affairs, as well as a trust budget from MITI. Its activities include technical co-operation, volunteers (similar to the US Peace Corps), recruitment and training of Japanese personnel, capital grants, soft loans (to the Japanese private sector in SCs) or services to immigrants.

THE CONCEPT OF 'ECONOMIC CO-OPERATION'

Although the DAC convened on a clearly defined terminology and Japan reports its flows according to these definitions, it has frequently been criticized that the distinction between aid and other flows is blurred. Hanabusa (1991, p. 96) remarks pointedly: 'Very few individuals, even in the aid officialdom, can tell what constitutes ODA and what does not.' According to Ozawa (1989, pp. 98f) Japan seems to regard any flow to SCs as 'aid', an attitude shared by all donors before Myrdal's critique of what passed as aid. On 14 March 1995, when the government announced the decision to merge JEXIM and the OECF, it also announced measures to establish clear distinctions between ODA and non-ODA.

The expression 'economic co-operation' (経済協力, *keizai kyoryoku*) seems to be more popular in Japan than 'aid' (援助, *enjo*). It encompasses almost all activities considered helpful to economic development, without distinguishing between official and private, commercial and non-commercial funds. This predilection might either be traced to what Ozawa (1989, p. 98) calls the concept of 'mutually beneficial economic assistance' or to what Goto (1994,

p. 8) calls 'comprehensive economic cooperation'. This is 'not just aid, but trade, investment, finance and science and technology in a broad approach' (ibid.). He also speaks of an 'active linkage' (ibid., p. 10) of aid, investment and trade. One might reformulate Goto, saying that Japan has apparently a very coherent view of development.

Close co-operation between the government and the private sector is thus characteristic of Japan's development co-operation. Ozawa (1989, p. 99) speaks of three basic components, budget determined official flows, market determined private flows, and hybrid flows, that is joint financing by the government and the private sector. The author calls this third type 'a unique feature of Japan's assistance that most sharply differentiates it from the other industrialized countries'. Historically quite substantial amounts of private funds have been mobilized in co-operation with official institutions. This connexion also shows in administrative structures. The OECF for example administers both ODA and Other Official Flows (OOF), and makes loans to and equity investments in private Japanese firms if projects are deemed to qualify as economic co-operation through the private sector. Or MITI proposed to expand its investment insurance facility with ODA funds to promote private capital flows (Yanagihara and Emig 1991, p. 57).

Kinoshita (1993, p. 119) calls Japan's aid 'economically orientated', that is higher priority is given to support economic development as opposed to 'commercially motivated', defined as strongly influenced by domestic commercial interests. He illustrates economic orientation by 'the frequent assertion of Japanese decision makers that ODA terms should be decided in the light of the development stage of recipients, and that a relatively higher share of loans might be allocated to infrastructure' (ibid., p. 121). The small number of development co-operation staff is also an incentive to prefer large scale infrastructure projects, which results in high amounts of dollars per head that each staff member must administer. This is a considerable disincentive to engage in a large number of small projects rather than one big project. The rapid increase in volume during the recent years has certainly reinforced this mechanism.

Critics are of course eager to point out that 'economic orientation' does not exclude 'commercial motivation'. The predilection for large infrastructural projects is frequently the aim of criticism. It is implied that tying of aid is widespread in these projects, although DAC figures document that Japan is no more restrictive than other donors. This perception of Japanese aid as being mostly tied seems to be a remnant from the early post-war period when it was actually so. In the meantime many authors (Islam ed. 1991; Healy 1991; Kinoshita 1993) have shown that this is no longer valid. Tokyo has gone as far as supporting seminars which teach non-Japanese how to do business financed by Japanese aid (Bloch 1991, p. 73), which is no doubt exceptional. After two successful seminars on Japanese procurement, US AID's office of International Trade and Investment lost its one officer with any knowledge of Japanese aid and did not think it necessary to replace him/her (ibid., p. 85). It goes without saying that after more than a decade of bilateral consultations with Japan, US AID's office responsible for co-ordination had no one speaking Japanese or knowing Japan. Nevertheless the US has been quite outspoken in criticizing the lack of access of US firms to procurement financed by Japanese aid.

The recent yen revaluations have put Japanese exporters at a disadvantage. Nuscheler (1994, p. 13) reports that the Japanese embassy in Bangkok put the share of Japanese firms in OECF loans in Thailand at 1 per cent. The OECF has, incidentally, committed most of its loans untied and the small remainder 'partially untied' in the recent past (OECF 1994, p. 16).

For the sake of fairness one must add that Japan's own experience since the Meiji Restoration in 1860 and after 1945 – possibly best illustrated by the Shinkansen railroad project financed by IBRD loans at near market conditions – obviously influences the view that loans might be better than grants provided they do not result in too heavy a burden on the balance of payments. Concentration on Asian neighbours, which are generally richer SCs, might also have corroborated this view.

THE EVOLUTION OF JAPANESE AID

Foreign aid has been part of Japan's official policy since the mid-1950s, and the country was one of the original members of the Development Assistance Group formed in 1960. 'Grants accounted for a fairly large share of the Japanese bilateral flows in the early years' according to Ohlin (1966, p. 48), but 'most of these grants constituted of payments under reparations agreements.' Ohlin's wording mirrors the understanding prevalent in the 1960s that any North-South flow automatically qualifies as aid, including even reparations. It deserves mentioning that Japan did not only pay reparations for war damages but also for its period as a colonial power (Serfas 1987, p. 211 for the case of South Korea). This difference must be emphasized clearly because European countries or the US have always steadfastly refused to recognize that colonialism was an exploitative and destructive system. Quite often it has been claimed that colonial transformations modernizing 'backward regions' were of advantage to the colonized, even if colonies were de-industrialized. Consequently the West has always insisted that aid must not and cannot be seen as a form of compensation or reparation for damages inflicted by colonialism. Nevertheless the roots of Western aid lie in the colonial past.

Japan's economic assistance programme originated in the reparations it paid to Asian countries in the early post-war period. Ozawa (1989, p. 97) points out:

> These reparations served to rebuild and strengthen economic ties between Japan and the recipient countries throughout the 1960s. Japan felt obliged to countries like India, which magnanimously declined to accept war reparations, and it extended economic assistance in the form of special loans and technical assistance as soon as it was financially able to do so.

The concentration of aid on parts of Asia, though declining gradually, is still a highly visible legacy of the 1950s and 1960s as well as the result of security concerns for the region's political stability. The oil price increases of the 1970s directed more Japanese aid to countries producing important raw materials. Nevertheless Tokyo gave more aid to Sub-Saharan Africa than Washington at the beginning of the 1990s (Islam 1991b, p. 211).

India received aid from early on. In 1954 Japan joined the Colombo Plan (Council for Technical Co-operation in South and South East Asia), where India, Pakistan and Ceylon were regional members, as a donor. In 1958, when the India Consortium was created as a rescue operation to meet India's balance of payments crisis, Japan was one of the founding members (OECD 1985, pp. 66f). India has remained among the major recipients of Japanese ODA ever since, although its share has declined over the decades.

Given a chronic balance of payments deficit during the 1950s and the early 1960s, scarce foreign exchange and the initially precarious economic situation, Japan used 'reparation payments and what little it could offer as new avenues of trade' (Ozawa 1989, p. 98). Official aid was seen as a means to promote exports with rigidly tied and relatively hard loans. The Ministry of International Trade and Industry (MITI) regarded economic co-operation as the new axis of post-war trade policy, with SCs as potential future markets (Rix 1980, pp. 23f). Kinoshita (1993, p. 120) characterizes Japanese aid until the 1980s as 'literally commercial and in sharp contrast to the aid of most other industrial nations.' This orientation showed in a relatively low grant element. Although it improved between 1965, the first year for which the average grant element was calculated, and 1984, Japan had by far the lowest grant element in 1984, 12.3 percentage points below the recommended DAC norm of 86 per cent (OECD 1985, p. 107).

Figure 8.1 shows the concessionality and tying status of Japanese ODA as percentages of the DAC average (defined as 100 per cent) during the period 1992–93. Two interesting differences *vis-à-vis* the average donor emerge: to a significant degree Japanese ODA is both less concessional and less tied. Furthermore the share of 'partially untied', or 'LDC-untied' loans as the OECF (1994, p. 16) calls them, is significantly above the DAC standard

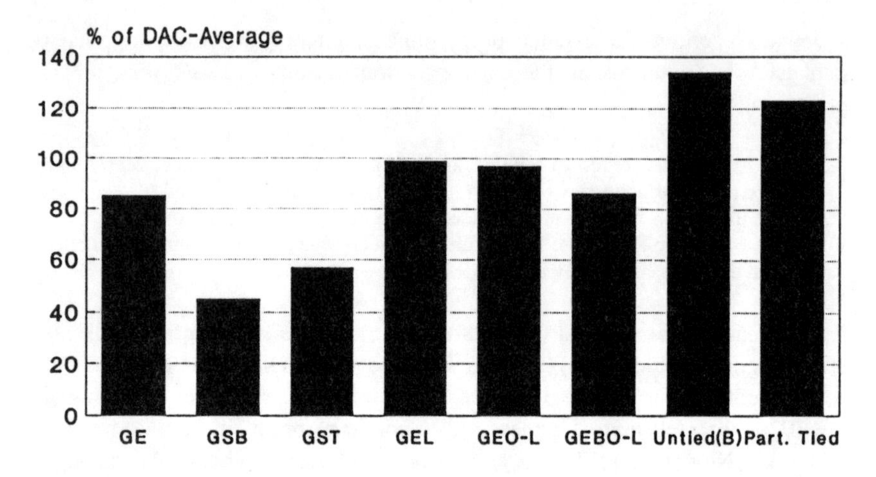

Notes:
DAC average for 1992 and 1993 = 100 per cent

GE	Grant element, total ODA
GSB	Grant share, bilateral
GST	Grant share, total ODA
GEL	Grant element, ODA loans
GEO-L	Grant element, ODA to LLDCs
GEBO-L	Grant element, bilateral ODA to LLDCs
Untied(B)	Share of untied bilateral ODA commitments
Part. Tied	Share of partially tied bilateral ODA commitments

Untied is defined as 'Fully and freely available for essentially world-wide procurement'. It is measured excluding administrative costs but including debt reorganization. Partially tied: contributions are available for procurement from the donor and substantially all SCs (also called LDC tied in Japan); data on tying status for the year 1992 only.

Source: OECD 1995

Figure 8.1 Terms of Japan's ODA, concessionality and tying, 1992–93

(OECD 1995). 'Partially untied' means that the money can be used for imports from the donor and 'substantially all developing countries' (ibid.). Finally Japan's bilateral ODA to LLDCs was relatively harder (the gap between its grant element and the DAC average wider) than its total aid to this group. Japan's bilateral ODA to LLDCs is of particularly low concessionality: 86 per cent compared with an average of 97 per cent for all ODA to LLDCs. This low grant element, originally resulting from Japan's commercial orientation, is justified nowadays on the grounds that repayable loans exert a discipline on the borrower to use the money efficiently, a discipline which is absent in the case of grants (Kono 1994, p. 14; Goto 1994, p. 8). The preference for loans over grants indicates a more businesslike approach. This does not necessarily mean that the recipient cannot benefit – it is in fact the essence of good business that all parties benefit – but partners still too weak to seize business opportunities need help instead.

Japan's low grant element results also from the way development co-operation is financed. Nuscheler (1994) points out that only half the OECF's resources are provided by the government. The other half is financed by tapping the postal savings system or pension funds, institutions which expect interest streams. Higher public contributions would be necessary to increase the grant element substantially, a solution disliked by the Ministry of Finance for budgetary reasons and which is not very likely to occur in the near future due to an increasingly critical public attitude towards ODA.

THE STEEP INCREASE IN ODA VOLUME

Although ODA doubling plans can be traced back to 1978 (Hirono 1991, pp. 173f), 1986 is often singled out as the take-off year of the steep increase in ODA and financial flows. In autumn 1986 ($10 billion) and in April 1987 before the Venice Summit ($20 billion) the government pledged a total of $30 billion in order to recycle part of the country's trade surplus. This package became known as the Capital Recycling Programme. The first $10 billion were channelled via IFIs, namely the IBRD, IDA, the Asian Development Bank (ADB) and the IMF (Kinoshita 1993, p. 122). The IBRD's Japan Special Fund to support technical assistance was established. The remaining $20 billion combined bilateral and multilateral financing. Establishing Japan Special Funds at the ADB and the IDB as well as funds for the IBRD, together with loans by the OECF and JEXIM were part of the $20 billion component (Yanagihara and Emig 1991, p. 65). The authors put the share of ODA at $4 billion, while the rest consists of other official and private flows.

Healy (1991, p. 107) remarks that the Recycling Plan 'evoked some scepticism because, in part at least, it is derived from a summation of ongoing programmes and a mere continuation of access to the Tokyo capital market' previously enjoyed by IFIs. It is not clear what exactly is supplementary over and above ongoing programmes. Islam (1991b, p. 199) calls recycling a 'catchall word' creating a great deal of confusion by covering all financial flows to the South although economic implications vary greatly. Grants do not recycle but reduce Japan's surplus, Islam remarks. Furthermore since a very substantial share of Japan's current account surplus is recycled to the US, 'redirecting' not recycling should be demanded.

By the end of June 1989 $28.5 billion had been committed and Japan announced a major expansion of the programme at the Arche Summit in July

1989, scaling it up to $65 billion over the quinquennium 1987–92, that is announcing an additional $35 billion.

On 25 June 1993 the government announced and launched a new programme, the Funds for Development initiative. It comprised the sum of approximately $120 billion for the quinquennium 1993–97, consisting of

- approximately $70 billion in ODA, provided in the form of untied yen credits (approximately $55 billion) and capital and other contributions to IFIs
- some $50 billion non-ODA, including $35 billion of finance provided by JEXIM and $10 billion of credits covered by the MITI's trade insurance programme (JEXIM 1993).

Financing 'environment related investments' is one of the main scopes of the funds administered by JEXIM. As Japan has earned itself an international reputation of high environmental standards at home and unrestrained environmental destruction in the South, this is a step in the right direction. During the first six months (July to December 1993) JEXIM committed $1.5 billion for ten 'cases', including guarantees for entirely private-sector funded loans to Greece and Venezuela and a short term 'bridge loan' to Vietnam for clearing arrears to the IMF (ibid.).

From additional explanation given by an executing agency, a main difference between the Funds for Development initiative and the Recycling Programme are the very names. While the latter indicates the pressure on Japan to make financial resources available to deficit countries, the name of the former clearly underlines a unilateral Japanese initiative for the benefit of the South. It documents a new more self-assertive role of the DAC's largest donor. This can also be seen by the way funds have been disbursed. Initially Japan channelled aid mainly through IFIs, but without trying to influence these institutions' policies perceptibly. The first $10 billion component of the Recycling Plan illustrates this very well. Now, a larger share of the new programme is administered by Japanese institutions and Japan has challenged IFI development perceptions.

The steep increase in financial flows to the South described above resulted directly from Japan's growing and increasingly strongly criticized balance of payments surpluses. The country was urged to react, particularly after German re-unification when Japan was left as the only important surplus country among OECD members. Deliberations as to how to reduce surpluses started on a massive scale. Drastic expansions of domestic demand and imports as well as increased flows to foreign countries, notably as aid, were recommended. Even a new island city built in the Bay of Tokyo was considered (Ozawa 1989, pp. 16f).

This pressure must be seen in the context of 'burden sharing'. The US had argued for quite some time that it contributed a disproportionate share of the burden of defending the West. Without comparable military expenditures other countries were said to enjoy a 'free ride'. During the 1980s Japan emerged as the main target of criticism, the 'top "unfair burden-sharer"' (Islam 1991b, p. 193), a point made particularly strongly during the Gulf War in the 1990s. This criticism was not entirely honest, but quite useful in making Tokyo 'pay up' generously for the Gulf War. It has been routinely and conveniently forgotten that the restrictions on military activities were not the country's own free choice.

Initially focusing on military spending alone, the US later started to refer to the costs of maintaining global peace and security by including foreign aid. This was possibly because Washington realized that it did not really wish Japan to increase military spending but preferred contributions of a non-military type. Not always without success the US tried to direct Japan's assistance according to its own priorities. As Islam (1991b, p. 196) puts it pointedly, 'Washington's foreign policy seems increasingly based on the principle of "take the yen and run the world"'.

Naturally, the US did not consider sharing political power with Japan, causing Islam to speak of a reverse free ride by the US exerting political power without shouldering the economic obligations associated with it. Japan on the other hand seemed willing to oblige the US with regard to aid, hoping to soften confrontations on trade issues.

Recycling Japanese money to problem debtors became an option rather popular outside the island empire. An IMF simulation using the Fund's Multimod-Model clarifies North American interest in Japan's aid. It shows that 'a $10 billion transfer from Japan to all SCs for one year would increase US exports by $2.26 billion, whereas an increase in fiscal expenditures of the same amount would result in increased US exports of only $620 million' (Sengupta 1988, p. 26). Moreover the transfer would also result in higher growth and more favourable balance of payments effects for the US, Germany and other major industrialized countries.

One may speculate to what extent the interest in recycling was influenced after 1982 by Washington's perception that Japan should perform the role played by IFIs in Latin America, where increased IFI inflows allowed (mostly US) commercial banks to receive higher debt service payments than otherwise possible and to withdraw partially from these countries. This resulted in higher shares of multilateral debts. Shifting larger shares of problem debts onto Japan as well would hardly have contradicted the policy of bailing out commercial banks via IFI exposure.

Apparently (and understandably) Japan was not prepared to pick up other people's problems. Rather than lending directly to problem debtors it channelled funds via IFIs. The relation between the so-called Baker Plan and the Recycling Programme is described by Kinoshita (1993, p. 124): 'The $10 billion recycling programme announced in 1986 was just to support it, an additional $20 billion programme following in 1987.' This 'Plan' describes the ideas of the US Treasury Secretary that Southern debtors would have to repay each cent of their debts, model their economic policies on the US example, and be subject to strict monitoring by IFIs in return for $29 billion in fresh money over three years to some 15 to 17 countries important to the US. Neither the exact number nor the names of 'Baker-countries' were known when the 'Plan' was presented. The amount of fresh money was noticeably less than debt service payments of either Brazil or Mexico alone.

After James Baker had become Secretary of State, the US administration's debt policy changed radically. Baker did not engage in debt policies any longer. *Time* magazine of 20 February 1989 claimed this was a result of 'the potential conflict posed by his holdings in Chemical New York Corp. , a bank that holds a significant amount of Third World debt'. The new Treasury Secretary, Nicholas Brady, presented another and historically remarkable plan. The US acknowledged for the first time that Southern debts could not be repaid fully, proposing debt relief – albeit only by commercial banks. Again Japan offered financial support. The expansion of the Recycling Plan to $65 billion in 1989 was aimed at increasing recycling efforts 'to support ... the Brady Plan' (Yanagihara and Emig 1991, p. 65). As Brady drew his ideas from a 'similar plan' (Kinoshita 1993, p. 125) proposed in 1988 by the Japanese Minister of Finance, Miyazawa Kiichi, one might say that Japan backed its own ideas financially. Nevertheless Miyazawa's initiative might be interpreted as a first departure from the previous policy of leaving the design of strategies for the South to others.

WHAT KIND OF MIRACLE IN ASIA?

The debate between Japan and the IBRD on appropriate development policies, which led to the IBRD study on East Asia (IBRD 1993), is an example of Japan's increasingly assertive role in international development co-operation. Comparing the elements of Structural Adjustment lending with both its own experience and that of successful East Asian economies, such as South Korea or Taiwan, Japan began to doubt the policies the Bank was forcing on debtor countries. In contrast to the strong anti-government bias and *laisser-faire* ideology of Structural Adjustment programmes, the 'miracle' in North-East Asia was achieved with substantial government intervention and within a framework of a wider industrial policy. Additionally Japanese aid had always been characterized by co-operation between a strong state and the private sector. Hanabusa (1991, p. 90) sums up this view very clearly:

> In the Japanese view, developing countries should manage and regulate their economies with the objective of achieving self-reliance as soon as possible. ... Also deeply embedded in Japan's philosophy of development is the idea that the public and private sectors must work not as adversaries, but as partners in development. Indeed, the countries that have succeeded in Asia have all embraced a policy of partnership between government and the private sector.

Both theoretically and with regard to practical success this approach is diametrically opposed to the ideology of state minimalism presently preached by the IBRD and other multilateral institutions. By the late 1980s Japan began to express disagreement with the IBRD. A dispute between the IBRD and its second largest shareholder over subsidized loans to assist private sector development, so-called 'Two Step Loans', highlights the basic differences between the two (Okuda 1992; Yanagihara 1992). The Bank insisted on the principle that credit should be extended on market terms. Drawing on its own and Korea's development experience, Japan believed that a directed credit policy is more effective under the conditions prevailing in South-East Asia. It might be of interest to add that Yanagihara sees Japanese decision makers as being heavily influenced by the German Historical School. Pragmatism instead of ideological creed is one further important distinction between Japan and the BWIs.

The difference between the two positions is drastically illustrated by Yanagihara (1992, p. 81), who reports that 'there is not even a word for "policy-based lending" in official parlance in Japanese ... official documents still use "commodity loan", the term long used to refer to Japan's emergency balance of payments support aid program'.

In an OECF occasional paper released in autumn 1991, officials of the Japanese government broadened their critique (Fishlow and Gwin 1994, p. 3). The paper argued that the government must adopt measures aimed directly at promoting investments to attain sustainable growth. These measures should be part of an explicit policy designed to promote leading industries of the future. Directed and subsidized credits should have a key role in promoting industries. This 'Proposal from a Major Partner' (to quote from the title of the OECF paper) was soon followed by a Japanese proposal to undertake a study of the East Asian development experience in order to document that successful development required a combination of market mechanisms and government intervention. Due to Japan's insistence and its readiness to finance, this study (IBRD 1993) was carried out. Its price tag was put at 'over $1.2 million' by Wade (1994, p. 56), but unofficially the study's costs are estimated to be much higher. Rumours have it that the East Asian miracle study has cost a lot more than $4 million.

The outcome might be considered predictable – 'the lessons of the East Asian success require virtually no modification of the Bank's recipe for development' (ibid.). It was conceded that 'Intervention resulted in higher and more equal growth than otherwise would have occurred' (IBRD 1993, p. 6). But the very next sentence warned: 'the prerequisites for success were so rigorous that policymakers seeking to follow similar paths in other developing economies have often met with failure' but did not specify which countries actually tried to copy Japan, South Korea or Taiwan. By enlarging the group of 'miracle countries' beyond South Korea and Taiwan the IBRD was able to detract a bit from the particularly refined mechanisms of intervention practised by Japan and these most successful cases. While the IBRD found that 'interventions did not significantly inhibit growth' in East Asia, it appeared 'difficult to establish causality' (ibid.) Having no such qualms with regard to its own liberalization ideology the IBRD recommended it wholeheartedly to other SCs as preferable to attempts to apply or adapt East Asian policies somewhere else. Truisms add to the length of the volume, for example: 'Fundamentally sound economic policies was a major ingredient in achieving rapid growth' (IBRD 1993, p. 5), or: 'It also teaches us that willingness to experiment and to adapt policies to changing circumstances is a key element of economic success' (ibid., p. 26). Finally the study stresses export push strategies, although it acknowledges that the conditions of market access will restrict this policy option (ibid., p. 25). Nevertheless such considerations on the North's willingness to allow substantially increased imports from SCs are not seriously considered. However the study obviously achieved the purpose of finding a compromise with Japan, without yielding to the idea of Japanese-type adjustment. Critics claim that it was perceptibly edited on its way up from researchers to the IBRD's higher echelons.

Although the results beg the question whether they could not have been produced more cost efficiently, it is not intended to go into details here nor into the criticisms of the study (for this see for example Fishlow et al. 1994; especially Wade 1994). The political meaning of this difference in opinions is much more important in the context of this book. Japan's debate with the IBRD stems from the Japanese perception of development and is a unique and extremely remarkable example of a donor's intellectual honesty. Seeing the glaring differences between their own experience or the policies of other late industrializing countries and the recipe of the BWIs, Japan spoke up, questioning their ideology. Although all Northern governments do in fact combine market mechanisms with government interventions, and none of them would even dream of applying to their own countries the same liberalization and adjustment policies forced on SCs, they have always supported the BWIs. Contrasting the Multi-Fibre Arrangement 'needed' by the North (see Chapter 2) with the demand that much less developed economies should adjust within an extremely short time reveals an unorthodox perception of honesty.

As the economic policies of industrialized countries are beyond the IBRD's or the IMF's reach, Japan also could easily have lived with the existing double standards for those controlling IFIs and those under their control. It could use subsidized and directed credits, also under the label of 'aid'. Speaking up on behalf of SCs – and indeed of the poorest people most severely affected by Structural Adjustment – the country differed from nearly all other donors. The lone exception was once the European Commission, more precisely its Directorate General VIII, which also tried to work out an alternative to present Structural Adjustment but could not find the necessary support among the EU's member countries, all of which strongly support the BWIs. It would have been interesting to see whether joint efforts by the DG VIII and Japan would have been able to challenge or even counterbalance the present political monopoly of the BWIs. Unfortunately for the South, these efforts were never joined.

THE NEGLECT OF POVERTY ALLEVIATION

Japan is strongly criticized for scoring low on support for human development and measures to alleviate poverty, or in sectors beyond its economic orientation. This is the most important shortcoming of Japanese ODA – a relatively pronounced lack of financial solidarity with the poorest. Compared with the low DAC average of 7.0 per cent of aid for human priorities as defined by the UNDP (basic education, primary health care, safe drinking water, adequate sanitation, family planning and nutrition programmes), only 3.4 per cent of Japan's aid was used for these aims during 1989/91 (UNDP 1994, p. 74). Japan is hardly a Santa Claus for the world's poor and needy yet, although it still ranked before Sweden and Germany.

Takayanagi (1993, p. 33) points out that 'Japan's ODA has a bad record on environment and the rights of local people, as evident in the cases of the Sardar Sarovar Dam in India and the Koto Pandjang Dam in Indonesia'. Although Japan's ODA Charter of 1992 commits the country to safeguarding the environment and human rights, there is still a long way to go in practice. The view of many NGOs is expressed in the open letter to the Prime Minister of September 1995 mentioned above. They demand clear resettlement guidelines at least meeting OECD standards, environmental impact assessment at least matching the IBRD's, more participation in planning by NGOs and affected people, an indigenous people's policy at least matching the IBRD's, creation of a formal appeals mechanism, and at least 20 per cent of total ODA for biodiversity preservation, women's health care and empowerment, child healthcare and basic human needs. It must not be forgotten though that Japan is certainly not the only donor to which these criticisms may be addressed and that IBRD practice has been under severe criticism for some time.

Whilst agreeing with Bloch (1991, p. 76) that Western critics too often overlook that a country having recently risen from the ranks of the developing world may hold a different view from Western donors, one must nevertheless criticize Japan's hard aid stance. The Meiji Restoration was pushed ahead by a functioning domestic system during a period of peace and enlightenment, as one might translate 明 治 時 代 (*Meiji jidai*). This was by no means the typical situation of a (former) colony. Very similar to Europe, the problem after World War II was money for reconstruction; functioning institutions and a well educated population were there. In many LLDCs these preconditions for successful hard aid under socially acceptable conditions have still to be created. The growing importance of Japan as a global source of aid should doubtlessly induce the country to finance 'non-economic' or humanitarian projects more readily, both to help the poorest and to help create the pre-conditions enabling the poorest 'to advance through hard work, efficiency, frugality and self-reliance', which Bloch (1991, p. 76) calls the hallmarks of Japan's development experience. Put into the language of the 'flying geese' model often used to describe East Asian development: the leader should also provide appropriate help to those members of the flock who need proper wings before they can fly along.

9. South-South aid: OPEC and other Southern donors

SOUTHERN DONORS

Although the bulk of ODA flows from North to South – or presently from West to South – the DAC definition does not exclude any developing country from qualifying as a donor. Countries on the DAC list of aid recipients may and do themselves give ODA to other recipients of OECD aid flows. Historically most of South-South aid has been granted by OPEC members, most notably by Arab countries. But there exist other Southern donors as well, such as India, China, Brazil, Israel, Egypt, Korea and Taiwan. While their ODA is very small in absolute terms and is therefore often overlooked, it should not go unnoticed. The OECD (1977, p. 92) once summed up the essence of this type of aid:

> While their aggregate contributions are only marginal in relation to total aid received by developing countries, they are nevertheless significant by their nature and by the effort it represents in relation to available resources.

South-South aid has indeed some special and interesting aspects. First, it is an exception to the usually assumed North-South pattern of flows. Second, it has often been declared a sign of political and economic solidarity among the South by donors themselves or by others. Third, what are the political implications if aid by some SCs is distinctly larger as a percentage of GNP than aid given by industrialized countries? Fourth, how should one measure SC contributions to multilateral institutions, such as capital subscriptions, which are considered to be ODA in the case of Northern countries?

Regarding SCs, the OECD (1977, p. 92) only considers flows '[I]n addition to their regular contributions to those multilateral institutions from which they receive aid and towards which they are not net contributors' as assistance. Literally this would mean that contributions, for example to the IBRD or regional banks, must be counted as aid since their loans are too hard to qualify as ODA. In terms of aid a Southern member of the IBRD (this does not apply to IDA) is by definition a net contributor, but the DAC is obviously not so literally minded.

As in the case of the former CMEA discussed in Chapter 4, reporting by other non-DAC members is below DAC standards:

> The diversity in types and sizes of donors makes it difficult to present a complete picture of all non-DAC aid activities, and the monitoring and analysis of non-DAC aid is further complicated by the absence of statistical and descriptive information comparable to that available from DAC-members. None of the non-members publishes comprehensive information on its aid activities although some do provide some information to the OECD. Information ... has to be compiled by the OECD Secretariat from a large number of sources – transaction by transaction.
> (OECD 1995, p. 107)

Thus DAC publications usually serve as sources on Southern ODA as well. It is an interesting point that SC governments are not keener to document their aid activities undertaken although they are often much poorer than rich countries in the North, but prefer the cloak of secrecy.

Traditional donors outside the OECD are OPEC or countries such as India or China. In the past China has been the most important non-OPEC donor from the South. The quality of its aid is described by the OECD as follows:

> The Chinese aid programme has usually been appreciated by recipient countries, in particular the poorer countries in Sub-Saharan Africa, because its technologies were adapted to the needs of those countries, particularly in the field of small-scale industries, agriculture and health.
> (OECD 1985, p. 119)

In spite of this official eulogy there have been no noteworthy attempts by DAC members to follow the Chinese example. Regarding statistics it should be noted that the much lower salaries of Chinese personnel in comparison with Northern experts result in lower project costs and thus lower ODA. The construction of the Tanzania-Zambia railway, for example, was financed by Chinese aid in the 1970s. The terms were quite favourable: no interest and 30 years maturity (OECD 1970, p. 34). The same railway built by Europeans would appear to be more generous aid simply because European experts are paid more generously. Considering that 90 per cent of the $12 billion a year in technical assistance is spent on foreign expertise (UNDP 1994, p. 76) these large differences in experts' incomes are worth mentioning.

In 1985 the OECD (1985, p. 119) called India 'a source of financial and technical assistance now for three decades'. Technical assistance was first provided under the Colombo Plan and it had traditionally been the second largest donor of the non-OPEC South until it was overtaken by Taiwan in the 1990s. South Korea and Taiwan have recently established co-operation funds and are likely to become greater donors in the near future.

In line with its political advocacy of Third World solidarity and non-alignment, Yugoslavia – like Israel a 'developing country' according to the DAC – was a donor for the duration of its existence. Its technical assistance programme dated back to 1954.

Countries such as Korea, Israel, Egypt, Brazil, Mexico (now an OECD, but not a DAC member) and Argentina have occasionally been mentioned by the DAC. More recently Taiwan and Turkey – an OECD but not a DAC member – have joined the ranks. Korea remains a fairly small donor but is, like Taiwan, expected to become more important in the future. The *1994 Report* speaks of a 'growing number of other countries [that] also provide technical assistance' (OECD 1995, p. 107). It does not mention any names though.

Interestingly the EU member Greece is on the DAC list of 'developing countries' (List of Aid Recipients, Part I; see OECD 1995, p. L6). Thus Greek aid is technically South-South aid. Flows to Greece, for example from fellow members in the EU, could be technically classified as ODA also according to the DAC definition. According to the OECD (GDF 1994) it received ODA from the Commission of the EC and fellow members during the period covered, which is 1989–92. Not surprisingly and in marked contrast to SCs with similar GNP/head, the grant element was 100 per cent precisely. Apparently not all the money flowing into Greece under EU arrangements is counted as aid, although it would perceptibly increase ODA flows of the EU and its member countries.

While Turkey had provided small amounts of aid before, its aid programme 'took on real momentum with the disintegration of the USSR in 1991' (OECD 1995, p. 109). The country was among the first providing assistance to the newly independent republics. According to the DAC (ibid.) 'Ethnic, linguistic and cultural affinities with several of these new states' were a strong motive for doubling ODA from 0.07 per cent of GNP in 1991 to 0.15 per cent in 1993. The Turkish International Co-operation Agency (TICA) was created to channel aid mostly to neighbouring countries. In 1993 Turkey's main recipients were, in order of magnitude, Azerbaijan, Uzbekistan, Albania, Kyrgyzstan, Georgia and Bosnia, mirroring Turkish interests in foreign policy quite closely. All in all some 30 SCs received Turkish aid in 1993.

Table 9.1 presents an overview of South-South aid flows estimated by the DAC. With the exception of Taiwan the 'lost decade' of the 1980s has left quite visible traces in the time series showing the evolution of aid. Even Korean aid declined although this country has been doing quite well.

Table 9.1 South-South ODA

	1980	1985	1989	1990	1991	1992	1993
In US$ million:							
Arab countries	9539	3609	1654	5955	2668	1173	n.a.
of which:							
Saudi Arabia	5682	2630	1170	3652	1704	783	539
Kuwait	1140	771	170	1295	390	202	381
UAE[a]	1118	122	65	888	558	169	236
Other SC donors	708	440	489	427	447	(387)	n.a.
of which:							
China[b]	334	167	169	141	120	(110)	n.a.
India[b]	126	144	109	110	81	86	34
Korea[c]	25	44	50	65	73	52	85
Taiwan	n.a.	n.a.	21	25	125	106	61
Venezuela	135	32	49	41	9	5	–
As % of GNP:							
Arab countries	3.26	1.28	0.56	1.81	0.85	0.36	n.a.
of which:							
Saudi Arabia	4.87	2.91	1.36	3.36	1.48	0.65	0.43
Kuwait	3.52	2.96	0.53	5.13	2.45	0.87	1.30
UAE[a]	4.06	0.45	0.24	2.64	1.64	0.48	0.66
China	0.12	0.06	0.04	0.04	0.03	(0.03)	n.a.
India	0.08	0.07	0.04	0.04	0.03	0.03	n.a.
Korea[c]	0.04	0.05	0.02	0.03	0.03	0.02	0.03
Taiwan	n.a.	n.a.	0.01	0.02	0.07	0.05	0.03
Venezuela	0.23	0.05	0.12	0.09	0.02	0.01	–

Notes:
[a] Data for 1985, 1989, 1992 and 1993 are incomplete
[b] Secretariat estimates
[c] Data subject to revision
n.a. not available
( ) Secretariat estimate in whole or in part
– Nil or negligible

Source: OECD 1995, p. 111

OPEC AID

Table 9.1 too shows that aid from Arab and OPEC countries has accounted for the bulk of Southern aid. This was particularly so during the 10 to 15 years following the oil price increase of 1973/74. During the second half of the 1970s OPEC aid accounted for some 22 to 30 per cent of ODA from all sources according to the OECD (1983, p. 14). Even considering the apparent manipulation of CMEA data, their share was quite substantial, resulting in OPEC replacing the CMEA group as the 'second largest donor group' (ibid.).

It is less well known that OPEC aid was already 1.18 per cent of OPEC GSP in 1970, well before the first oil price increase (ibid.), when the corresponding DAC average was 0.34. As in the 1990s the high average GSP share of the group was accounted for by three countries: Saudi Arabia (5.6 per cent), Kuwait (6.21 per cent) and Libya (2.01 per cent), while all other members gave much less or no aid. For 1971 the OECD (1983, p. 21) reports 1.1 per cent. Two years later the OECD (1985, p. 93) downgraded the OPEC average substantially to 0.78 per cent for 1970–71, a pre-oil boom figure less embarrassing to the rich North than a value above 1.1. One further comparison is quite interesting. While OPEC's ODA is put at 1053 million 1983 dollars for 1971–72 by this latter source, ODA from China, India, Israel and Yugoslavia totalled $1149 million. The average GSP share of these four countries is however not provided by the OECD.

In 1973 and 1974 aid from OPEC rocketed to 2.25 and 2.53 per cent of GSP respectively. For the Gulf states (Kuwait, Qatar, Saudi Arabia and UAE) 12.76 and 7.78 per cent were recorded by the OECD (1983, p. 21) for these two years. Qatar (15.62 per cent of GSP in 1973, 15.59 in 1975), Saudi Arabia (14.80 in 1973), and the UAE (1973: 12.67; 1975: 11.69) even surpassed 10 per cent of GNP (OECD 1983, p. 21).

Nevertheless aid from OPEC was by no means identical with Arab aid after 1973. Iran, Venezuela and Nigeria were also donors, accounting for slightly less than one-sixth of total OPEC aid in 1976 (ibid.) These countries' GNP shares were 0.19 (Nigeria), 0.34 (Venezuela) and 1.13 (Iran). The First Gulf War between Iraq and Iran led to the virtual disappearance of these two countries' aid programmes at the beginning of the 1980s. During the 1980s the sharp fall in oil prices, often called the 'Third Oil Shock' or 'reverse oil shock' resulted in sharp cuts of financial flows from all OPEC members. Some, such as Nigeria, ceased to be donors. At the moment, aid from OPEC is again basically aid from (some) Arab countries (see Table 9.1).

It is worth mentioning that aid by Nigeria and Venezuela consisted exclusively of grants in most years (ibid., p. 29). Generally the OECD remarked on a close correlation between size of aid and softness. Relatively small donors offered softer terms. Thus Saudi terms were the hardest among OPEC commitments at the beginning of the 1980s.

OPEC's average level of concessionality, measured for instance by the overall grant element, was usually lower (terms were harder) than the DAC's according to the OECD (1983, p. 16), although the share of grants and the grant element of loans fluctuated considerably. On the other hand aid by OPEC – with the main exception of loans and grants for the supply of oil – was untied. This is a main difference to DAC or CMEA members, allowing recipients to procure goods and services at lowest world market prices. Considering the production structures of OPEC members this is no surprise: major donors exported little else but oil. Nevertheless this fact is inconvenient enough for the OECD (1983, p. 12) to defend the tying practices of its members: 'there is no way to quantify the presence or absence of tying on the value to the recipient of a given aid transaction with any degree of acceptable accuracy.' This is not quite so. One could measure price differences between tied goods and the best world market price as easily as one compares domestic and foreign prices to determine distortions by protectionism. Also there is no mathematical difficulty in calculating increased costs resulting from a larger loan due to overpricing. OPEC however has never carried out such calculations of the costs of tying by DAC countries, and the DAC has, understandably, no real incentive to do so or encourage them.

The astonishingly high GSP percentages of some OPEC countries call for comment. The GSP of an OPEC member results mainly from the depletion of a non-renewable resource. A swap of assets (crude oil for cash) results in high liquidity and is wrongly measured as income, although only the composition of assets changed, not their total value. Due to the definition used in the framework of national accounts this results in GNP growth. Reductions in the stock of wealth are measured as earnings while in fact the family silver is sold off. This argument is often used to criticize the GNP concept. This factor is unimportant in industrialized countries with a very low share of extractive industries but particularly valid for major OPEC donors due to their distorted, one-sided economic structures. Shihata (1982) therefore concludes that GNP percentages understate OPEC's real performance. If a 'depletion factor' were applied, the author argues, OPEC performance would be even better than it looks.

The OECD (1983, p. 12) mentions this problem of GNP comparability, but simply goes on to say that GNP as presently defined has long been accepted as a measuring rod. It adds that no economically viable and internationally recognized method of gauging depletion of non-renewable resources exists. However when OPEC took up this challenge and Stauffer and Lennox (1984) presented a viable method worth discussing, the OECD preferred not to react. Reducing OPEC GSP by whatever depletion factor would make the comparison of performance by GSP percentages even less favourable for the DAC. During the period of extremely high GSP ratios of OPEC aid the DAC was obviously not too keen to popularize such a method.

Allocating bilateral aid geographically is difficult because necessary details have often been withheld. Traditionally Arab countries have had a relatively large share of unallocated aid. Saudi Arabia has always been particularly secretive; for 'nearly half' of its aid no geographic allocation was available (OECD 1983, p. 30). The Saudi Ministry of Finance, whose co-operation is acknowledged by the OECD Secretariat in this publication, chose not to give more information on the geographic distribution of its aid. During 1971–81 34.9 per cent of bilateral concessional disbursements by OPEC remained unspecified. While there might be political reasons for secrecy, it is difficult to check figures properly if recipients remain secret.

With this caveat the OECD (1983, p. 31) draws attention to an extreme concentration of bilateral Arab aid. This was especially so in the early 1970s when 90 per cent of net disbursements went to Egypt, Syria, Jordan, Gaza and the West Bank (OECD 1983, p. 31). This is a clear sign of the financial support for the fight against Israel. Later the share of these recipients declined substantially until 1981, averaging 'over one half' (ibid.) for the decade 1971–81. However since ODA from Arab OPEC members literally exploded after 1973, this did not mean less generous help was available to them.

Concessional multilateral flows were similarly skewed. Egypt accounted annually for 60 to 80 per cent of total concessional receipts by all SCs from multilateral Arab/OPEC aid agencies between 1976 and 1978. Resources were mostly provided by the Gulf Organization for the Development of Egypt (GODE), a rare example of a multilateral institution created for the sole purpose of supporting one single country financially.

Disregarding GODE the following countries were the five largest recipients of Arab aid according to the OECD (1983) up to and including 1981: the Sudan, Egypt, the Arab Republic of Yemen, Somalia and Syria. The Sudan, Yemen AR and Somalia belong to the group of Least Developed Arab Countries (LDACs). The largest non-Arab recipient was Bangladesh, a country joined together with Arab OPEC members in a common faith, Islam.

As a result of Egypt's peace talks with Israel, President Sadat's visit to Jerusalem in 1977 and the signing of the Camp David Agreement in 1979, aid from Arab countries to Egypt plummeted. Bilateral aid fell from $ 2070.8 million in 1975 to $744.5 million (1977), $166.4 million (1979), $4.8 million (1980), resulting in a net outflow in 1981 (OECD 1983, p. 32). A parallel evolution is documented in multilateral flows. On the other hand US and DAC aid to Egypt, which had been negative in 1972 and 1973, turned positive, that is from net outflows to net inflows. US ODA was $82 million in

1975, jumping to $401 in 1977, $913 million in 1981 and $1.117 billion in 1982 (OECD, GDF 1978; 1981; 1984). ODA by all DAC members rose to nearly $2.9 billion in 1982 as other Western governments followed the US example. Japan for instance roughly trebled its ODA to Egypt between 1977 and 1980 and France increased it nearly ninefold. Meanwhile Egypt is the largest recipient of US aid along with Israel. During 1992–93 Israel accounted for 13 per cent and Egypt for 10.5 per cent of US aid. In 1980–81 Egypt received an even higher share of US aid (12.6 per cent) than Israel (11.5 per cent; OECD 1995, p. H29). During both periods Egypt was also the main aid recipient from DAC taken as a whole. In the period 1991–92 29.0 per cent of US ODA went to Egypt, dwarfing Israel's share of 9.9 per cent (OECD 1994, p. 227). But the last Gulf War can also be discerned very clearly by looking at the aid disbursements of Arab countries in Table 9.1.

The history of aid to Egypt is a particularly good illustration of the evolution of world politics and the interrelations between politics and aid. At one time it was a main recipient of Soviet and CMEA aid as a result of President Nasser's independent policies of non-alignment, as the Aswan dam still testifies. Subsequently its fight against Israel was generously supported by rich Arab nations. Finally it became the favourite of the US and the West. The US attempt to include substantial amounts of military debt cancellation granted to Egypt because of its participation in the Gulf War in its ODA statistics was described in Chapter 1. In the 1990s finally, after Egypt had joined the anti-Iraq alliance it became again the main recipient of Arab aid (OECD 1994, p. 103). In 1990 its receipts were slightly higher than those of all other five main recipients mentioned in this source. Turkey, the only non-Arab nation among the six countries but also a member of the allied forces against Iraq, was the second largest recipient.

A similar, even swifter change occurred in the case of another traditionally large recipient, Yemen. When the country supported Iraq in diplomatic fora after its invasion of Kuwait in 1990, aid was cut. Yemeni citizens were violently kicked out of Saudi Arabia, even though each citizen does not always support his or her country's official policies. At the same time 'the major Arab Gulf states disbursed large amounts to countries which supported the liberation of Kuwait' (OECD 1992, p. 113).

The correlation between oil-based balance of payments surpluses and OPEC aid has often been mentioned (OECD 1985, p. 113; OECD 1983, p. 19). There was a sharp increase in OPEC ODA during 1973–75 and a distinctive peak in 1975 immediately after the first price increase for crude oil. After falling slightly it peaked again in 1980 after the second rise in oil prices, at over $9 billion (OECD 1985, p. 113). As these peaks occurred immediately after the two oil price increases, political consideration should not be overlooked as an important factor in the evolution of OPEC aid. Large aid flows to SCs cushion the effects of higher oil prices and might be seen as a strategy to secure political support for higher prices from SCs affected by price increases and to avoid confrontation. After 1973–74 OPEC was indeed seen as a model by the South and as a protagonist in the fight for a New International Economic Order. The creation of 'many more OPECs' was demanded and other commodity exporters tried to replicate OPEC's success.

OPEC AID AND THE IMPACT OF OIL PRICES

The role of OPEC aid in alleviating the effects of higher oil prices on net importers in the South is an interesting issue. The net effect (increases in oil import bills minus inflows from OPEC) was estimated by Raffer (1992) for the fifteen year period 1973–87. The results are shown in Table 9.2.

Net Importers (NIs) comprise all net importers of oil in the South except so-called refining centres, that is countries importing huge amounts of crude oil to export it after refining. As three so-called NICs (Brazil, Taiwan and South Korea) usually accounted for well over 40 per cent of the total impact of higher oil prices on NIs, the group NIs without NICs (NI–NICs) shows the impact on the other net importers. LLDCs is the group of Least Developed Countries as defined by the UN.

Data on OPEC flows and OPEC ODA must be treated with caution. Big changes occur for the same year from one edition of the OECD's *Geographical Distribution of Flows* to the other without any explanations. Data may differ considerably between OECD, IBRD and UNCTAD (1987; 1988), which started reporting on OPEC flows and ODA for the period 1981–86. Neither OPEC itself nor the OPEC Fund publish data on their own concessional and unconcessional flows, as is done by the OECD, which makes an objective assessment more difficult. Comparing data of the OECD's *Geographical Distribution of Flows* with the IBRD's (1989) *World Development Report* reveals large discrepancies in ODA disbursed by Arab countries. For example the IBRD shows ODA by OAPEC of $7246 million (OPEC: $7365 million) for 1979, while the OECD discloses $5190.5 million for Arab Agencies and Countries, a difference of more than $2 billion. Arab (OAPEC) aid was nearly $2 billion more according to the IBRD than the OECD's total receipts. In 1980 the difference between the sources is more than $3 billion or over 50 per cent! The neglect of non-Arab OPEC members as a result of the OECD's concept of Arab countries and agencies explains a very small difference from the IBRD's OPEC group. Using the IBRD series reduces net effects perceptibly, although differences are not always as large as in the quoted examples (for example within the $300 million range in 1987, which is still around 10 per cent of the OECD value). Interestingly the IBRD (1989, p. 241) explains

Table 9.2 The effects of oil price changes on groups of SCs, ODA and total receipts from OPEC, 1973–1987 (US$ million)

Group	1973	1974	1975	1976	1977	1978	1979
Direct effects of oil prices							
NIs	748.8	8596.7	9211.2	11 397.9	13 350.6	14 994.2	23 508.8
NI-NICs[a]	452.2	4912.6	5225.1	6247.6	7482.6	8410.0	13 025.2
LLDCs	63.8	350.7	333.8	590.1	753.5	792.2	982.6
Total receipts (net) from OPEC[b]							
NIs	1352.1	4072.8	6659.2	6760.5	6333.5	5379.3	5409.0
LLDCs	78.3	632.4	797.1	831.7	941.7	769.0	793.2
OPEC-ODA[b]							
NIs	1208.2	3131.9	5106.3	4955.3	5173.5	4212.8	5190.5
LLDCs	78.3	632.4	797.1	831.7	881.8	607.7	691.4
Net effect: direct price effects minus total receipts							
NIs	**–603.3**	4523.9	2552.0	4637.4	7017.1	9614.9	18 099.8
NI-NICs[a]	**–899.9**	839.8	**–1434.1**	**–512.9**	1149.1	3030.7	7616.2
LLDCs	**–14.5**	**– 281.7**	**– 463.3**	**–241.6**	**–188.2**	23.2	189.4
Net effect: direct price effect minus ODA							
NIs	**–459.4**	5464.8	4104.9	6442.6	8177.1	10 781.4	18 318.3
NI-NICs[a]	**–756.0**	1780.7	118.8	1292.3	2309.1	4197.2	7834.7
LLDCs	**–14.5**	**– 281.7**	**–463.3**	**–241.6**	**–128.3**	184.5	291.2

Notes:

[a] Net importing SCs minus Brazil, South Korea, and Taiwan

[b] As defined by the OECD; the sums in the Table were obtained by adding the figures for 'OPEC' (after 1983 'Arab Countries') and 'Arab Agencies' (initially 'OPEC Financed Agencies')

Source: Raffer 1992

1980	1981	1982	1983	1984	1985	1986	1987
41 716.3	45 082.6	37 345.7	37 711.0	32 516.2	30 250.0	19 171.7	16 618.2
22 989.1	24 947.5	19 614.4	22 190.4	19 166.3	18 846.9	12 896.2	8384.2
1804.5	2093.3	2438.0	2071.0	1914.6	2170.4	1302.6	738.6
6797.3	9403.5	6071.6	4899.3	4191.2	2963.3	3872.6	3211.4
1038.8	1199.2	1121.2	1142.2	675.0	714.6	641.3	565.1
6382.7	7916.5	4922.6	4603.1	3800.0	3104.2	4018.9	3031.8
951.5	968.7	1171.0	1106.7	669.6	684.2	667.7	565.1
34 919.0	35 679.1	31 274.1	32 812.5	28 325.0	27 286.7	15 299.1	13 406.8
16 191.8	15 544.0	13 542.8	17 291.9	14 975.1	15 883.6	9023.6	5172.8
765.7	894.1	1316.8	928.8	1239.6	1455.8	661.3	173.5
35 333.6	37 166.1	32 423.1	33 108.7	28 716.2	27 145.8	15 152.8	13 586.4
16 606.4	17 031.0	14 700.8	17 588.1	15 366.3	15 742.7	8877.3	5352.4
853.0	1124.6	1267.0	964.3	1245.0	1486.2	634.9	173.5

in its technical notes that 'ODA data for OPEC and OAPEC are also obtained from the OECD' – a fact not necessarily increasing confidence.

UNCTAD has also published data under the title *Financial Solidarity for Development*. The data provided by UNCTAD (1988) covering the quinquennium 1982–86 differ from both other sources: total concessional flows to SCs and multilateral institutions were more than $2 billion higher in 1982 than OECD figures and around $1.2 billion above IBRD figures, differences declining to about $1 billion to the OECD in the following years. Total bilateral concessional flows were however roughly of the size of OPEC ODA according to the DAC as shown in Table 9.2.

Data problems apart, which are usually considerable for non-DAC donors, these differences seem to result from diverging conceptual approaches. Shihata (1982, pp. 6f.) complains that the OECD discriminates against OPEC by including flows as ODA in the case of member countries 'which are not readily included in OPEC flows'. He also mentions non-concessional flows of a 'mainly ... private character' which are reported for OECD members but not for OPEC countries. This exclusion of private flows however is quite probably the result of precarious databases. Finally Shihata mentions that contributions to IMF facilities – including the oil facility, which was expressly created to soften the effect of higher oil prices – are not recognized as non-concessional flows (which UNCTAD does). Considering that private investments, loans by private banks and flows from the multilateral sector to SCs are expressly mentioned as non-concessional flows in the case of DAC members, this is certainly remarkable.

To avoid underestimating the impact of crude prices, Raffer (1992) consistently used lower rather than higher OECD values for OPEC flows, even when substantially increased figures for the same year exist in later OECD publications. To illustrate this point: according to OECD (GDF 1984) OPEC aid for 1979 would have been more than $7 billion, or roughly $2 billion more than shown in OECD (GDF 1981). Also the nominal oil price of 1972 was used as the basis of comparison, disregarding the likely increase of nominal oil prices without OPEC's intervention. Thus the estimation introduces a distinct anti-OPEC bias, leading to 'maximalist' results exaggerating the real impact of price increases.

Two concepts of net effects are presented in Table 9.2. The first measures the net outflow caused by oil, while the second shows the difference between increased costs of oil and ODA by OPEC according to the OECD's *Geographical Distribution of Flows*. A minus sign characterizes a net inflow. These figures are also shown in bold type.

The absolute gross effect on LLDCs was surprisingly small. However this does not exclude a relatively heavy additional burden on some LLDCs' balances of payments as OPEC aid was by no means distributed according to oil price effects but determined by other criteria, such as ethnical proximity, political calculus and whether Islam was a country's official religion.

During the 1970s LLDCs as a group were sheltered from balance of payments effects caused by oil prices by inflows from OPEC members, mostly Arab countries, as can be seen by simply summing up the net effects until 1979. Even though adjustment is not easy for countries with the inflexible and distorted structures of the typical LLDC that is unable to offer products benefiting from high income elasticities in OPEC countries, this gave LLDCs some time to adjust. In the case of NI–NICs cumulative total receipts were nominally higher than direct effects until 1978. Occasionally net ODA is larger than total net receipts. In 1986 for instance LLDCs received ODA net disbursements (by so-called 'Arab Agencies' and 'Arab Countries') of $667.7 million, while total net receipts from both were $641.3 million (OECD, GDF 1989).

The figures labelled OPEC ODA and OPEC Net Receipts in Table 9.2 are the sums of flows from what the OECD called Arab Agencies and Arab Countries (called 'OPEC' prior to 1983). Contributions to international financial institutions, such as the IBRD or regional development banks, are not provided by the OECD although they should be available. The concept of 'Arab (Financed) Agencies' covers only four Arab institutions but not for instance IFAD, where OPEC countries have played a leading role both politically and financially. In short, the amounts shown in Table 9.2 are lower than actual flows from OPEC or even from Arab countries.

Due to the data and the method used there is reason to suggest that flows from OPEC have been somewhat higher and net effects correspondingly lower than shown in Table 9.2. Furthermore remittances from foreign labour employed in OPEC countries after 1973/74 have been a major source of income for several countries in Africa and Asia. Foreign labour was employed from as far afield as the Philippines, India, Pakistan and even Korea. Substantial amounts of money were sent home by people working in the Gulf region, as the last Gulf War documented. While this effect cannot be isolated from international statistics – except for the group of LDACs where these resources have played an especially important role – one must be aware that it reduces net effects further.

Due to traditional links and geographical proximity, the impact of O(A)PEC's increased incomes on LDACs differ perceptibly from the effects on other SCs. This group consists of five (six before the reunification of Yemen) countries, namely Djibouti (until 1977 a French colony), Mauritania, Somalia, the Sudan and Yemen. Available data suggest that balance of payments effects of Arab ODA, other flows and remittances by migrant workers were higher than the direct effects of increased oil prices for LDACs as a group (Raffer 1992). Effects varied significantly between countries but as a group these countries experienced a net inflow of foreign exchange, thus actually gaining from oil price increases.

A possible exception is Djibouti, where data are even more defective than in other LDACs. The significant increases in these flows are clearly a result of increased oil income in OPEC member countries. Not surprisingly the conservative AR Yemen was by far the largest beneficiary, accounting for up to 88 per cent of the group's net inflows (ibid.) This remarkable concentration illustrates the point that flows from OPEC were not correlated with the direct effects of higher oil prices on net importers.

The two Yemens were traditional sources of foreign labour to oil rich neighbours, in particular to Saudi Arabia. Up to 1.2 million Yemenis of the AR Yemen and 'perhaps half the domestic labour force' (Arab Banking Corporation 1990, p. 169) of the PDR Yemen worked in neighbouring oil-producing countries during the boom years, mostly in Saudi Arabia where for instance up to 800 000 Northern Yemenis worked according to this source. For the Sudan Murtada Mustafa (1983, p. 281) quotes figures according to which 75.5 per cent of migrants worked in Saudi Arabia in 1978. Nearly all migrants worked in Arab countries with the exception of 1.7 per cent quoted under 'Others'. Only 1.5 per cent worked in non-OPEC countries: 1 per cent in Oman, also an oil exporter, and – surprisingly – 0.5 per cent (800 people) in Northern Yemen. In this latter case their employment might have been an indirect result of increased oil incomes from which Yemen benefited more directly. Arab Banking Corporation (1990, p. 121) estimates the number of Somalis employed abroad to be 100 000, 'mostly in other Arab countries'. Furthermore the movement of private unrequited transfers over the period 1973 to 1987 suggests a strong correlation in all four cases with the development of oil prices and the income of rich oil exporters.

While it is undeniable that increased oil bills were one important factor influencing the balance of payments of SCs, the usual practice of singling out oil prices as *the* explanation for imbalances and increasing debts needs to be put into perspective. GATT (1980, p. 8f) compares the effects of the two 'oil crises' on the whole South with other factors:

> The overall trade deficit of the non-oil developing countries grew steadily from \$15 billion in 1973 to \$40 billion in 1975. *The largest part of this increase resulted from an increased deficit in manufactures, essentially in trade with industrial countries; the rise of the deficit in fuels, while substantial, was relatively less important.* Between 1974 and 1978, the overall deficit of non-oil developing countries levelled off, the further rise in the manufactures deficit being offset by a higher surplus on trade in non-fuel primary-products. In 1979, however, the overall trade deficit increased once again reflecting a *sharp rise in the deficit on trade in both manufactures (to \$71 billion) and fuels (to \$21 billion).*
> (emphases added)

Even if one excludes net exporting non-OPEC SCs from this group (which GATT subsumes under 'non-oil developing countries') the combined deficit of these countries is estimated at 'nearly $35 billion' (ibid.), or less than half the deficit in manufactures alone.

The impact of interest rates is shown by the findings of the IMF's Padma Gotur (1983) quoted in Chapter 2. In spite of the 'second oil crisis' the impact of interest rates was 1.33 times the impact of oil.

Finally a few lines on OPEC money and the Euromarket are necessary, as the problem of Southern debts has so often been presented simply as the result of OPEC surpluses. Commercial banks drowning in liquidity, a popular Northern line of argument runs, could not help 'recycling' this surplus cash to SCs.

According to data published by the Bank of England, $130 billion of the petrodollar surpluses accumulated between 1974 and the end of 1983 were channelled to private banks and thus available for credits to SCs via the international banking system (Reichmann 1988, p. 230). As SCs were not the only borrowers during the 1970s one cannot argue that this money was exclusively lent to SCs, while other borrowers, for example Northern governments, did not borrow petrofunds. Direct loans from OPEC countries to other SCs amounted to US $55 billion during this period.

Singer and Roy (1993) rightly point out that the responsibility for Southern debts was widely shared. In addition to OPEC and commercial banks, some responsibility also attaches to the IMF and the IBRD, two institutions which strongly encouraged and advised SCs to borrow, and Northern and Southern governments.

Quantitative evidence apart, the recycling argument is theoretically wrong. If doubtful loans would not have been urged upon SCs, excess supply of international money would have driven interest rates down towards an equilibrium interest level which would have allowed investments unprofitable under actual rates of interest. The assumption that sovereign debtors can at most become illiquid, but not insolvent, and the knowledge that their claims would be protected against the market by their governments, on which basis commercial banks operated during the 1970s without obeying the most elementary rules of banking, led to massive misallocations of resources, both directly in borrowing countries and indirectly by preventing otherwise possible investments elsewhere. Obviously the imperfections and interventions that kept the market mechanism from functioning properly can hardly be blamed on OPEC.

Assessing the role of OPEC aid in alleviating effects created by OPEC's price increases puts these effects in the proper perspective as one, but by no means the main or the only, factor responsible for balance of payments problems and increasing debts.

10. Aid and NGOs

WHAT IS AN NGO?

Although the activities of Non-Governmental Organizations (NGOs) deserve attention as an important and special feature of development co-operation, giving them the attention they deserve is difficult. There seems to be nothing with regard to NGOs on which people can agree, starting with how these organizations should be named. Sometimes it is even disputed whether and to what extent NGOs are really non-governmental. Although a number of names have been used, such as voluntary organizations, private development organizations, people's organizations, private voluntary organizations or the third sector, Smillie (1993, p. 14) concludes: 'It is the unsatisfactory term "non-governmental organization" that seems most intent on not going away, and perhaps for good reason.' The reason is that NGOs, by and large, see themselves as being what governments are not. They define themselves, as Smillie argues, as 'not bureaucratic, not rigid, not directive, and not stultifying of local initiative' (ibid., pp. 14f).

The UNDP (1993, p. 84) restricts the use of the term NGO to 'voluntary organizations that work with and very often on behalf of others'. It differentiates NGOs in this sense from people's organizations, which it defines as 'democratic organizations that represent the interests of their members and are accountable to them. They are formed by people who know each other, or who share a common experience, and their continued existence does not depend upon outside initiative or funding.' If one accepts this definition, many organizations in the South usually subsumed under NGOs would have to be called people's organizations, while organizations from the North active in development co-operation could only be NGOs.

The dispute as to whether and to what extent NGOs are really non-governmental has two roots. First, there exist formally independent organizations with extremely close connections to the government or the ruling party, particularly in the South. The UNDP (1993, p. 88) gives examples from Zimbabwe, such as the President's Fund where the very name explains the connection, or Child Survival operating under the patronage of the president's late wife. In Japan many organizations have been formed by, or in close co-operation with, various government ministries. They have close links with the government through subsidies, personnel exchange and with regard to policy formulation and implementation. Smillie and Helmich (1993a) argue that, although technically non-governmental in the strict legal sense, they must be distinguished from real NGOs. To do so they call them 'public interest corporations', a term also used by the Japanese government. In other countries the term quasi-NGOs, or quangos, is more popular (Bratton 1989, p. 579). Government-inspired NGOs seem to be so frequent in the Philippines that a special acronym recalling the Wild West – GRINGO – was coined for them.

The second root is that many NGOs, even though neither quangos nor GRINGOs, depend critically on government funds. NGO-government co-operation dates back to the 1960s. By 1970, when the DAC began collecting data on grants by private voluntary agencies, a number of DAC members had already established mechanisms for financial collaboration with NGOs. By 1979 virtually all DAC countries had adopted some system of co-financing projects designed and presented by NGOs. Working as executing agencies for bilateral projects, NGOs may sometimes get so large a chunk of their budgets from government ministries that the very survival of an organization becomes dependent on government funds. To avoid this situation, those NGOs having other substantial sources of finance, such as commercial operations, donations from the public, self-taxation of members or a sponsor (as is very often the case with NGOs connected to and financed by a religious community), sometimes choose to limit the amount of government money they accept. Oxfam for instance has a policy of restricting support from government sources to 20 per cent of general income.

This quagmire of definitions is easily explained. Since being non-governmental in the strict, formal sense is the only characteristic common to all NGOs, they are a motley collection of organizations of all different types. Negatively defined as not being in the government sector, they represent civil society, but one cannot speak of a typical NGO. There is a distinction between NGOs in donor countries (Northern NGOs) and in recipient countries (Southern NGOs). NGOs are not necessarily or mainly concerned with aid but as charities they are also concerned with the welfare of poor or vulnerable groups in their own countries. This is of course particularly true of Southern NGOs. The relationship between Northern and Southern NGOs may also vary greatly. Some of the larger Northern NGOs such as Oxfam (UK) maintain their own overseas staff and engage in widespread projects both in emergency and development aid; others like Christian Aid (UK) prefer to work in partnership with overseas organizations such as Southern NGOs. Yet other Northern NGOs sub-contract projects and activities. In this Chapter we are mainly concerned with Northern NGOs directly involved in external aid.

In addition to the distinction between Northern and Southern NGOs, there is the distinction between large multi-purpose NGOs, which work simultaneously in many different countries and many different areas of assistance, and small single-purpose NGOs whose objectives are limited for example to problems of blindness among children due to lack of vitamins, or aid to elderly people. The distinction of large versus small and multi-purpose versus single-purpose tends to overlap as there are large single-purpose NGOs such as Médecins sans Frontières. An example of a large multi-purpose NGO would be the International Red Cross.

Some NGOs specialize in assistance in emergencies, others more on long term development; some of the larger NGOs combine both. The work of NGOs reflects the general trend in aid of increasing importance of emergency assistance and also of increasing concentration on Africa given the economic marginalization of that continent.

The word NGO is usually associated with one particular type of organization in people's minds, namely a private, voluntary, non-profit organization with altruistic and philanthropic motives. The present Chapter concentrates on NGOs in this sense. Given the diversity of organizations and activities it is of course neither possible nor intended to present an exhaustive survey, but we limit ourselves to a few issues which seem important to us. One main focus is on public advocacy, efforts to influence governments and the public at large on key development issues. Remembering the relation between NGO aid, ODA and other North-South flows shown in Table 2.1, advocacy in fields such as debt reduction or lobbying for more and better ODA is definitely a task of great importance. It should for example be remembered that NGO pressure was the most important factor making the EU Commission change beef export practices (see Chapter 7).

NGO AID AND ODA

Comparing ODA/GNP ratios with privately collected grants by NGOs between DAC members, the OECD (1992, p. 97) found a 'leading role of Sweden, Norway and the Netherlands in both cases'. Although warning that it would be difficult to establish causal conclusions the OECD drew attention to the fact that 'active public education has contributed to create a positive public opinion towards development assistance' (ibid., p. 98). Raising awareness for development issues is one central and important matter of NGO concern. The OECD saw 'support for aid on the part of political élites and broader public opinion, based on humanitarian concern and understanding of the need to contribute to international economic and social stability' (ibid., p. 96) as one main factor explaining differences in ODA/GNP ratios between

DAC members, particularly the very low ODA/GNP ratios of some of the wealthiest countries.

On the other hand the country raising most money in absolute (dollar) terms and having the most impressive ODA/NGO aid ratio (0.20:0.05 in 1991, compared with Norway's ratio of 1.14:0.12) is the US. Although private grants declined to 0.04 per cent of GNP after 1991, the ratio improved since US ODA fell more dramatically. Of the $5634 million grants by NGOs (private voluntary agencies in OECD terminology) recorded for 1993, $2567 million came from the US (OECD 1995, pp. C3f). In 1992 this sum was $2812 million. One factor explaining this glaring difference between public parsimony and private readiness is surely the different role played by the government in the US and its much smaller economic involvement in comparison with Europe. North American NGOs have also played a crucial role in lobbying on behalf of the South with regard to issues such as the environment, gender issues and debt reduction.

Table 10.1 ranks DAC countries according to their average GNP percentages of NGO aid and ODA during the biennium 1992–93.

High variations from one year to the next can be observed at the national level. High resource flows of both ODA and NGOs can only be observed in Norway, Sweden and the Netherlands. Ireland, the US and the UK show NGO activities far ahead of official development co-operation, if measured by their ranking. For all DAC members the correlation between NGO aid and ODA is positive but rather weak: r^2 is only 0.268. The Spearman rank correlation coefficient is 0.304. Apparently a high level of private activities may complement as well as (to some extent) substitute official aid. Naturally the amount of private funds that can be raised depends quite substantially on income tax laws, or more precisely on whether such donations are tax deductible or not.

Not surprisingly Japan, a country with a 'small, young and fragile' (Smillie and Helmich 1993a, p. 182) NGO community, ranks as last but one. Nevertheless in Japan there exists a very interesting scheme of fund raising which also illustrates quite well the co-operation between the private and the public sector, or, if one wishes to put it that way, the blurred line between official and private activities. In 1970 the Ministry of Post and Telecommunications initiated a scheme known as the 'Voluntary Deposit for International Aid'. This scheme is based on ordinary postal savings deposit accounts, of which there were 85 million in 1992 (ibid., p. 191), and is a form of self-taxation. People signing up for the programme donate one-fifth of their after-tax interest earnings to a special fund for development NGOs. The scheme is simple to operate, no great financial burden to the individual donor and has already outpaced the support offered to Japanese NGOs by the government. In 1991 the average contribution was $2.97 and in its second year of opera-

Table 10.1 The relation between ODA and NGO aid, 1992–93

Country	NGO aid (% of GNP)	Rank[a]	ODA/GNP (% of GNP)	Rank[a]	Rank difference
Norway	0.12	1	1.09	1	0
Netherlands	0.08	2	0.84	4	2
Sweden	0.06	3	1.01	3	0
Switzerland	0.06	4	0.39	8	4
Ireland	0.06	5	0.18	20	15
Canada	0.05	6	0.45	7	1
UK	0.05	7	0.31	14	7
US	0.04	8	0.17	21	13
Germany	0.04	9	0.38	10	1
Austria	0.04	10	0.30	15	5
Belgium	0.04	11	0.39	9	–2
New Zealand	0.03	12	0.25	19	7
Denmark	0.03	13	1.03	2	–11
Luxemburg	0.03	14	0.29	16	2
Australia	0.03	15	0.36	11	–4
France	0.02	16	0.63	5	–11
Spain	0.01	17	0.26	18	1
Finland	0.01	18	0.56	6	–12
Italy	0.01	19	0.33	12	–7
Japan	0.00	20	0.28	17	–3
Portugal	0.00[b]	21	0.32	13	–8
OECD average	0.03	–	0.32	–	–

Notes:
[a] ranked according to following decimal places if amounts rounded to hundredths of percents are equal
[b] grants by NGOs literally zero in 1993

Source: OECD 1995

tion 250 projects by 185 organizations, worth approximately $18.4 million, were financed (ibid.). Smillie and Helmich (1993a, p. 192) wonder how the fund can be effectively used by 185 NGOs if only 53 NGOs have the 'recognised delivery capacity overseas' according to the Japanese NGO Centre for International Co-operation. Besides raising money this scheme is an excellent mechanism for direct development education as reports on how the money is used are available at any post office. Although one might discuss to what extent it is an NGO activity it is certainly a model which deserves to be copied in other countries.

Grants by NGOs experienced a drop similar to ODA in nominal terms between 1992 and 1993. The latter fell by 8 per cent and NGO grants by 6.2 per cent (OECD 1995, p. C19). This might be explained by the economic situation in the North.

THE ROLE OF NGOS IN AID

While the quantitative volume of NGO aid is limited, NGO projects are nevertheless an important part of North-South relations. As the OECD (1985, p. 153) points out, NGOs have evolved pioneering approaches in some sectors, such as primary health care and rural development approaches focusing on self-help, and have advantages in reaching the grassroots. One might add other approaches evolved by NGOs rather than state bureaucracies, such as empowerment.

Another important class of NGO projects takes place in the North itself. Development education projects explain development issues to the public in donor countries and try to integrate them into the curricula of schools and into adult education.

Last but not least some NGOs engage in alternative trade which is characterized by higher prices paid to producers in SCs. Although no 'aid' project in the technical sense, this is highly innovative, tackling the problem of global inequalities of factor remunerations or, more technically formulated, of unequal exchange.

Naturally the heterogeneous character of NGOs must never be forgotten. Whatever is said about 'NGO projects' is valid for some but hardly ever for all organizations. Thus one can find both the claim that NGOs do reach the poorest and the claim that they do not in the literature. Both assertions are right for some NGOs. The success of a project depends in the end on the motivation of the NGO's staff.

The UNDP (1993, p. 96) estimates that while governments and official aid usually fail to reach the poorest 20 per cent, NGOs 'probably miss the poorest 5–10 per cent', although 'Many interventions do, however, reach such people'. NGO results in tackling poverty are judged to 'have often been outstanding'. Nevertheless the UNDP cautions that even people helped by successful projects remain poor, although the worst forms of poverty are reduced. Looking at both the total amounts of money moved by NGOs and the very small amount of money per person assisted (less than 60 US cents according to the UNDP 1993, p. 94) one can hardly expect the non-profit sector to change global or national economic structures. Furthermore value-driven NGOs often take on tougher tasks than official aid in very inhospitable environments. The UNDP rightly points out that what might seem modest achievements can thus be very significant to the people helped.

NGOs have also been strongly criticized as Smillie (1993) points out, but one cannot understand why he attacks the UNDP's evaluation of NGO activities so fiercely and unjustifiably. He quotes only passages where the UNDP draws attention to the drawbacks and problems of NGO activities or where it puts these activities into quantitative perspective but omits quotes showing NGOs in a very positive light. On this basis he qualifies the UNDP's chapter on NGOs as 'one of the most recent and dismaying examples' of NGO bashing.

By any standards the role of NGOs in aid has been increasing in importance. The number of NGOs increased substantially during the 1980s. Government funding has grown relatively fast. In 1993 Northern NGOs alone accounted for $5.6 billion or approximately 15 per cent of what the OECD calls 'bilateral grants and grant-like flows' from DAC countries. In India NGOs handled 25 per cent of foreign aid. In total they reached 250 million people. Within this rising share of NGOs in aid expenditures, the share of Southern NGOs has increased even faster – they thus represent a rising share of a rising share.

Indicative of the increased importance of NGOs the communiqué of the G7 summit in Halifax (June 1995) specifically acknowledged their importance as separate actors in aid for the first time, when it requested 'improved coordination among international organizations, bilateral donors, and NGOs …'.

The increased role of NGOs is directly connected with the increased emphasis now being given in aid, and in development policy generally, to poverty reduction as the major objective. NGOs are acknowledged as being in a better position to reach the poor than governments or large financial institutions. They are perceived as having a more 'human face'. They are in a better position to work at the grassroots and involve the participation of local people in development projects – factors now considered essential for poverty alleviation. Their ability to refer to their grassroots project experience is an important factor in their capacity to raise funds and public consciousness. Additional reasons for their increased role are that they are perceived to be less bureaucratic, cheaper and more cost effective than governmental sources of aid – all factors which are increasingly emphasized in recent thinking about aid.

Big aid agencies are increasingly looking for ways of reaching the very poor, especially women, by way of 'micro-loans'. Invariably the agencies act through NGOs as intermediaries, accepting that they themselves are not suitable for administering micro-loans directly. The most quoted successful model is the Grameen Bank in Bangladesh with an almost 100 per cent repayment rate. The NGOs involved often also provide technical assistance to the borrowers. In a successful scheme in Kenya, the average size of the loan (in a Nairobi slum area) was $3500 and the repayment rate was 98.2 per cent.

The role of NGOs has also been highlighted by an increasing emphasis on preventive action and early warning in case of threatening disasters, whether natural or man-made. With their decentralized structure and local contacts, NGOs are in a good position to pick up the early warning signals of impending famine due to lack of rainfall, such as farmers reducing their stocks of food, slaughtering or selling their cattle, getting into debt or beginning to move away from drought-stricken areas. This also applies to early local signals of ethnic conflicts which can lead to civil wars and genocide. The recent reports by the UN Secretary General on *Agenda for Peace* and *Agenda for Development* both emphasize the importance of early preventive action, which requires early information. Preventive action is infinitely cheaper and more effective than dealing with major troubles after they have developed. In the same way rehabilitation after disasters should be built into the humanitarian relief work and here again the NGOs have been leading in developing experience.

In disaster situations governments are usually only too willing to subcontract to NGOs and leave the humanitarian action to them. Here again the danger is that many NGOs may compete with each other for such government subcontracts and act without co-ordination. For example in the Rwandan refugee camps in Zaire it is reported that there are over 100 agencies active in work among the refugees, competing with each other for funds, transport, local staff, housing and so on. This also leads to the creation of spurious NGOs without real links with local communities (Watkins 1995, p. 86). All this points to the need for co-ordinated action by NGOs but this is not easily achieved in view of their large numbers and heterogeneity.

There are further reasons for the increase in NGO activities. First, official aid had increasingly come under heavy criticism and bureaucracies saw increased NGO involvement as a way to avoid it. Second, the ideas of 'small is beautiful' and the 'barefoot revolution' (Schneider, 1988) of the poor gained currency. NGOs were seen as better able to provide aid fulfilling these demands, particularly as a means to overcome institutional restrictions on official aid favouring large projects. Third, the political swing away from government involvement towards the private sector and privatization in all DAC countries since around 1980 has also led to a stronger emphasis on NGOs. Meyer (1992) found evidence of a 'major shift' in US aid policies toward the non-profit sector. Delegating the execution of projects to NGOs allows the implementation of more projects with fewer civil servants. Switzerland is a good example. Since the Swiss civil service was capped in 1976 while funding for development co-operation increased after 1976, the number of so-called 'en regie' projects (NGOs implementing a project for the government) increased perceptibly.

Fourth, as Structural Adjustment by the BWIs was imposed on debtor governments, NGOs were increasingly seen as a channel for funds aimed at mitigating the effects of BWI policies. To the extent official donors do this they heal the wounds their own policy within the BWIs has inflicted.

This shift towards NGOs differs from donor to donor. The Austrian government for example has never had an implementation agency, always depending on NGOs and even private business firms to implement bilateral aid projects.

There are also some dangers for NGOs involved in this expanding role. As they obtain increasing resources from donor governments and donor institutions, they may have to accept governmental priorities and agendas for their work which may differ from their own. They might be forced to become more bureaucratic to satisfy the perception of professionalism held by government ministries or agencies. Similar dangers exist in relation to the governments of the developing countries in which they operate: if they are too outspoken or go against the wishes of those governments they risk being thrown out. As NGOs grow larger there is also a danger that they themselves may become more bureaucratized and thus lose their special advantages. It may also become more difficult for those wishing to do so to maintain a neutral and purely humanitarian stance and avoid getting involved in politics.

This latter point is a matter of debate among NGOs. Some of them, especially the larger ones, positively welcome greater involvement in debates on broader issues of economic and social policies. They feel they have their own more human-oriented development paradigm to put in the place of the growth- and market-oriented paradigms of many major bilateral and multilateral aid donors. They increasingly realize that good work at the grassroots (micro) level may be frustrated by harmful and poverty-increasing policies at the macro level. This applies both to donor governments and institutions as well as to the recipient governments. In some donor countries the political activities of NGOs are limited by their preferential tax status as charitable organizations, which is given on condition that they refrain from political activities. This is a grey area, much debated in some donor countries.

Moreover it has been the experience of NGOs that their involvement with humanitarian aid in areas of conflict inevitably amounts to some degree of political involvement. In Rwanda, for example, feeding the Hutu refugees in their camps in Zaire means acting in opposition to the Rwandan government which wants the refugees to be repatriated. Similarly in Bosnia humanitarian relief to Sarajevo inevitably means the strengthening of the Bosnian Muslims against the Bosnian Serbs. The same would apply to NGO work in the

Southern Sudan and elsewhere. NGOs rightly put the humanitarian objective of saving lives above any worries about possible political involvement but it has led to intensive debates within the NGO community. Some NGOs wish to preserve a 'purely humanitarian' non-political stance as far as possible, while others feel that it is impossible to help effectively without addressing unequalizing political structures.

SOUTHERN NGOS

Self-help and various forms of common activities by villages or other communities have a long history in the South, particularly so in rural areas. However less traditional forms of NGOs have also existed for quite some time. This can be illustrated with a few more widely known organizations, such as the Sarvodaya Sharamadana Movement in Sri Lanka (founded in the late 1950s), the Groupements Naam in Burkina Faso (founded in 1967), the Self-Employed Women's Association in India (1972), the Grameen Bank (founded in 1976) and the Vicaría de la Soledaridad in Chile (established in the 1970s).

Southern NGOs committed to empowerment and democratization are often regarded as subversive by their governments and subjected to control and harassment. The line drawn between normal legal requirements and repression can be quite blurred, as the example of registration illustrates. Once detailed information on activities and income are available it requires only a short step for the government to control income and expenditures. The Foreign Contributions Regulation Act in India gives the government the legal base for far-reaching investigations of NGOs whose views and actions challenge the governments' own (Farrington and Bebbington 1993, p. 51). Foreign exchange control has been used to prevent NGOs (particularly those operating in tribal areas or in regions with unrest) from receiving foreign funds. Nevertheless Fernandez (1987) saw the Indian situation as relatively liberal compared with Bangladesh, where the government demanded to review and approve NGO programmes. Nepal uses a co-ordination council to control, co-ordinate and decide on the NGOs' priorities (ibid.). According to Farrington and Bebbington (1993, p. 51) the council is also used to offer employment to the government's political allies.

Repression of NGO activists in the South includes violence perpetrated by the government or vested interests and even murder. The speaker of Brazilian rubber collectors, Chico Mendes, is the most famous example. NGO work in the South is thus frequently much more difficult and dangerous than in the North, where the killing of a Greenpeace photographer by agents of the French government in 1985 appears to be a lone exception.

Large Northern NGOs collaborate increasingly with local Southern NGOs by sub-contracting some of their activities, attaching their staff to local NGOs and even helping to set up local NGOs. In this way NGOs also satisfy another development priority now increasingly emphasized, namely the need for institution-building or capacity-building in SCs and the importance of strengthening the role of civil society as an alternative both to unregulated markets and state intervention.

The relationship between Northern and Southern NGOs is by no means free of problems and frictions. The UNDP (1993, p. 89) points out that Northern NGOs typically refer to the relation to their Southern counterparts, which is mostly characterized by heavy financial dependence, as 'partnership'. It adds: 'But seen from the South, this relation is often far removed from the equality the term implies.' Kajese (1987, p. 80) perceived the nature of the partnership between Southern and Northern NGOs much more critically as 'at its most benevolent, that of "junior/senior" partner or at its most malevolent, that of "horse and rider"'. Kajese called it 'a fact, not an accusation' (ibid.) that money and know-how of Northern partners lead to unequal partnership.

According to the UNDP (1993, p. 89) participation is not only a central tenet for almost all NGOs, but 'mostly' they also promote it in practice. Nevertheless different perceptions may exist even with regard to what the most urgent need of a group of people is, which has to be financed by the project. Furthermore Northern partners who are themselves exposed to bureaucratic demands very often pass these on to the South.

The wide range of different approaches in co-operation can be illustrated with two examples from Elliott's (1987, p. 60) fieldwork. A tiny NGO in Bangladesh showed him the quarterly accounts demanded by German donors contributing $200 000 per year. They weighed over two kilograms and included, at the donor's request, a line item and supporting vouchers for the food supplied to the guard dog. At the other end of the spectrum a British NGO thought they had financed a school and a community centre in Lebanon until field investigation could find no trace of either.

The *Oxfam Poverty Report* recommends that: 'Northern and international NGOs should concentrate more on building the advocacy capacity of community-based organisations and Southern NGOs working for change at national and international levels' (Watkins 1995, p. 219).

ADVOCACY BY NGOS

One of the major functions of NGOs in the aid business is that of advocacy, raising public awareness of the extent of poverty and human exploitation in poorer countries and lobbying their respective governments for more aid or more effective aid. In a broader sense Northern NGOs have a role in educating the public in the donor countries on the perceptions and priorities of the South. They form the strongest domestic constituency of the South in the North – and one might well add the only one.

In democratic countries the pressure of public opinion as a result of NGO publicity has on occasion proved very important in forcing governments to act. However this has proved more effective in the case of emergencies than in the less dramatic but essential case of the 'permanent emergency' of underdevelopment. The advocacy function of NGOs was particularly strongly demonstrated at the UN summits, for example the Rio Summit on the Environment and the World Social Summit in Copenhagen. On both occasions many hundreds of NGOs were represented in parallel 'NGO summits' putting pressure on the government delegates to take strong and constructive action.

IFIs are a good, though by no means the only example for NGO advocacy. Their disregard for the environment, indigenous peoples, human rights and their way of 'managing' the debt crisis have focused NGO attention on multilateral institutions. NGOs lobbied politicians, commercial banks and IFIs, demanding fundamental changes in IFI policies. More recently they have concentrated on the issue of IFI debts, which are an increasingly heavy burden for most of the poorest countries.

NGOs have forced the IBRD to become substantially more transparent than it had been. NGO pressure in the US was particularly important and successful, no doubt also because of the greater responsiveness of politicians to public pressure than in other OECD countries. In 1983 Washington environmentalists persuaded the House Subcommittee on International Development Institutions and Finance to hold the first hearings on multilateral development banks and the environment. Representatives of indigenous peoples' rights organizations were able to speak up, charging 'that much development financed by the [World] Bank in the name of the poor was a catastrophe for the earth's tribal peoples, verging in some cases on genocide' (Rich 1994, p. 114). On 22 May 1985 the IBRD was for the first time forced to account to outside NGOs and a parliamentarian of a member country, the US, for its catastrophic Polonoroeste project in Brazil (ibid., p. 125). On Easter Sunday 1987 the Bank's vice president for external relations was confronted before 20 million television viewers with internal documents from 1979 and 1983 in which Bank staff warned management continuously and consistently that 'the project was a disaster in its very conception and predicted uncontrollable deforestation and virtual genocide of the Indians if the project went ahead' (ibid., p. 141). This happened after he had claimed that according to the Bank's knowledge at the start of the Polonoroeste project it was believed to be better for the environment, indigenous people and migrants if the Bank were involved.

In the case of the Narmada dam, Indian NGOs fought this project from the start, later on supported by a wide international network of NGOs.

The unique although still insufficient institution of the IBRD's in-house Inspection Panel (see Chapter 3) largely owes its existence to this continued NGO pressure. NGOs have thus become a small yet not always unsuccessful countervailing power against the IBRD's preference for speedy disbursements regardless of environmental, social or human rights aspects. NGO pressure has thus saved many people from hardship inflicted by the kind of project implementation described by the Wapenhans Report or the Morse Report on the Narmada project. NGO opposition prevented the IBRD from taking control of CGIAR and its biomaterial.

On the other hand NGOs are only too aware that their countervailing power is still relatively small and will have to be increased substantially to allow civil society (and taxpayers, who legally own IFIs) to force IFIs to obey the principles of good governance. Swiss NGOs however were already able to go one step further towards accountability and democratic participation.

MONITORING THE BWIS: THE CASE OF SWITZERLAND

The case of NGOs officially monitoring their country's participation in the Bretton Woods Institutions is a unique and extremely laudable example of public participation in decisions regarding development co-operation. The principles of participation and transparency, so dear to donor governments when preaching to SCs, are realized within a donor country itself. Switzerland, a country with a tradition of direct democracy preserved over centuries, is certainly an exceptional case, but its example can be copied and/or even improved in any other OECD country. One might suspect that other governments are likely to be perceptibly less prepared to introduce similar participation and democratic accountability in their own countries, being used to eschewing accountability to and public scrutiny by taxpayers or the public at large with regard to decisions on aid projects or voting in international institutions. This makes popularizing the Swiss example all the more necessary. In doing so this book draws substantially on Gerster's (1994) unpublished description of the Swiss case, as well as on Gurtner (1994).

Switzerland had refused to join the BWIs for decades, before the government decided to become a member at the beginning of the 1990s. Unlike any other country this decision had to be submitted to a referendum, which became necessary because of opposition to BWI membership by some development NGOs. The NGO community was split. While most members of the Swiss Coalition of Development Organizations (Swissaid, the Catholic Lenten Fund, Helvetas and Caritas) campaigned in support of membership subject to three conditions, one of its members (Bread for All) joined the group of NGOs opposing membership. On 17 May 1992 the Swiss voted in favour of membership by a majority of 56 per cent.

The three conditions under which many NGOs were prepared not to oppose BWI-membership were:

- additional funds; the costs of membership must not be shifted onto the regular development budget,
- a stipulation that the goals and principles of Swiss development policy should be the guiding principles for Swiss participation in the IMF and the IBRD group,
- the establishment of a broadly based advisory body to monitor Swiss development co-operation within the BWIs.

While the first condition might sound quite self-evident it is by no means so. When Austria for example joined the EU in 1995 the high burden of membership payments to Brussels in general and the legal obligation to contribute financially to (multilateral) EU development co-operation in particular, led immediately to extremely harsh cuts in bilateral Austrian ODA. These severe cuts were effected even though politicians trying to influence voters in favour of accession before the referendum on joining the EU gave NGOs to understand that EU membership would lead to increased ODA, because there would be a 'moral obligation' to increase Austria's performance to the 'EU level'.

In Switzerland NGOs had demanded as early as 1982 that the government should introduce a development policy amendment if the country should decide to join the BWIs. Although the Swiss National Bank and parts of the business community disputed it, the second condition was enacted as part and parcel of the Swiss Bretton Woods Agreements Act of 4 October 1991, demanding that the principles and goals of Swiss development policy have to be heeded by the representatives of Switzerland within the BWIs. This outspoken legal obligation is unusual for a donor. Although practice might not always live up to this formal commitment, this is a step towards coherence which should be copied by other DAC members.

The third condition of consultation with extra-parliamentary circles – or civil society, as it is called nowadays – is the most important point, particularly as regards possible emulations of this model. A special committee on the BWIs ('BWI Committee') was formed, a sub-committee of the Advisory Commission for International Development Co-operation and Humanitarian Aid. Initially the Committee had six members chosen equally from politics (the chairwoman, a former member of the Parliament's Lower House, and one member of the Senate), the NGO and business communities. NGO members are the Swiss Coalition of Development Organizations and the Declaration of Berne. In 1995 the number was increased to seven. The chair was taken over by Klaus Leisinger, an academic affiliated with the Ciba-Geigy Foundation for Development Co-operation.

The three Federal offices directly affected (the Federal Finance Administration, the Federal Office for Foreign Economic Affairs and the Directorate for Development Co-operation and Humanitarian Aid) as well as the Swiss National Bank participate in the meetings. The Committee has the right to discuss directly with Swiss representatives at the BWIs and to consult external experts. The Committee's task is to advise Swiss authorities on their participation in the BWIs, as far as these affect SCs. General as well as specific questions may be brought up by Committee members and the administration. Consultations should occur before decisions of a fundamental nature are made. Furthermore discussions on pending problems in development policy and the respective Swiss positions should be held before the spring and autumn meetings of the BWIs. The BWI Committee usually meets every other month.

The members of the Committee have the right to obtain all documents and all the information necessary to fulfil their mandate. This includes confidential documents, which are identified as such. Naturally Committee members have to respect the confidentiality of classified information obtained in and because of this function.

NGOs in particular represented in the BWI Committee can thus influence the government's position on a range of items on the agendas of the BWIs at quite an early stage. However the amount of operations carried out by the BWIs does not allow NGOs to comment on all operations and decisions, as Gerster (1994) points out. Attention has therefore focused predominantly on some significant projects such as the Narmada dam in India or the Arun dam in Nepal, on SCs of particular interest either to NGOs or the Swiss government, as well as on issues such as resettlement policy, the allocation of Special Drawing Rights, ESAF and the Wapenhans Report (see Chapter 12). Furthermore Swiss NGOs are committed to institutional reform including improved access to information, greater transparency, independent evaluation and inspection, improved possibilities of participation for both BWI member countries and NGOs and greater financial accountability. Naturally the two NGO representatives depend strongly on NGO personnel responsible for a country or a project to 'tip them off' and to prepare and provide the information necessary to bring a case up and advocate it successfully.

According to Gerster (1994), who was himself a member until 1994, the BWI Committee's influence can be traced in cases such as the Narmada dam, the information policy of the Swiss government in matters related to the BWIs, ESAF contributions and Article IV consultations.

The lack of symmetry of IMF influence with regard to Northern and Southern members made Swiss NGOs focus on 'Article IV' consultations between the IMF and Switzerland. This term describes the 'surveillance' of member countries' economic policies pursuant to Article IV of the IMF's Articles of Agreement. The Swiss Coalition of Development Organizations had the possibility to participate in this process for the first time in 1993. Because of the secretiveness of the Fund and because members of civil society are normally not listened to during the formal proceedings this is quite an achievement. Naturally NGO demands were practically not reflected in the IMF report.

As Article IV reports had never been published before, although major conclusions have been made known on very rare and exceptional occasions, the Swiss Coalition pressed for publication from the start. In January 1994 the Swiss government decided to do so, a unique step which provoked harsh criticism by the IMF and other member countries but stimulated new discussions on IMF transparency. Only the US was in favour of publication at that time (Gurtner 1994, p. 3). Jean-Daniel Gerber, an executive director of the IBRD, commented most trenchantly: 'Withholding these reports from the public contradicts two principles of good governance that we readily preach to developing countries – transparency and accountability' (ibid.). Although each member country has the right to ask the IMF's board formally to approve publication, the Fund does not like applying the cherished new aid principles of participation, accountability and transparency to itself. Gerster (1994, p. 8) sees a reason for the Fund's reluctance to publish: 'To be frank, the IMF report was rather poor, and we think publication of it might be an incentive for the Fund staff to improve it.'

It was a small victory, particularly as no further reports were published in full, only the final remarks by the staff delegation. Although of little importance to Switzerland itself, this precedent brought about by NGO lobbying is a commendable step in the right direction towards breaking the present IFI privilege of undemocratic secretiveness. In the case of Mexico, demands to publish the IMF report were reportedly made. If the present practice of excluding the affected population in this most undemocratic way should finally be changed, the poor in SCs forced to accept IFI programmes will benefit enormously from it. Strong pressure to do so must emanate from the North, whose governments have the power, although not yet the will, to change present practices.

PART THREE

New Trends in Aid

11. Aid conditionality

CONDITIONALITY IN HISTORICAL PERSPECTIVE

'Conditionality' today is largely associated with the 'support' given by the BWIs to countries in payments difficulties. IMF conditionality is associated with 'stabilization programmes' and IBRD conditionality is associated with Structural Adjustment programmes. Both types of programmes are subject to conditionality or, more precisely, policy conditionality. Such policy conditionality was not envisaged in the constitutions of the IMF and IBRD when they were set up at Bretton Woods in 1944, so perhaps the first step should be to consider when and why such policy conditionality was introduced.

To take the case of the IBRD first, the IBRD was initially confined to financing specific projects. It is true that in 1944 the IBRD was supposed to take part in post-war reconstruction of war-devastated countries (as the name still documents), which might have required programme lending as well as project lending. In the event however the reconstruction function was taken over by the Marshall Plan and other specific bilateral US aid measures so that for the first 25 years of its existence the IBRD was in fact limited to financing specific projects. This was not at the time supposed to be a strong limitation; in early post-war development thinking it was optimistically assumed that the capital scarcity of poorer countries relative to labour and natural resources meant that capital must have a high rate of return, and there would be a multitude of such high-return projects only waiting to be identified, formulated and financed.

Project aid also involved conditionality, but such conditionality was initially limited to the specific project rather than the general policies of the recipient country. Typical conditions of this kind, embodied in project agreements, included commitment by the recipient government to provide local finance or otherwise co-finance the project, to make complementary investments (for instance provide roads in connection with an irrigation project in order to enable the agricultural surpluses to be marketed) and to provide budgetary resources for operation and maintenance of the project after completion. Such project conditionality – which also applies to bilateral project aid – was taken for granted and not questioned.

Why then did the IBRD abandon project limitation and shift to programme lending with policy conditionality? There are a number of reasons.

Firstly the limitation to project lending turned out to be more restrictive than originally envisaged or intended. High yield projects in developing countries were by no means easy to find or develop. Moreover project aid is a very labour intensive and time consuming activity. Technical feasibility studies have to be made, economic and social benefits and costs have to be investigated, construction work may lead to lengthy delays, there may be frequent cost overruns and crucial deadlines may be missed. As a result, under project limitation the IBRD remained a relatively small and unimportant institution, at least as measured by the amount of money that was actually disbursed. This was very irritating to the Bank's staff, and particularly so to Robert McNamara when he became President of the IBRD in 1968. In his previous capacity as US Secretary of Defense, McNamara had been used to handling much bigger budgets than that of the IBRD under the regime of project limitation. As a result he was searching for ways of enlarging the activities of the IBRD and he seized eagerly upon an academic doctrine by the name of 'fungibility'. This doctrine pointed to a fallacy involved in project lending: if you provide finance to a government for a high priority project, this sets free the government's own resources which otherwise would have gone into the high priority project. The resources thus freed will then finance some other project – a low ranking marginal project – which could be military expenditure, additional salaries for high ranking civil servants and so on. Thus in effect the IBRD's money would finance projects which it had not examined and which it was not even aware of.

Secondly experience soon showed that the success or failure of projects depended not only, or not even mainly, upon the virtues of the project itself but rather on the general efficiency of the recipient government and its policies. As the rising tide lifts all boats, so a dynamic and growing economy can absorb and turn to advantage even a doubtful project and vice versa: where the economy is stagnant and macroeconomic policies counterproductive, even the best designed project will fail to yield its expected benefits and will be engulfed in the general failure. Projects are not carried out in a policy vacuum. It is for this reason that project lending has become more and more policy conditional and has shifted over to programme lending.

There was however a third reason to account for the shift to and the present importance of programme lending coupled with severe policy conditionality. This is a general undermining of the concept of sovereignty of developing countries on which the United Nations Charter is based (reflected in its voting system of one-country-one-vote) and which originally also governed bilateral aid and, in particular, the operations of the IMF and the IBRD. This undermining of the concept of sovereignty can be attributed partly to the collapse of OPEC after riding high in the 1970s and the building up of the debt burden for most developing countries, arising from high international liquidity and the recycling of the huge financial surpluses of some OPEC countries through the commercial banks of the Western industrial countries. It must be a matter of criticism of the BWIs that they were encouraging this method of recycling as proof of the 'strength of the international financial system'. If there was a time to impose strict conditionality it was in the 1970s before the debts were building up, rather than in the 1980s after the bubble had burst and unsustainable balance of payments deficits and levels of debt had emerged.

The dependence and weak international position of SCs created by the debt situation (and also by deteriorating terms of trade) was combined with increasing scepticism about the nature and role of governments in the South; this was part of the neoclassical paradigm or 'Washington Consensus' which became dominant in the 1980s. In the earlier period, the governments were supposed to be the Platonic guardians and best judges of national interests and the IBRD, as a UN organization, was designed to serve them. As late as 1971, in his David Owen Memorial Lecture on 'The Evolution of Foreign Aid', W. Arthur Lewis took it for granted that there could be no policy conditionality in foreign aid since SCs would consider this an infringement of their sovereignty and would never accept it. More recently though there has been a remarkable reversal of this relationship: governments are depicted now as centres of corruption, policy failures, rent seeking, ignorance and so on, while the Bank has acquired a self-confident status of being in possession of the secret of 'good governance' and an ability to sort out the 'good boys' from the 'bad boys'. Conditionality was the instrument to discipline the 'bad boys', teach them a stern lesson and convert them into 'good boys'. Under the Washington Consensus, as confidence in governments decreased, the self-confidence of donors and especially of the BWIs increased (to a point where critics accuse them of being arrogant). The strict conditionality imposed by the IBRD and donors is based on a firm confidence that they know what is best for recipient countries, that they have got hold of the sacred truth, that is the market-ruled principles ('basics') of neoclassical economics.

The case of the IMF is different. From the very beginning the IMF was directed towards programme support – there was no question of project limitation. In the original vision of the IMF there was no specific provision for conditionality, but from an early stage the IMF applied it implicitly, at least in milder form, in its actual operations. Its original role was to provide liquidity for countries in balance of payments deficit and shift resources from countries with balance of payments surpluses. In Keynes's original vision this was supposed to be achieved mainly by pressure on surplus countries – Keynes proposed an international tax on balance of payments surpluses at the rate of 1 per cent a month. In the interest of full employment – which was the main concern at the time of Bretton Woods – it was quite logical that the pressure should be on surplus countries which have a deflationary impact on the rest of the world, rather than on deficit countries which by their excess demand for imports create employment in the world economy. As visualized at Bretton Woods, the IMF was to exert at least equal pressure on surplus as well as deficit countries and it was hoped that it would play the role of a world central bank by providing liquidity where needed, that is mainly to deficit countries, without much question of conditionality.

In the event, largely as a result of the increased dependency of most SCs because of the debt problem but also partly as a result of the Washington Consensus where control of inflation rather than full employment became a chief objective, IMF pressure today is almost entirely on the deficit countries and accompanied by harsh conditionality. The IMF has virtually no influence on the affairs of the richer countries – these are looked after by the G7, the group of the seven major industrialized countries. The contents of IMF conditionality are highly controversial but most SCs have no alternative to accepting them.

THE IMF-IBRD RELATIONSHIP: CROSS-CONDITIONALITY

The difference between IMF and IBRD conditionality is often expressed by saying that IMF conditionality refers to the demand side of the economy while IBRD conditionality refers to the supply side. IMF conditionality aims at reducing inflationary pressures in the economy by cutting government expenditure, raising taxation, encouraging saving, monetary discipline, trade liberalization and stable sustainable exchange rates. IBRD conditionality aims to improve the supply efficiency of the economy by such measures as privatization, promotion of free markets and competition, promotion of investment, flexible labour markets, training of labour and so on. In practice this distinction has become blurred and there are overlapping activities, for instance trade liberalization plays a role both in IMF and IBRD conditionality.

Similarly the traditional distinction between IMF conditionality aiming at short-run reforms and IBRD conditionality at long-run reform has also become blurred. Both institutions have aimed for the middle ground and thus have become less clearly distinguishable in their functions. Logically however IMF 'stabilization' is a prior and relatively short-term adjustment compared with IBRD 'Structural' Adjustment.

IMF and IBRD conditionality are tied together by so-called cross-conditionality. This means that in order to qualify for IBRD Structural Adjustment programmes – subject to IBRD conditionality, countries must first also have accepted an IMF stabilization programme – subject to IMF conditionality. The reverse is also the case, although usually demand adjustment under IMF conditionality precedes supply adjustment under IBRD conditionality, and is certainly quicker to implement. Thus under the regime of cross-conditionality the initiative usually lies with the IMF which has become the leading actor in the conditionality business.

There is another important type of cross-conditionality although it is not usually referred to by that name. This consists of the fact that bilateral aid, and private investment to some extent also, is conditional upon countries being given the 'seal of approval' by the BWIs. This type of cross-conditionality is not formally embedded in any constitution or agreement but is still quite effective. Bilateral aid from major donors is often facilitated by the IMF or IBRD seal of approval. It can also be cut off quite suddenly if a country fails to implement the BWI conditions. In fact the relatively small amount of direct financial assistance given by the IMF or IBRD under stabilization/Structural Adjustment programmes is specifically assumed to have a 'catalytic effect', that is to mobilize additional bilateral or private financial flows.

CRITICISM OF IMF/IBRD CONDITIONALITY

The BWIs understandably claim that the programmes embodying their conditionality are essentially 'owned' by the recipient government. They are supposed to be their client's programmes, freely negotiated in equal partnership between the government and the BWIs. The critics claim that this is a fiction. The governments are under extreme pressure, with pressing debt obligations, no foreign exchange reserves and unsustainable budget and balance of payments deficits. Thus they have no choice but to submit to conditions which are in effect imposed on them unilaterally by the BWIs. The truth may well differ between different countries and often lies somewhere between these two extremes. Nevertheless even the BWIs are worried about a general 'lack of ownership'.

The question of 'ownership' is very important. If conditionality is imposed on countries against their wishes and against their own judgement of what is best for them, the government of the recipient country is unlikely to persevere with the programmes and fulfil all the conditions. This is a real problem and is proved by the fact that many of the programmes are not fully implemented and many of the conditions remain unfulfilled. This is admitted and deplored by the BWIs. It cannot be doubted that in fact many governments are under great pressure when negotiating conditions of funding by the BWIs and aid donors in general. The bargaining advantage is clearly not on the side of the recipient. The BWIs retort that this could be avoided if governments came to them at an earlier stage, before they came under extreme pressure. The dilemma is that if countries are not under pressure they have no need to go to the BWIs – additional financial resources can be obtained from bilateral programmes or private capital markets with less or no conditionality. By the time the BWIs become involved, the situation is usually quite urgent, and often desperate.

The question of ownership affects the relationship between SC governments and the BWIs. If the programme fails or is abandoned, the government will blame them and say that the conditions were wrong or unfulfillable and unrealistic. They will also then claim that they never really wanted the programme to which the conditions were attached and that it was forced upon them by the BWIs. Bank and Fund on their part will claim that the failure or abandonment of the programme was due to a lack of political will or competence on the part of the government or the result of political manoeuvring and instability in the recipient country. In this way governments may use the BWIs as scapegoats, pinning the blame for failure on them, whereas the BWIs will use the governments as scapegoats blaming them for failure rather than the programmes and conditions.

This is clearly an unhealthy situation and it gives rise to much worry and thought on the part of the BWIs. They are therefore very keen that the programmes should be genuinely 'owned' by the recipient countries and that the conditions attached to the support for these programmes should be freely accepted as being in the best interests of the country itself. But this is easier said than done. It also raises the question of why conditionality should be imposed: if the recipient country genuinely considers the conditions as in their own best interests, then there would seem to be no need to impose these conditions in the first place. A simple declaration of intent would be sufficient.

The fundamental dilemma is that if a government is utterly dishonest and incompetent and cannot be trusted at all, conditionality will be futile because the conditions will not be fulfilled. On the other hand if you have a highly trustworthy and competent government whom you can trust to do the right things, there would seem to be no need for conditionality. Here again many cases will fall between these two extremes and in those intermediate situations some kind of conditionality would be appropriate.

In the wider context of aid the difference between conditional aid and unconditional aid is not as clear as it might appear. It is complicated by the fact that much aid – whether in the form of project aid or programme aid – represents tied aid. For instance aid may be in the form of food aid in which case it is tied to food; aid may be tied to use in a certain sector only, for example a sectoral loan for the power sector or the transport sector; bilateral aid may be tied to the use of inputs from the aid-giving country only, thus limiting the choice of the recipient. It is a question of semantics whether we call such tying of aid conditionality or not. It is certainly a condition of the aid that it should be taken in the form of food, or used in the transport sector, or use capital goods from the aid-giving country. However this form of conditionality does not claim to affect the overall policies of the recipient government. It is not seen as a limitation of sovereignty by the recipient countries and the right of the donor to tie aid in this manner is generally recognized and not contested. In the current debate the term 'conditionality' is usually reserved for the type of policy conditionality typically applied by the BWIs.

Apart from the controversial matter of ownership and equality in negotiation, there are other criticisms of the BWI type of conditionality.

Firstly, the conditions are criticized for being too much influenced by a common ideology, failing to make sufficient allowance for different circumstances, political systems, objectives and cultures of individual SCs. It is certainly true that to a considerable degree the conditionality package contains identical features, such as greater outward orientation, control of inflation, reduced role for the government, removal of subsidies and import liberalization. It can be estimated that perhaps three quarters of the conditionality packages are common to all stabilization and Structural Adjustment programmes. The critics would say that this does not make sufficient allowance for the great differences between SCs. They would add that this may be connected with the fact that the IMF and IBRD missions which negotiate (some critics would say impose) policy-conditional programmes do not stay in the country long enough and do not know enough about the real conditions in the countries to do justice to country differences (the typical length of a mission is perhaps three weeks). To some extent this criticism would also apply to bilateral aid programmes, especially dominant aid programmes (such as US aid in Latin American countries). The BWIs and aid donors might reply that their emphasis on a number of common policies and measures is based on experience which has shown that various common features ('basics') are essential for sound economic policies everywhere. Currently these common features are embodied in the Washington Consensus based on neoclassical teaching. Many of the critics would not accept neoclassical teaching and the Washington Consensus based on it; they consider it a passing phase or fashion and point to the fact that not long ago we had a different kind of consensus, the Keynesian Consensus, embodying quite a different view of the 'basics' of sound economic policies.

There are in fact signs that the pendulum is swinging back from the Washington Consensus to something like a compromise with the earlier Keynesian Consensus, but also embodying new concerns with the environment, poverty reduction, human resources and human rights. The type of conditionality suggested by this new approach, represented for example by the UNDP *Human Development Reports*, would lead to a different kind of conditionality than is presently the case under the Washington Consensus.

The foregoing may be summarized by saying that the policy conditionalities imposed by the BWIs are not sufficiently country-specific. Paradoxically there is also an important line of criticism which maintains that in another sense the policy conditions are too country-specific. The programmes containing policy conditions are negotiated country by country, by country missions from the IMF or IBRD negotiating with the governments of the individual countries, without any attempt to co-ordinate the various missions. To illustrate: a country mission in Ghana will recommend 'outward orientation' which in effect means a number of measures such as devaluation, higher prices for producers of export crops or import liberalization for inputs needed for exports. In effect all this will mean in practice is increased exports of cocoa. Yet at the same time there are country missions in the Ivory Coast, Brazil, Ecuador, Indonesia and other exporters of cocoa, all recommending outward orientation resulting in increased exports of cocoa. Given the inelasticity of world demand for cocoa the result is predictable – a collapse of cocoa prices and general impoverishment of cocoa-exporting countries, a case of what economists call 'immiserizing growth', in this case growth of exports. The resulting deterioration in terms of trade of cocoa-exporting countries is then treated by the BWIs as an 'external shock' to which SCs will have to 'adjust'. Yet the deterioration in terms of trade is not external but is inherent in the policy conditionalities applied on a country-by-country basis.

The case of cocoa has been picked out as an example, although in this case (and in the similar case of coffee) the fallacy involved in making the small country assumption when applied to many countries simultaneously is now becoming more generally recognized (including by the BWIs themselves). This fallacy is known as the 'fallacy of composition'. The remedy would lie either in complementary measures of commodity stabilization – for instance the promotion of an effective International Cocoa Agreement – or else in the BWIs establishing more cohesion and co-ordination between their different country programmes. However the BWIs have been sceptical about commodity price stabilization as constituting interference with free markets, and have refused to acknowledge any tendency for commodity prices to be vulnerable with a tendency to deteriorate. There are also no signs that the country-by-country method of negotiations is being abandoned. The ultimate remedy would be for the Bank to qualify its emphasis on 'outward orientation' – but this would remove one of the main pillars of the Washington Consensus and one cannot see this happening in the immediate future. Such qualifications would apply chiefly to primary commodities but might be relevant for textiles and other simple manufactures also. What would be needed would be emphasis on export diversification into higher technology manufactures in which the global market for SCs is still far from saturated.

The same criticism regarding a fallacy of composition also applies to the case of devaluation, which forms part of many stabilization and Structural Adjustment programmes. Devaluation in country A is equivalent to overvaluation in other countries competing in exports with A.

The criticisms that the Structural Adjustment programmes with their policy conditionality are on the one hand too country-specific and on the other hand not country-specific enough might be assumed superficially to cancel each other out. This however is not the case. It is perfectly possible for the programmes to be too country-specific in one direction and yet not country-specific enough in another direction.

A third criticism relates to the way in which the conditionalities of Structural Adjustment programmes are presently being negotiated in a very narrow financially-oriented framework. This is particularly true of IMF stabilization programmes. On one side of the table you have macroeconomists from Washington, highly likely to be monetary or financial specialists, whilst on the other side of the table you have the representatives of the ministry of finance and central bank, also likely to be monetary and financial experts (and also quite possibly former staff members of the BWIs). Yet in this financially oriented group, decisions are made which deeply affect the agriculture, industry, health, welfare and all other sectors of the economy of the country concerned. For example devaluation may appear as a monetary measure but it has a great impact on the real sectors depending on whether they produce for export or are import substitutes or produce non-tradables; similarly cuts in government expenditure will affect health, education, agriculture and so on, depending on the extent to which the cuts in government expenditure fall on health, education or agricultural subsidies. Yet the agricultural experts from the FAO, the health experts from the WHO and the education experts from UNESCO are not there in the negotiations, nor on the government side are the ministries of agriculture, health and education. The narrow framework in which conditionalities are negotiated has a deep impact on the nature of the conditions themselves. The critics ask for a broadening of this framework and have some good arguments on their side.

Fourthly, and partly connected with the narrow financially oriented framework in which conditionalities are negotiated, there is the criticism that the conditions and criteria are too narrowly macroeconomic and economistic. Typical targets include exchange rates, control of inflation, reduction of government deficits and privatization. Success is measured by growth of per caput GNP, rates of inflation, ratio of exports to GNP and ratio of investment to GNP. This neglects such possible targets as reduction of poverty, greater equality of income distribution or more employment, although these are the real objectives of economic development. The displacement of fuller employment opportunities by control of inflation among the conditions and objectives is all the more remarkable since the original Terms of Agreement of the BWIs as established at Bretton Woods specifically mandate these institutions to aim at high and stable levels of employment as objectives, while control of inflation does not figure at all. The BWIs might respond to these criticisms by saying that the original Terms of Agreement reflected the Keynesian Consensus of 1944 but that the world has changed during the 50 years since then and it is the Washington Consensus which is now valid. If this is true however, it would be better and more honest to change the Terms of Agreement openly – which is not on the practical horizon.

The above list by no means exhausts all the criticisms but would seem to include the most important ones.

CONDITIONALITY: SUCCESS OR FAILURE?

Are these policy-conditional approaches successful? That is a hotly debated question. Understandably the BWIs claim success, although they themselves admit that even by their own measurements and criteria results are somewhat mixed. For example most analysts find that these approaches have had a negative rather than positive impact on the rate of investment. This is a particularly serious matter because the programmes claim to lay the foundations for sustainable future growth – and investment today seems to be one of those conditions for sustainable future growth. (The same is also or even more true of investment in human capital – better education, better health and so on – but human capital is not included in the targets of these programmes.) The BWIs might retort that while the volume of investment or its ratio to GNP may have declined, the efficiency of investment has increased as a result of better market-oriented allocation of resources. This is difficult to prove or disprove, since increased efficiency of investment could only be tested by long term future growth.

In general testing success is difficult because of the problems involved in counterfactual evidence. If it is shown that countries accepting the conditions and following the lines of the conditional programme are doing better than before, this may well be due to factors quite different from the conditionality in the programmes, for instance an upturn in the world economy or improved market conditions for a principal export commodity. Improved performance could also be due to the additional financial support given to countries obeying the new prescriptions rather than the prescriptions themselves. Would the countries not have done just as well if the money had been given without conditions? Such questions can only be decided on the basis of judgement rather than scientific analysis, at least in our present state of knowledge.

To some extent, but only partially, this problem may be avoided by asking a different question, namely not whether individual countries have done better as a result of policy conditionality but whether countries which have adopted the conditions are doing better than countries which have not adopted them, or have abandoned such conditional programmes. In other words, the 'non-adjusting countries' are used as a control group for observing the impact of conditionality in the 'adjusting countries'. With this approach, often adopted by the BWIs, two problems remain: (1) whether the control group of non-adjusting countries is really identical in all other respects with the adjusting countries and (2) whether the adjusting countries do better because of the inflow of finance associated with the conditionality. The borderline between adjusting and non-adjusting countries is also to some extent a matter of judgement and difficult to define.

CONDITIONALITY AND HUMAN RIGHTS

Conditionality in aid and in trade concessions has not remained limited to questions of strictly economic or even social policies. Instead it has been extended from what might be called 'economic governance' to 'good governance' in general, and by a further logical extension the concept of 'good governance' has been extended to include not only honesty and accountability, but also democracy and observance of human rights. There remains a fragile connection between this extension and the original economic governance or economic efficiency conditionality: it can be argued that non-democratic governance without popular backing and with governments violating the human rights of their citizens do not have the moral or political authority to undertake and implement the adjustments required by economic aid conditionality. In other words in the case of undemocratic or inhumane governments the programmes would be unsustainable in the long run. This is a possible connection although doubtful in the light of historical experience – in some ways authoritarian regimes may be in an even better position to enforce strict adjustment programmes and maintain them through the inevitable initial period of disruption and sacrifice, while fully democratic governments depending on the results of the next election might not be able to afford such a long term outlook. There is no evidence of any clear connection between the degree of democracy and the record of implementation of adjustment programmes.

One of the points under debate relates to the meaning of 'democracy'. The BWIs, as well as bilateral donors, are often suspected of imposing a westernized version of multi-party democracy on countries with different political and social cultures. In countries with ethnic divisions for example, as is the case in many African countries, there is a danger that different political parties will be associated with different ethnic groups, hence the legitimate struggle between political parties may all too easily result in ethnic strife and ethnic conflict. Genuine democracy in such countries may perhaps be expressed better by having good rules of law and order, even-handed treatment of ethnic and other minorities plus democracy and self-determination at the local or regional level. However such variations on the western type of multi-party democracy are not easy to identify or measure when considering aid or trade concessions.

In a further logical extension the concept of good governance has then been broadened by including the observance of human rights. This extension has been facilitated by recent progress in international agreements in defining and codifying the observance of human rights. The latest examples of such international efforts were the UN Declaration of Universal Human Rights and the recent UN conference on human rights (Vienna, 1993). The recipient or developing countries would not argue against such human rights conditionality, but they would point out, with a good deal of justification, that among the basic human rights are the rights to survive, to eat and to have the chance of earning an income. In other words they would argue for inclusion of the right to development among the basic human rights. Certainly such concepts as food security, job security, access to basic health and education facilities are now recognized as the legitimate objects of development and therefore the right to development which includes all of these would also be a legitimate part of human rights.

SCs tend to be somewhat suspicious of the inclusion of human rights as part of good governance and hence one of the conditions for aid and trade access. They point out, again with some justification, that the acceptance of such human rights conditionality may well be used as a pretext by donor governments or funding agencies to deny aid or trade access to a politically unacceptable regime. Human rights conditionality is also felt to be an even greater infringement of national sovereignty than economic conditionality. Such worries came to the surface during the UN Human Rights Conference when several delegates talked about 'human rights imperialism'.

The move towards conditionality related to democracy and human rights on the part of the BWIs raises a latent inconsistency with the non-political mandate of these institutions. The Terms of Agreement of the BWIs mandates them to make their decisions on purely economic and non-political grounds and to behave as international technocrats rather than politicians. The BWIs have been very conscious of this problem and have explicitly justified their shift to policy conditionality by pointing out that, ultimately, the sustainability of efficient development policies depends on the political stability which only democracy and observance of human rights can bring. However doubts must remain about the extent to which insistence on good governance and observance of human rights is compatible with the Terms of Agreement. This problem does not of course apply to bilateral aid programmes which are free to take political and humanitarian considerations into account (unless specific domestic legislation says otherwise). On the other hand under the 'seal of approval', bilateral donors are giving backing to BWIs programmes and to that extent they are forgoing separate bilateral political conditionality.

DILEMMAS OF CONDITIONALITY

Some doubts have also arisen as to whether the shift to policy-conditional programme lending has interfered with or reduced the quality of project lending which remains the chief mode of operation of the IBRD. The Wapenhans Report, an authoritative document written from inside the IBRD, provided evidence that the number and proportion of faulty IBRD project loans has sharply increased since policy-conditional programme lending was introduced. There is a plausible connection: for efficient project work you need technicians – irrigation engineers, sanitation experts and so on – whereas for programme lending and the associated policy conditionality you need macroeconomists and perhaps political scientists. Thus the two types of work are not readily combined in one and the same institution. The earlier implicit policy conditionality during the Cold War did not raise the same problem: all you had to decide was whether the country was on 'our' side or whether it was on the 'other' side – you did not need macroeconomists for that!

There is another inherent contradiction: the shift to policy conditionality is justified by pointing out – quite correctly – that aid cannot be given in a policy vacuum. Economic efficiency and political stability cannot be easily separated. In the case of the BWIs the people imposing and operating policy conditionality are unelected technocrats without direct democratic political mandate, lacking significant political accountability to any kind of electorate and without any economic accountability. This problem is not resolved through control of the BWIs staff by the board of directors representing governments. The directors are paid by the BWIs and by all accounts have for all practical purposes been absorbed in the administration of these institutions. They are given the 'mushroom treatment': keep them in the dark and feed them garbage!

There is a further dilemma involved in the shift to policy conditionality. This revolves around the question of military expenditures. Policy conditionality invariably involves measures to reduce government expenditures or to increase the efficiency of government expenditures so as to minimize budget deficits and control inflation. In many SCs military expenditure accounts for a big chunk of government expenditure. Yet the BWIs – and to some extent bilateral aid donors also – usually find it very difficult to suggest cuts in military expenditure and they meet strong resistance against raising this subject. Military expenditure is justified by the governments as necessary for their national security and it is not easy for outsiders to question this. Hence in practice military expenditure tends to be a taboo subject in negotiations concerning policy conditionality. Yet without cuts in military expenditure the cuts in government expenditure usually involved in policy conditionality will fall disproportionately on development expenditures and particularly on social expenditures on health, education and sanitation, clearly contradicting any insistence on observance of human rights: less education and health expenditure violates the human right to access to education and health facilities. Moreover military expenditure, although justified by reference to external security, is in fact often used to suppress internal opposition and ethnic groups, thus violating human rights. The ultimate solution would of course be to eliminate the argument of external security through universal disarmament and effective guarantees against any external aggression for all countries, but this is clearly a task for the UN rather than for the BWIs or bilateral aid agencies. Ultimately therefore the logic of policy conditionality will call for a more active involvement by the UN in development matters than is now the case. This raises the question of the relationship of the Bretton Woods system to the rest of the UN, a matter in urgent need of reconsideration.

REFORM AND FUTURE OF CONDITIONALITY

There is general agreement that realistically there has to be some form of conditionality. Except on purely political and humanitarian grounds, we cannot expect economic aid – whether on a project or programme basis – to be given without conditions. On the other hand there is equally wide agreement that the present type of conditionality is in need of reconsideration and reform and a lively debate has arisen about the reforms required.

First of all, there is a widespread belief that conditions should be less rigid and more allowance should be made for contingencies or external factors beyond the control of the recipient government. Alternatively there must be compensatory mechanisms to help recipient countries in the event of such external contingencies, for example deterioration of terms of trade, increased debt obligations as a result of rising rates of interest or crop failures. Where such compensatory facilities now exist, for instance the IMF's CFF, the support should be given on more generous terms, more automatically, and without imposing further additional conditionality.

Secondly, the conditions should be made more in terms of objectives rather than instruments. These objectives should be reduction of poverty, employment creation and improvement of human resources. The record of recipient governments should be judged by these criteria rather than by their compliance with such economic instruments as the size of the government deficit, monetary discipline or outward orientation. This means that governments should be given greater leeway in selecting the instruments for achieving those objectives according to the particular circumstances of each country.

Thirdly, conditionality should be a two-way business. The commitments of recipient governments must be matched by commitments by the international community to provide support. There should be more of a development contract between donors and recipients rather than unilateral conditionality. One example would be the 20/20 proposal: this is a mutual contract under which recipient countries commit themselves to devote 20 per cent of government expenditure to social sectors, while donor countries commit themselves to devote 20 per cent of their total aid to the same puposes (see Chapter 13). This would apply to multilateral as well as bilateral aid.

Fourthly, when Structural Adjustment programmes run into trouble and the initial targets and conditions are not reached, it should not be automatically assumed that this indicates failure on the part of the recipient government, to be punished by withdrawing support. An independent investigation would be needed to determine whether and to what extent such difficulties are the fault of external factors beyond the control of the government, or due perhaps to the inappropriate and unrealistic nature of the initial conditions. To that purpose an independent monitoring service is needed consisting of experts independent of aid-giving institutions and governments and of recipient countries. Such independent experts could also be involved in the original negotiations when conditions and targets are fixed.

Finally, conditions should be more pragmatically adjusted to the specific circumstances of each country and each situation. As explained above, there is a widespread feeling that the conditions are too ideologically determined and drawn from a preconceived set of tools. For this purpose, as well as for other reasons, it would be desirable for the staff of the BWIs to be less concentrated in Washington and to have greater knowledge of actual field conditions within SCs. Staff should also be recruited from a wider field than at present and not limited to people with a financially-oriented training and adhering to given economic ideologies.

12. Political conditionality – illustrating double standards

The shift of conditionality mentioned in the previous Chapter is an interesting new development deserving closer attention. In perceptible contrast to the decades of the Cold War, donors have increasingly emphasized good governance, human rights, democratization, participatory development, transparency, accountability and, more recently, environmental issues. These political demands are now manifestly present both in bilateral and multilateral development co-operation. Aid has become increasingly conditional on appropriate observation of these new demands. In a recent document the DAC declares:

> The agendas for good governance, participatory development, human rights and democratisation are clearly interlinked. They include elements which are basic values in their own right, such as human rights and the principles of participation, and others such as accountability, transparency and high standards of public sector management, which are also means of developmental ends. Some of the objectives, such as the rule of law, must be viewed as both ends in themselves and means to viable development.
> (OECD 1993, para. 4)

However practice differs from official declarations, as the UNDP (1994, p. 76) points out:

> rhetoric is running far ahead of reality, as a comparison of the per capita ODA received by democratic and authoritarian regimes shows. Indeed, for the US the relationship between aid and human rights violations has been perverse.

Multilateral donors also seem not to have been bothered by such considerations. They seem to prefer martial law regimes, quietly assuming that such regimes will promote political stability and improve economic management.

Naturally this change of mind gave rise to sceptical and critical voices. The new political conditionality is a distinctive U-turn in donor theory, which is not accompanied by a corresponding redirection of actual aid. As colonial powers, donor countries ruled very undemocratically. After decolonization all Northern donors have supported dictatorial and undemocratic regimes, in some cases extending their 'assistance' as far as training special police forces how to torture most efficiently. Baby Doc, Mobutu, Bokasa, Pinochet, Somoza (qualified as a 'son of a bitch, but our son of a bitch' by a US president), the Shah of Iran or dictators in South Korea and Taiwan have all been pets of Northern donors for decades.

This historical record as well as present policies make it difficult to believe that donor governments are honestly committed to this issue. Not surprisingly fears have been voiced that political conditionality might finally end up being a new and even more efficient instrument of interference applied selectively as a means of achieving other political goals. Pointedly put it might simply increase the 'implicit price of aid to recipients' (Murshed and Sen 1995, p. 499). The use of the expression 'policy dialogue' by the OECD in this context might not have been conducive to alleviating such fears either.

Apparently aware of these reservations, the OECD document points out the importance of donor behaviour and credibility. It specifically mentions both the 'record of respect for human rights in donor countries' (OECD 1993, para. 82) and 'a donor country's stance in good governance and participatory development' (ibid., para. 85).

Human rights, good governance and political conditionality in general are of course worthy goals. Enforcing them worldwide would certainly be in the interest of the repressed as well as of humankind in general. Stopping financial flows to torturers and dictators while increasing funds to countries where the population, especially the poor, are allowed to benefit is no doubt something that needs be done.

Stopping aid to dictators should not necessarily mean halting aid to that country totally. From a moral point of view aid that benefits governments systematically violating human rights must be stopped. However projects benefiting groups that have no connection with the government or do not support it should go on. Cutting off this aid just because people live in a country whose government violates their human rights systematically would amount to punishing the population for the actions of their government. It would affect those groups already suffering repression from the government, thus further deteriorating their lot. Briefly put, it may matter less to which country aid is given than to whom within that country.

As a result Gunnar Myrdal (1985) recommended supporting opposition movements as well as freedom fighters trying to improve the lot of their peoples. On the purely technical level this implies intervening in the internal affairs of other countries, as donors have done quite often but for much less justified reasons. Nevertheless it might be difficult for one government to support opposition in another country openly. However Myrdal's proposal to give aid to opposition forces fighting repression is unlikely to be followed by OECD governments with a history of supporting right-wing guerilleras and military dictators not at all concerned about improving their peoples' lives.

Unfortunately the current most vocal advocates of political conditionality as well as their practice strongly corroborate fears (characterized by the catchphrase 'human rights imperialism' in the previous Chapter) that it is simply a cleverly devised new tool to enforce political agenda. This covers a field sufficiently wide to enable donors to find fault in any country if that should be convenient. It appears more likely that something might be found in a small country where donors have no or little interests (such as Myanmar) rather than in a large, economically interesting country (such as China).

The fact that OECD practice does not match declarations is manifestly evident. Rhetoric rightly accuses excessive military expenditure of diverting 'scarce resources away from development needs' (OECD 1993, para. 53), demanding 'DAC Members must conclude that their aid is helping to sustain such expenditures and in such cases envisage a number of actions' (ibid., para 61). In practice these same donors export arms and weaponry and would not be pleased to lose these markets. This situation is presented as a double moral hazard in a principal-agent model by Murshed and Sen (1995). Not only are the recipient's (agent's) efforts to meet the requirements of political conditionality not fully known to the donor (principal), but the action of the donor is also not fully transparent to the recipient. Moral hazard on the donor side is illustrated by the 'recent allegations made about the linkage between British aid and arms exports to Malaysia' (ibid., p. 501). It relates to insufficient action by the donor to promote good governance and demilitarization in the recipient country. This situation is shown to create economic inefficiencies and serious equity problems and allows donors to shift the burden of action on recipients. Unless asymmetric information is reduced by a frank dialogue where donors and recipients can express their genuine concerns regarding security and development, the authors fear that the impression will remain that the main concern of donors is not disarmament but the reduction of the share of aid in donors' GSPs.

In practice high military spenders got two and a half times as much ODA per caput from bilateral donors as low military spenders in 1992 (UNDP 1994, p. 75), a figure which hardly confirms a desire to disarm. Compared with 1986 when this ratio was five, this can be seen as an improvement but it still indicates that words and deeds diverge substantially in the case of OECD donors.

Furthermore military assistance was again – for the first time since the 1960s – explicitly included in aid figures in 1990 (see Chapter 1). It must be recalled that military aid, officially banned by the DAC after Myrdal's (1970) criticism, is again fully acceptable as ODA if granted indirectly via loans and debt forgiveness. Only the fear of negative reactions by public opinion kept donor governments from labelling it ODA. As pointed out in Chapter 1 it is technically correct according to the official DAC definition to include military expenditure, as long as soldiers kill mainly to promote welfare and development.

A telling illustration of this discrepancy between rhetoric and reality is the Dutch-Indonesian case. After a massacre in East Timor in 1991 the Dutch government decided to freeze its aid, a move that met heavy criticism by other donors. In 1992 Indonesia cut its relations with the Dutch and requested the IBRD to take over as the organizer of the Intergovernmental Group for Indonesia, which the Bank did with the consent of the other donors. The Netherlands and Canada, which also cut its aid to Indonesia because of human rights abuses (Randel and German 1993, p. xii) were left totally isolated (Uvin 1993), with 'other donors queuing up to take their places' (Randel and German 1993, p. xii) without any concern for the victims.

A much less drastic example of the reality of participatory government is provided by the EU. It has a nearly powerless Parliament, laws are made and relevant decisions are reached behind closed doors by the executive branch and unelected bureaucrats. Taxpayers are not even allowed to know their own government's arguments. This deprives them of any possibility of holding their governments responsible for what they have done. Elected representatives of national Parliaments have no choice but to accept decisions from Brussels. While democracy has been rolled back in Europe, the EU and its member governments insist on democracy and participation in SCs, as shown in Chapter 7, although they are themselves not meeting their own standards.

This double standard is particularly clear in the case of IFIs controlled by the North, such as the IMF or the IBRD. If principles such as participatory development, transparency, accountability, the rule of law and good governance were indeed believed to be integral to effective development co-operation, vital and urgent and factors enhancing the efficient use of resources for development – as the OECD (1993) contends – there is convincing scope for applying them not only to recipient governments but also to donors' administrations in charge of development co-operation and to international agencies. Efficient management by public institutions, be they government departments or public finance institutions, is immensely desirable everywhere. Thus logic would demand these principles be applied to bilateral aid and multilateral sources of finance controlled by OECD countries with equal fervour as it is proposed to the South. This example set by donors would provide a most powerful argument against any scepticism about the honest intentions of OECD governments. It would also allow Northern bilateral and multilateral institutions to reap the social and economic benefits to which the OECD draws attention, such as better use of scarce resources or relieving delays and distortions of development. These reasons apart, any efficiency gains are welcome from an economic point of view.

The BWIs have been among the most vocal advocates of good governance in SCs, particularly emphasizing its economic aspects. More recently however critics of these IFIs, especially NGOs, have started to call for good governance and accountability by the Bretton Woods institutions themselves. There is in fact no reason why good governance or high standards of public sector management should not be useful for the donor side as well. The IBRD in turn published the rather self-critical Wapenhans Report (IBRD 1992) stressing accountability, participation by beneficiaries, transparency and 'prudent' governance. It urges the Bank to reconsider management procedures in a way apparently inspired by the new OECD principles of sound management.

As the IMF has not been equally open-minded to publish official criticism (if any exists) this Chapter will focus on official publications by the Bank. It must be pointed out though that the Fund has failed to show any proof of success so far, even though it has been engaged in Structural Adjustment of SCs for about 20 years. According to *Finance & Development*, the official BWI quarterly, adjustment policies by the IMF in Africa started already after 1973 (Kanesa-Thasan 1981). During this early phase when the Fund was apparently glad to find clients, conditionality was lenient 'in relation to the required adjustment effort' (ibid., p. 20). In the 'third phase' starting in 1979 it became stricter. Eighty-eight arrangements were approved by the IMF between January 1979 and December 1981, to support adjustment policies, particularly measures to reach a sustainable balance of payments position (Crockett 1982). All countries asking for reschedulings in 1981 (nine within the framework of official creditor clubs plus several outside these clubs) 'had adopted an adjustment program' with the Fund when negotiating with their creditors (Nowzad 1982, p. 13).

Regarding efficiency it must be noted that BWI adjustment measures – they were essentially the same as they are today, though expressions and lingo have changed a bit – did not prevent the debt crisis. The BWIs, particularly the IMF, did not arrive on the scene after 1982 to solve the debt problem created by others but they had been part of the process leading to it (Raffer 1994c). A critic of the BWIs might even say, with justification, that the first unsuccessful adjustment programmes existed before the debt crisis. The Fund might counter by pointing out that it did not have sufficient leverage before 1982 (the Bank started in 1980) to force countries into necessary reforms. Naturally this would be at odds with the claim that SCs 'own' their programmes only 'supported' by BWIs. This claim of country 'ownership' is heard more often recently than it was in the past, when more pride was expressed on how tightly one was able to control SCs.

As can be shown from both official sources and from publications by leading BWI staff, the claim that countries own programmes cannot be reconciled with the truth. J.J. Polak for instance, a leading theoretician of the IMF, illustrates the strengthening of conditionality very clearly, using the example of the CFF. Initially introduced to compensate shortfalls in export earnings beyond the control of SCs its

> conditionality was limited to an obligatory statement by the member to 'co-operate with the Fund ... to find, *where required*, appropriate solutions for its balance of payments difficulties. ... Over the years, however, the Fund has increasingly come to the realization that *even though a country's export shortfall was both 'temporary' and largely beyond its control the country might still have balance-of-payments difficulties attributable to inappropriate policies and that large amounts of unconditional credit might cause the country to delay adopting needed policy adjustments.*
> (Polak 1991 p. 9; emphasis added)

Put in plain English, even if the country's economic policy is not at all the reason for the temporary problem the country still has to change it if that is what the Fund wishes. Put another way, the claim that programmes are owned by the countries and only supported by BWIs is not true (for further proofs of who designs Structural Adjustment programmes see Raffer 1993; 1995a) and the blame for lack of success cannot be simply shifted onto the victims.

Existing evidence as well as the fact that SAF and ESAF are administered jointly by the Bank and the Fund (which contributes to the blurring of theoretical distinctions described in the last chapter) show that the IMF cannot be more efficient than the IBRD in this respect. This chapter will focus on the IBRD as an illustrative example of how little importance OECD governments give to their own demands for participatory development, transparency, accountability, the rule of law, good governance and efficient management by public institutions, when it is their responsibility to act, even when mismanagement means hurting vulnerable groups lethally. One reason is the flagship role claimed by the IBRD itself. Another reason is that there exist official publications on its efficiency, in contrast to the IMF which is still much more secretive. The criticism that sources inimical to the Bank are quoted can thus be avoided.

The Wapenhans Report released at the end of 1992 (after nearly double the time initially expected by the Bank's president for completion) calls for important basic changes in Bank policy, as the existing system of management has led to grave and, seen from the perspective of an economist or a business administrator, simply unbelievable shortcomings. The Report (IBRD 1992, p. iii) speaks of an 'approval culture' characterized by 'the Bank's pervasive preoccupation with new lending', which led to 'promotional – rather than objective' appraisals. To avoid misunderstanding it should be mentioned that references to projects include operations of all types (including programmes) according to the Wapenhans Report (IBRD 1992, p. 1, footnote 4). This emphasis on getting loans approved (and disbursed) resulted in 'poor design, poor management and poor implementation' (ibid.) and contributed eventually to a steady deterioration in the performance of the Bank's portfolio. Trying to include as many novel features as possible to secure favourable management and board response, scant attention is paid to 'on-the-ground benefits' or the actual development impact, in contrast to loan approvals, good reports and disbursements. Warning the staff off 'many temptations to introduce embellishments' during the review process (ibid., Annex A, p. 7) the Report found it necessary to state expressly – in the case of an institution calling itself a bank – that 'the perception that the literary quality of the SAR [Staff Appraisal Report] is in itself a criterion of performance', is wrong, reaffirming:

> It is not, and that point would be driven home if managers and Board were to agree that the SAR, as a working - i.e., a staff - document is intended to (i) assess the intrinsic quality of the project, (ii) evaluate the critical risks to which it is exposed, and (iii) demonstrate its applicability.
> (ibid., Annex A, p. 8)

In other words, managers and Board still prefer good English to good economic results. Staff confused by lack of clear guidelines, giving advice without adequate knowledge of relevant guidelines and practices, frequently unrealistic financial covenants, inconsistent approval of procurement actions, inadequate flexibility in adapting project designs to changed circumstances or new insights, insufficient staff experienced in financial and general management or public administration, project conditions conflicting with Structural Adjustment conditionality imposed by the IBRD and the IMF, and insufficient attention to financial risks are just examples of gravest shortcomings mentioned by the Wapenhans Report. According to this source borrowers allege that featuring conditions favoured by the Bank's management and the Board are included even 'where these may complicate projects so as to jeopardise successful implementation' (ibid., p. iii). More detailed and equally appalling reactions from representatives of borrowers (not speaking in their official capacities but for themselves, but chosen by the Bank and approved by the appropriate executive directors) corroborate this (ibid., Annex B).

Not surprisingly personnel are used inefficiently, or in the wording of the Wapenhans Report:

> Task Managers are asked to take on administrative, managerial, liaison and negotiations responsibilities far removed from their areas of experience and technical proficiency. Second, skill constraints in the Bank's workforce are felt most often

> in such areas as accounting and auditing, procurement, organization, management, and environmental assessment. Third, staff believe existing skills are often inefficiently deployed ...
> (ibid., p. 19)

Briefly put, cumbersome red tape, misallocation of personnel, economically dubious bureaucratic goals such as pleasing one's superiors' fancies, channelling a certain amount of money 'out in time' to reach 'targets', or even the beauty of style of memos have been given priority over economic results and benefits to borrowing countries at the borrowers' expense. Not surprisingly the Report complains that '*portfolio management work* [or controlling the effects of one's decisions] *should receive the same feed back from managers and the same recognition and rewards as other operational work*' (ibid., Annex A, p. 18f; emphases as original).

The Wapenhans Report is usually quoted as a completely new and more self-critical approach by the Bank, which is a widespread but wrong perception. The Bank's Operations Evaluation Department (OED), answering directly to the president, established because of US insistence and frequently quoted by the Report, has published the same criticisms, for quite some time, very often even in the same wording. Quite often, as the OED itself states, this has not affected the actual implementation of projects, although only about half the projects could be judged likely to sustain their benefits (OED 1989, p. xv or p. 9). Unrealistic scheduling and objectives at the time of appraisal, excessive expectations leading to huge gaps between appraised and re-estimated economic rates of return, enduring errors in implementation rate forecasts (even called 'embarrassing' by the OED 1989, p. 14), insufficiently detailed engineering prior to approval, inappropriate expertise in procurement – an issue the OED could, for instance, not elaborate on in 1989 because of inadequate statistics – lack of training, will or motivation by 'most operations staff' were all found as well. In the sector water supply and waste disposal, critique was not heeded since the earliest appraisal in 1970 – a 'sobering' result as the OED correctly remarked in 1989 (ibid., p. 70). Not surprisingly the Wapenhans Report (IBRD 1992, p. ii) quotes water supply and sanitation as a particularly problematic sector with 43 per cent of projects facing major problems in their fourth or fifth year of implementation.

The meaning of 'success' of projects can only be understood if one looks at the method of measurement. The OED introduced a new methodology in 1985–86, based on a greater degree of subjectivity and increased 'weight given to evaluators' perceptions, some of which were difficult to explain fully' (OED 1989, p. 15f). This switch of methods was very 'successful', producing – in contrast to the old method – an apparent upward trend. While 28 per cent of projects were unsatisfactory for the 1987 cohort according to the traditional method, this new technique found only 12 per cent with unsatisfactory or uncertain performance – the worst category. 'Uncertain' is in itself a euphemism defined as: 'Project achieves few objectives, if any, and has no foreseeable worthwhile results'(ibid.). The possibility of damage done by a project is not considered by the classificatory definitions at all. The perceptible decline in the share of satisfactory operations in spite of this new method and its greater subjectivity must be seen with this knowledge in mind.

The great publicity given to the Wapenhans Report is the main difference *vis-à-vis* the OED. Both are official sources and both point at more or less the same grave shortcomings. The Report's disturbing result, which can be corroborated by other sources including the Bank's own, is that available knowledge and evidence have simply not been used to avoid financial consequences disastrous to borrowers. Like the OED before, it shows an appalling lack of appropriate care and concern by the management. One has to concur with the Wapenhans Report that 'The cost of tolerating continued poor performance is highest not for the Bank but for its Borrowers' (IBRD 1992, p. 5).

Finally, the Report (IBRD 1992, p. 9) establishes a perceptible negative correlation between time devoted by the Bank to a project and its success. Based on statistical analysis of 1478 projects rated by the OED, satisfactory projects differ from 'average' projects by 21 per cent less staff-weeks for preparation, 20 per cent less for appraisal, and 4 per cent less needed for negotiations. This can be interpreted that the less IBRD staff get involved, the greater a project's probability of success.

This raises the problem of risk, accountability, and 'ownership' of operations. Echoing other IBRD publications the Report qualifies Bank operations as being substantially risky, stating on its very first page that the 'projects the Bank supports – as a lender of last resort – entail substantial risk taking' (IBRD 1992, p. i). The OED (1989, p. xiii) even expressed concern that a 100 per cent success rate, if ever achieved, 'would invite questions about whether an appropriate level of risk was being faced in development investments'. Echoing this passage the Wapenhans Report defends the share of projects in difficulty, worrying that a very low rate 'could imply the Bank was not taking risks in a high-risk business' (IBRD 1992, p. 3). The wise remark about who actually has to shoulder the greatest risk is forgotten.

Passages like these, which can be found quite often in IBRD publications of the last two decades, give a fundamentally wrong impression, veiling the fact that the Bank itself has never been and still is not taking risks at all. In sharp contrast to important economic decisions taken by it, the financial risk is entirely the borrower's. All borrowers must service their debts unconditionally both according to legal stipulations and to avoid being penalized by the whole donor community. As can be shown, poor countries and mostly the poor within these countries have been forced to pay for the Bank's errors and learning-by-doing so far. Nowadays the IBRD likes to point out that they are learning, but fails to mention at whose cost. The Wapenhans Report (IBRD 1992, p. 5) states clearly that the IBRD's limited use of remedies is sending the wrong signals to both borrowers and staff. It follows logically from this passage that costs could be avoided if the Bank used remedies more appropriately and acted with greater care.

This exemption from financial accountability is *the* important factor explaining IBRD performance. It should be pointed out that similar and not necessarily better results were found with regional development banks. The pressure to lend (or what the Wapenhans Report called 'approval culture') was present in all three cases (IDB 1993; Asian Development Bank 1994; African Development Bank 1994). With the IDB, which had a relatively good report or possibly a less frank task force, a history of tensions between borrowing and non-borrowing members was identified as a specific problem, resulting from the majority of regional votes and the perception of regional members that the IDB is their bank.

The similarity of all other problems is no surprise. It is difficult to imagine how any management could become more attentive to the economic effects of its decisions under such circumstances. Unless decisions are linked with financial accountability, in other words unless the most basic mechanism of a market-friendly economy is introduced, one cannot expect a real and fundamental change in the IBRD's (or other IFIs') business culture.

The present total lack of accountability precludes in principle and unconditionally any liability, even in cases of gross negligence or malicious intent (which is hopefully a purely theoretical possibility). This privileged position of the IBRD, and generally all IFIs, denies those damaged by negligence or intent and – in the cases of imposed and prescribed decisions to paraphrase an executive director of the IBRD (Raffer 1995a) – against their own volition any claim of damage compensation. A privilege of standing above basic legal and economic principles is conferred on IFIs, which is absolutely alien to democratic legal systems where even governments are not as a matter of principle above any judicial and financial accountability.

Economic theory suggests that inefficiencies and politically motivated decisions are fostered by the market-unfriendly environment of riskless deciding. It provides a logical explanation of IBRD performance. Without financial risks other factors become more important, such as disbursing enough to meet country lending targets or pleasing political predilections of one or more big shareholder(s) and other fancies. The de-linking of decisions and risk, an arrangement irreconcilable with a market economy must lead to economically sub-optimal practices. Mosley et al. (1991, vol.I, p. 72) present an extremely telling but by no means singular example revealing how country lending targets may put pressure on officials to disburse. Although the whole division including its chief agreed that Bangladesh could not absorb any more money, the lending programme was not slowed. The division chief explained that if he advised slowing down he would be fired. In some cases adjustment conditionality ran counter to the policy changes the Bank itself was trying to bring in at the project level or the Bank prescribed Structural Adjustment in cases where it was not needed, according to the IBRD's own analysis (ibid., p. 300). Such shortcomings also addressed by the Wapenhans Report or the OED make it difficult to discard the possibility of negligence without further examination.

To avoid being misunderstood as another case of 'IBRD bashing', it might be helpful to state expressly that this is simply an obvious economic truth, valid for any management anywhere. To an economist it is no surprise that firms and institutions exposed to financial accountability have fared better than those in the Eastern Bloc, where this link was severed. Interestingly many shortcomings exposed by the Wapenhans Report strongly recall Eastern Bloc type management procedures. To make a particular point, one of the last communist-type Planned Economies seems to be located in H Street, Washington DC.

In friendlier language the Wapenhans Report (IBRD 1992, p. 17) contends that the present incentive system is distorted and acts as a barrier to desirable changes. In the light of facts this is misleadingly cautious and polite. At present IFIs, such as the Bank, can gain financially from their own failures or negligence at the expense of their clients. If and when damages occur because of failures by IBRD staff, the country has to service their loan fully and might even have to get a second loan from the Bank to repair damages done by the first. As this second loan must of course be serviced as well, the Bank increases its income stream.

Brazil's Polonoroeste project, already mentioned in Chapter 10, clearly illustrates this point. *Time* (12 December 1988) reported that a loan of $240 million had caused considerable environmental damage. Bank officials admitted that they had erred. Another $200 million were lent to Brazil to repair damage done by the first loan. Brazil's debts increased by nearly half a billion US dollars and the IBRD nearly doubled its income stream from interest payments. There is no reason to doubt the IBRD's claim that Brazil did not live up to its obligations too, but while the country had to face the consequences the Bank placed a new, profit-earning loan. Briefly put, the present incentive system is exactly the opposite of an efficient arrangement, allowing the Bank (or other IFIs) to gain from its own errors at their clients' expense.

The question of success or failure of projects is of some importance for Structural Adjustment too, since economic flops increase a country's debt burden. This is especially important in poor SCs with high shares of IFI activities. A sufficient amount of IFI failures will render Structural Adjustment necessary which in turn is administered by IFIs, just as failed Structural Adjustment programmes are likely to call for new Structural Adjustment programmes, as long as unconditional repayment to IFIs is upheld. This logical relation might be described somewhat cynically as IFI flops securing IFI jobs.

This absurd incentive structure, irreconcilably inimical to the very idea of the market mechanism and to any principle of sound management, produces a systemic bias towards accommodating other goals. These may be internal to the Bank or external political demands at the expense of economic efficiency and the client. As the Wapenhans Report rightly formulated, staff feel compelled to address many or all programmes of special emphasis in each project, while there is no countervailing incentive to keep projects designs and conditions down to sensible and manageable dimensions. This can be illustrated by the over 100(!) conditions of the IBRD's second Structural Adjustment Loan to Thailand. The host of conditions supplies 'supportive' arguments to both lines of criticism described in Chapter 11. Those claiming that loans are not country-specific (enough) can point out that essentials remain the same. Those positing that they are, will always find differences. Naturally it becomes impossible to fulfil all conditions and stipulations made, particularly so if some conditions contradict others.

This impossibility or frequently demanded unrealistic financial covenants allow the Bank to decide whether or not to ignore slippage. In other words, the rule of law is substituted by the Bank's arbitrary decisions. The IBRD's (or the IMF's) long history of political lending aggravates this problem substantially. Seen from the angle of increasing leverage, a vast amount of conditions that cannot be fulfilled does in fact make sense. On top of financial impunity it allows the Bank unrestrained arbitrariness in deciding whom to call to account for non-compliance. This situation is certainly not in line with the objectivity criteria for decision-making processes espoused by the ideas of good governance or the rule of law.

Although the Wapenhans Report or the OED's long standing criticism document that the very principles imposed on SCs under the label political conditionality, such as good governance, are clearly violated by the IBRD itself, OECD countries have not thought it necessary to encourage the Bank to adopt these principles. Controlling the majority of votes they could easily do so. They have not even considered introducing the most basic principle of civilized legal systems, namely that those inflicting damages must pay compensation. The Bank is by no means the only institution where this attitude shows. Some time ago the Republic of Trinidad and Tobago (1989) documented grave irregularities and deficiencies in the IMF's assessment of its economy, which created the impression of economic mismanagement and led to a Structural Adjustment programme. After the IMF became aware of these substantial errors no correction was published, in spite of the importance to the country. Because of the government's need for the IMF's 'seal of approval' Trinidad's own expert advised them not to pick a fight with the IMF. It is of interest to note that no OECD country, which as a non-borrower and relatively big shareholder could have acted without any fear of consequences, bothered to ask for a detailed enquiry although this case became famous as the so-called 'Budhoo affair'. Good governance is obviously only a political weapon against unpopular governments and no real, honest concern of OECD governments.

The fact that it took the IBRD nearly half a century to realize that the effects of its operations are no less important than simply spending money or that known problems have not been systematically addressed defy even the most basic rules of economics, business administration and good governance. Nevertheless the Bank's president, Lewis T. Preston, apparently saw no cause for alarm. As its main shareholders seem prepared to allow the IBRD to go on as before, he is absolutely right. In his letter introducing the Report officially he writes: 'While Mr. Wapenhans, in his memorandum to me, finds no cause for alarm in the state of the portfolio, the report validates my initial concerns that all is not well with the results of Bank-financed projects …'. In the light of the sharp criticism by the Wapenhans Report this seems a strong understatement.

The effects of the Report have remained limited. The in-house 'independent' inspection panel with a restricted mandate mentioned in Chapter 3 was created, which, though unique for a multilateral institution, is a rather weak reaction to the untenable situation described by the Report. Without an external authority independent of the IBRD itself and able to award damage compensation (Raffer 1993; 1995a) the Bank is essentially allowed to remain unaccountable. Given the increasing weight of the BWIs as co-ordinators of aid and in setting trends in development co-operation this appalling lack of good governance is all the more alarming.

As countries undergoing Structural Adjustment under Bank and Fund rule are not in a position to address this topic the responsibility remains wholly with 'donor countries', presently embracing the principles of good governance much more by rhetoric than by appropriate action.

13. Aid and human development

HELPING THE VICTIMS OF PROCESSES OF TRANSITION

Describing involuntary poverty as an unmitigated evil persisting in spite of decades of development efforts, Paul Streeten (1994, p. 13) makes a trenchant distinction between development narrowly defined in the economic sense and human development, which comprises other dimensions in addition to income such as longevity, access to knowledge, human rights and so on: 'Yet all too often in the process of development it is the poor who shoulder the heaviest burden. It is development itself that interferes with human development.' Poor people, women, children and vulnerable groups are the victims of processes of transition, such as from subsistence to commercial agriculture or from traditional to market relationships. There is thus a need to help the victims of transition, to cushion the frictions of social and economic changes on those who would otherwise suffer unduly. This very pithy presentation of human development shows an important shortcoming of present development and aid strategies, that is their insufficient focus on and help for the poor. The author points out that protecting vulnerable groups is not only fully justified as an end in itself, as the ultimate purpose of development is to promote human well-being, but it also increases the productivity of the poor and improvements in living conditions result eventually in lower population growth. Human development is thus thrice blessed. Logically one would therefore expect development co-operation to earmark a certain amount of funds for human development purposes.

The UNDP's *Human Development Report 1994* proposed this in the form of the 20:20 compact on human development already mentioned briefly in Chapter 11. All nations should pledge to ensure the provision of at least very basic human development levels for all their peoples. While most countries can achieve this by adjusting their budgets, some of the poorest countries would need substantial financial help from without. The UNDP (1994, p. 7) however underlines that 'No new money is required, because the compact is based on restructuring existing budget priorities'. In other words, an increase of present ODA, more or less stagnating during the last few years and declining slightly since the beginning of the 1980s (OECD 1994, p. 160) would not be required. It would require a shift in favour of the poor though, which means against the interests of SC élites and against donor's export and other interests. This shift has become even less likely after the perceptible fall of ODA in 1993.

The expression 20:20 derives from the suggestion that SCs should earmark at least 20 per cent of their budgets for human priority expenditures, while donors should devote 20 per cent of their ODA to them (UNDP 1994, p. 7; p. 77). The compact's most important targets include:

- universal primary education (for both genders alike)
- adult illiteracy rates to be halved (the female rate must not be higher than the male one)
- primary health care for all
- elimination of severe malnutrition
- family planning services for all willing couples
- safe drinking water and sanitation for all
- credit for all to ensure self-employment opportunities.

This list, considered to be the 'very minimum targets' (ibid., p. 7), may sound universally acceptable. The DAC definition of aid states that the promotion of economic development and welfare must be the main objective of aid. Answering the question 'What is development?' the *World Development Report 1992* states:

> Development is about improving the well-being of people. Raising living standards and improving education, health, and equality of opportunity are all essential components of economic development. Ensuring political and civil rights is a broader development goal. Economic growth is an essential means for enabling development, but in itself it is a highly imperfect proxy for progress.
> (IBRD 1992, p. 34)

In fact we might expect that no donor would speak out against these targets, even if that donor might actually be more concerned with using aid as a convenient outlet for exports than with human or any other kind of development. Nevertheless the UNDP's proposal sparked a brief yet important debate with the OECD.

While the desirability of human development remains officially unchallenged, the question whether and to what extent aid actually promotes it is strongly debated. The UNDP (1993; 1994) presents data showing that although the range between Denmark's 25 per cent and Germany's 2 per cent is substantial, only 7 per cent on average of bilateral DAC aid goes to human 'priority areas such as basic education, primary health care, rural water supplies, nutrition programmes and family planning services' (UNDP 1994, p. 73). Regarding donor countries it therefore finds 'considerable scope for changing the allocation priorities in their aid budgets in the post-cold war era' (UNDP 1994, p. 7). A similar picture emerges for multilateral aid, although multilateral institutions allocate around 16 per cent on average. UNICEF spends 77.8 per cent on human priorities. The African Development Bank is singled out as the multilateral institution devoting the smallest share (4 per cent) to this purpose.

THE DEBATE BETWEEN THE OECD AND THE UNDP

Naturally such figures are not very popular with donors, always eager to claim altruistic motives for their actions as the expression 'aid' itself documents. The OECD (1994, p. 98) defended its aid policy against the UNDP (1993), arguing that human priority concerns 'have long been prime areas of interest for the DAC and its Members', and were at the heart of the 1989 DAC's Policy Statement on Development Co-operation in the 1990s.

After confirming its total support for human development, the DAC tackles the problem of aid allocation. It argues that the average figure of less than 7 per cent quoted above is based on aid loans recorded transaction by transaction in the Creditor Reporting System administered by the DAC Secretariat. As loans only account for 20–25 per cent of bilateral ODA and the 'sectoral allocation' (ibid.) of grants is substantially different, the DAC believes the allowance made by the UNDP for this discrepancy is inadequate. This belief though cannot be supported by any data. The OECD refers vaguely to 'other reporting to the DAC (the aggregate reporting system)'. As only donors report to the DAC this means that donors themselves are not able (if not unwilling) to produce more precise data on how much of their aid goes to prime areas of interest at the heart of their policy concerns. One must agree with the OECD (1994, p. 98) that this 'demonstrates also the importance of improving the capacity of the aid reporting system to track the sectoral allocation and impact of aid'.

The OECD goes on to argue that aid to the water supply sector was even the subject of a special DAC meeting held in 1994. Its thinking in terms of sectors and the wording 'sectoral allocation' show a further fundamental discrepancy between the DAC and the UNDP with regard to the concept itself. The UNDP (1993, p. 68) clearly, though briefly, criticized the wrong weights attached within sectors. Demanding that ODA allocation be based on levels of poverty it stated that 'ODA should be allocated to people rather than countries' (ibid., p. 7). The *Human Development Report 1994* repeats that it is not allocation to sectors that matters but allocation to people, that is *within* sectors. While the presentation and definition of human development priorities could have been carried out in a more precise way in the UNDP *Report* of

1993, thus possibly avoiding misunderstandings, the following quote for instance is absolutely clear:

> The problem here is not so much the proportion of aid they [donors] give to the social sector (16% on average) as the distribution within the social sector. Less than one-fifth of education aid goes to primary education, and a similar proportion of aid for water supply and sanitation is earmarked for rural areas, with very little for low-cost-mass coverage programmes.
> (UNDP 1994, p. 7)

The *Human Development Report 1993* (UNDP 1993, p. 67) explicitly criticized the fact that higher status projects get preference and that aid does not go to poor people, a criticism repeated in more detail in 1994. Thus urban water supply and sanitation receives about 80 per cent of sectoral funds, or roughly four times as much as rural areas. Higher education is favoured *vis-à-vis* primary education (which receives less than 20 per cent of sectoral expenditure), urban hospitals get preference over primary health care which is only allocated about one-third of total aid expenditure on health (UNDP 1994, pp. 73f). This citicism had already been made by the UNDP in its *1993 Report*, but less clearly. Higher visibility of larger and more modern projects in not too remote areas is one reason mentioned by the UNDP for this allocation. It appears in fact to be more attractive to donors to finance a new, modern hospital in the capital – where a plaque at the entrance informs that this was financed by country X's ODA or which is worthy to be given the name of the minister of development of country Y – than to finance 200 health stations for paramedics or barefoot doctors somewhere in the bush, which are appropriate for their purpose and look it.

The UNDP's focus on need cannot be invalidated by pointing at sectoral figures. Aid to any sector may go to the rich or the poor. Irrigation projects for instance might be exclusively in the interest of the rich, strengthening their economic position, even enabling them to exploit the poor more thoroughly. The example of deep tubewells in Bangladesh – well digging projects, quite often undertaken with good intentions, were quite popular in the donor community some time ago – illustrates this very clearly. Access to water was immediately controlled by the rich and even used to the detriment of the poor in the village (Jansen 1979). The famous 'Green Revolution' benefited the rich, exacerbating social disparities.

It must be pointed out that the UNDP might have contributed to the misunderstanding. It argues for example that ODA distribution is not linked to human development objectives, basing this conclusion on those shares of ODA or development finance going to SCs with two-thirds of the world's poor, to countries with the highest numbers of poor people, or to high military spenders (UNDP 1993, p. 7; 1994, pp. 72f). Apart from possibly blurring the real focus –

helping the poorest people – this is not logically convincing. Allocating more aid to Brazil, Indonesia, Vietnam or the Philippines would have resulted in more flows going to SCs with two-thirds of the world's poor, but would this money necessarily have reached the poor in these countries? The OECD's logical flaw of arguing with sectoral expenditures might thus have been provoked, at least to some extent, by the UNDP. The OECD's assertion that neither the DAC nor its members know how much money did benefit the poor explains these attempts by the UNDP to argue via sectors or countries, simply because no adequate figures exist. A plausible correlation between the regional distribution of aid and the global distribution of the poor is apparently seen as a necessary though not a sufficient condition for actually reaching the poor. The UNDP should have pointed out clearly that this is all that can be done with existing data. The absence of appropriate data in turn does not support the claim of donors that human priority concerns have long been prime areas of their interest. Goals to which governments have been committed for a long time are invariably well covered by statistics, true or crooked.

Defending its allocation, the OECD confuses the UNDP's developmental concept of high human priority with humanitarian concerns, a mistake which might not have occurred if the UNDP (1993) had been as clear as its *Report 1994*, although it is quite possible to recognize what the UNDP meant in 1993. It is true that aid to refugees and disaster victims is necessary and of high human priority, and it is highly commendable to help in such cases. But this is relief, and by no means what is meant by the UNDP's concept of development. The former helps in emergencies or after disasters while the latter is committed to long term development and to changing economic and social structures. To describe it with the help of the old adage of the fish – relief means giving fish to people, human development means equipping them better to catch their own food. Both activities are necessary, important and laudable but they are different. They should be properly linked, as will be explained in the next Chapter, but they must not be confused.

While part of the confusion could be accidental and arguments might have been phrased differently if things had beeen clear from the start, there remains a most important and fundamental divide between DAC donors and the UNDP concept. The last counter argument of the OECD brings it to light:

> Even more problematic is the question of how broadly the definition of 'human priority concerns' is drawn and how the various forms of aid interact with human priorities. The UNDP covers only aid going directly to the sectors identified above. But aid which assists general economic development, including aid to support economic stabilization, policy reforms and adjustments to public expenditure priorities, can have a wide impact on the access of poor people to basic education, primary health care and family planning services.
> (OECD 1994, p. 98)

This view qualifies everything as potentially of human priority concern. This would make the UNDP demand to allocate 20 per cent to human priority concerns obsolete and in fact unduly modest. Logically of course virtually anything *can* have positive effects on anything and anyone, including the poor. But in plain English this means that the OECD considers that the very concept of special projects aimed at the poor or other special groups is flawed and logically unnecessary. By this passage the OECD implies that whatever is done by donors is likely to benefit the poor anyway. If this point is accepted there would be no need to target any projects specifically on them. Quite conveniently there is then no need for detailed statistics on the actual impact of aid, nor for criticism either. If accepted this view destroys any logical basis to criticize actual aid policy on the grounds of its (lack of) impact on the poor.

The OECD's argument is particularly interesting with regard to the attempts to include military assistance under ODA. Figures of aid including military expenditures (OECD 1994, p. 82) are published a few pages before the OECD's worry about too narrow a definition of human priority concerns.

The thesis of the two opposing concepts is supported by the *Chairman's Report* on 1994 (OECD 1995). Within about a year the OECD reconsidered the 'policy importance of the UNDP recommendations' (OECD 1994, p. 98) and simply refused to discuss them. Instead it restricted itself to one paragraph in its most recent DAC *Report* blaming the UNDP for undermining 'public and parliamentary support' (OECD 1995, p. 10) for aid. The debate with the UNDP is specifically referred to as 'an unfortunate fact' (ibid.) and as 'much more difficult to clarify and resolve with factual analysis than is often assumed', even by the DAC Secretariat

> with all its access to the most authoritative information in the field. Obscurantism in this field would, of course, have the effect of undermining public understanding and confidence, but so does the kind of debate that poses deceptively simple questions or unrealistic expectations to which donors cannot satisfactorily respond.
> (ibid.)

Comparing the two DAC *Reports* on 1994 and 1993 one cannot help noticing a clear contradiction. The bottom line is that the OECD is unwilling to commit itself to the 20:20 compact but has no good arguments to back that decision, particularly so considering its acceptance of humanitarian goals. Refusing further discussion it falls back upon ill-founded accusations.

To some extent the OECD's perception recalls donors' attitudes before Myrdal's critique of the undifferentiated use of 'aid' for any North-South activity. Nowadays it is again implied that any ODA or development finance activity benefits the poor. Thus aid is again given the philanthropic notion of the 1950s and early 1960s, although we have seen that it is simply a technical term covering helpful activities as well as greed or – at worst – 'lethal aid'.

Economically the two opposing views may be represented by two questions: (a) should aid target the poor directly or will the benefits of development at large eventually trickle down to all members of society, and (b) does one have to embark on a bottom-up strategy for development or are top-down projects better. Within this dichotomy the DAC position is a reformulation of the old 'trickle down' model. It argued that growth would finally benefit everyone since its positive effects, such as higher incomes, would eventually trickle down to the poor. Thus helping the rich was not only necessary for development but would actually amount to helping the poorest as well. Similarly there is no need for special support of minorities, vulnerable groups or women as gender and all other issues will be benevolently solved to anyone's liking anyway. Of course benefits may and even do sometimes trickle down to the poor, but empirical evidence shows that this has not happened on a scale envisaged by the supporters of this approach.

The trickle-down model might sound cynical but it was essentially accepted by neoclassicists as well as by orthodox Marxists, a fact which induced Dudley Seers (1979) to write a paper on the congruence of Marxism and other neoclassical doctrines. According to basic neoclassical teachings the propensity to save increases with income. Poor people, especially if living around subsistence level, are very likely to consume all additional income. The rich on the other hand save a larger part of their income. They can and should invest their savings. In countries where savings and capital are scarce, causing a large gap between domestic savings and necessary investment, redistributing income to the poor would therefore compromise future growth.

Kuznets's findings on income distribution were immediately – and against the warnings of the author himself not to generalize them uncritically – seen as the empirical validation of this reasoning (Kuznets 1955). The inverted U symbolizing increasing inequality during the first phases of development (measured as GNP per head) and a trend to greater equality after that period was fully in line with theory. Irrespective of the author's own reservations it thus acquired the status of an economic law. Many other models fitted this perception perfectly as well, such as the famous Lewisian model of growth with unlimited supply of labour. Once the modern sector had grown large enough surplus labour and disguised unemployment would disappear. Beyond this Lewisian turning point benefits would spread widely and speedily, wages would increase, workers would have a better standard of living and the economy would emulate the structures of developed countries.

To avoid an undue caricature of past thought it should be mentioned that economic growth was also emphasized as the key to poverty eradication.

Streeten (1993, p. 16) points out that sensible economists and development planners saw quite clearly in the 1950s:

> that economic growth is not an end in itself, but a performance test of development. Arthur Lewis defined the purpose of development as widening our range of choice, exactly as the UNDP's Human Development Reports do today … Even in the early days some sceptics said that growth is not necessarily so benign.

It was thought necessary first to build up capital, infrastructure and productive capacity in a 'backward' economy in order to improve the lot of the poor later. For some time though the poor would have to tighten their belts and the rich would receive most of the benefits. However if the rewards of the rich were incentives to innovate, to save and to accumulate capital, this could eventually be of benefit to the poor and the early hungry years would turn out to have been justified. Classical, neoclassical and palaeo-Marxist economists all agreed on this. Caveats on growth were thus eclipsed by a pervasive emphasis on the technics of growth.

Orthodox Marxists, such as Bill Warren (1979), advocated helping capitalism to develop, sharing Karl Marx's view that the best way to abolish capitalism would be to help it develop more quickly. Marx (1967) argued that the stage of socialism can only be reached after capitalism has developed fully, the latter creating thus the material base for the former. Consequently Marx saw capitalist developments in the South as a progressive factor helping to bring about the final doom of the system, as his views on India show. Seen from this perspective, investment and the creation of industries (and thus of proletarians) were of paramount importance as well. Until Lenin had to explain why a revolution could happen in relatively underdeveloped Russia, rather than in England or Germany, this was generally accepted wisdom by Marxist thinkers. After Lenin (1973) turned Marx topsy-turvy by claiming that capitalism would first be overcome in a not fully developed capitalist country – just as the weakest link of a chain is the first to give – scientists in 'really existing socialist states' were well advised not to cling to this view of Marx's.

In the West there were occasionally authors such as Nurkse (1952) and Adler (1952) who expressed concern that the rich might use their income for luxury consumption rather than for investment. This of course questions the logical justification for trickle down as a pro-poor growth strategy. However this concern was by no means the ruling view, nor the view of those ruling in North and South engaged in 'development aid', who were all for the *status quo*. This idea was taken up later on by *dependencia* thinkers, who argued that the rich – or in their wording the bourgeoisie – did not behave in a properly capitalist way because they did not invest their revenues in the country, thus depriving the South of needed development stimuli.

The fear that philanthropic approaches might 'waste' resources urgently needed for growth by taking from the rich, was so strong that more direct policies for the benefit of the poor needed substantial technocratic justification. Paul Streeten (1993) describes briefly how direct policies in favour of the poor had to be defended. One fabric going into basic needs is the argument that nutrition, health and education are important for fuller labour utilization and hence greater productivity. Better nutrition, health, education and training can be very productive forms of developing human resources.

Redistribution with Growth (Chenery et al. 1974) published for the Development Research Centre of the World Bank and the Sussex Institute of Development Studies was a first attempt to find a compromise between promoting growth and helping the poor. A proportion of incremental income would be taxed and channelled into public services to raise their productivity.

Briefly put, strategies to help the poor had to be specifically justified by saying that they will (at least indirectly) increase productivity. In other words, they are not only consumption but (often with a lot of roundaboutness) investments. The basic needs approach was presented as an approach 'to growth, employment, income redistribution and poverty eradication' (Streeten 1993, p. 24). Just helping the poor was not considered a legitimate aim of aid. In contrast to export promotion, the incorporation of relief for military debt or other forms of ODA, this particular use had to be explicitly and cumbersomely justified as legitimate.

Naturally the concept of basic needs was no more popular with those ruling in the South, a group who benefited from the trickle-down idea that anything helps the poor eventually. To the rich in the South the idea that increasing their standard of living is a developmental necessity and in the long term interest of the poor was exceedingly appealing.

The view that helping the poor means wasting resources remained so influential that the first *Human Development Report* by the UNDP in 1990 had to justify putting people back at centre stage. The basic arguments used to defend the concept are the same as in the basic needs approach:

> Human beings are both ends in themselves and means of production. Human development, properly interpreted, is thrice blessed. It is an end in itself; it is a means to higher productivity; and it reduces human reproductivity, by lowering the desired family size. This has been widely recognized, though it is odd that institutions like the World Bank accept without questioning Hondas, beer, and television sets as final consumption goods, while nutrition, education and health services have to be justified on grounds of productivity.
> (Streeten 1993, p. 27)

Seen from the *dogmengeschichte* of development the OECD thus advocates a somewhat simplified (pre-Lewisian) 1950s view, which is apparently preferred to the UNDP's demand of widening choices. Both administratively and politically it happens to be the more comfortable view for donors.

What differs decisively from the 1950s is the OECD's implication that financing Structural Adjustment – 'aid to support economic stabilization, policy reforms and adjustments to public expenditure priorities' (OECD 1994, p. 98) – benefits the poor as well. Thus by cutting food subsidies to the poor, hitting vulnerable groups in the ways described by the seminal UNICEF study *Adjustment with a Human Face* (Cornia et al. 1987) one only acts in the very interest of the poor. This opinion is maintained in spite of and after the publication of the great shortcomings of IFIs, as well as the incapability of proving reasonable success of Structural Adjustment measures by the BWIs described above.

THE BWIS AND THE POOR

This OECD argument is identical to the stance of the BWIs at the beginning of the debt crisis, a stance which – due to facts and public pressure – is no longer upheld by them. They insisted then that carrying on Structural Adjustment had positive impacts and was in the very interest of the poor. Special measures to protect them would thus be superfluous if not harmful. Emphasizing human needs might even obstruct needed reforms (Jolly 1991, p. 1811). The IBRD (1980, p. 62) described the 'major drawback' of efficient food subsidies as costly, often using up 'scarce foreign exchange or aid'. The usual arguments are nicely summed up by the IMF's Tseng (1984): 'Structural Adjustment costs are inevitable and lower than the costs of not adopting timely adjustment. Efficiency gains will more than make up for Structural Adjustment costs and financial help by the BWIs mitigates these costs. Bringing down inflation is of particular benefit to the poor who are likely to hold their assets in cash. Successful economic reforms benefit everybody, including the poor. Subsidies have to be abolished as they are a huge part of public outlays. They discriminate against the rural poor and create incentives for low wage industries, thus leading to rapid urbanization (and slums)'. To be on the safe side Tseng adds that the IMF has no mandate regarding the poor anyway.

Beckmann (1986), to quote someone from the Bank, concurs, explaining the change in the IBRD's policy away from the poverty focus of the McNamara years as triggered by a change in SCs' needs. A balance of payments equilibrium reached by growth of GDP and exports benefits the rich as well as the poor while relying on market mechanisms does not mean less attention to the poor, planned adjustment is better than unplanned adjustment and sacrifices are necessary for a better future. The growth crisis made advances in poverty alleviation practically impossible. In line with his employer, the Bank, he adds that many projects benefited the poor as well, even though the political climate of the 1980s does not favour the poor. To prove this he mentions that most IDA and IBRD funds went to poor countries and sectors, whose projects are supposed to benefit the poor in particular – a statement that, as we have seen, may raise objections from statisticians. As the Bank's policy is guided by its members and in consultation with borrowers, the IBRD itself has – according to the author – limited room for manoeuvring. Summing up, there was no reason for catering to special vulnerable groups, gender issues and so on. It might indeed be harmful to do so.

Basically this view was held until UNICEF's two volumes on *Adjustment with a Human Face* (Cornia et al. 1987) were published, although the BWIs had been confronted with the effects of Structural Adjustment on the poor as early as 1984 (Helleiner et al. 1991). After rejecting the study at first, the BWIs now accept special programmes to help those affected by Structural Adjustment. It is argued that they would make Structural Adjustment more acceptable and thus more efficient – the very point denied wholeheartedly a short time before. But whatever the BWIs did, they always claimed that they were helping the poor. In practice though little was done by the them. Stewart's (1991, p. 1847) finding that 'while there was a big change in rhetoric, little action has so far followed' still holds. Arguments and titles of publications have changed while Structural Adjustment has essentially remained unaffected, in spite of severe criticism and even though it could not be proved empirically that it works. Quite on the contrary, the successful 'tigers' in Asia have done the opposite of what the representative debtor country is forced to implement.

For quite some time the IBRD has agreed that they have learned, a view valid for the Bank as well as for all other IFIs engaged in this activity. So far it has failed to specify at whose cost. The poorest, who are most severely hit by Structural Adjustment, had to pay for the IBRD's and other IFIs' tuition. In spite of this change of opinion in the IBRD, brought about by public pressure and NGOs, the OECD still champions the old position now considered untenable by the BWIs. Given the relatively large amount of resources controlled by DAC members this bodes ill for the poor. Particularly so as similar tendencies towards less participation by the people, greater influence of donors and less concern for alleviating the lot of the poor can be seen within the EU's Lomé framework (see Chapter 7).

THE DANGER OF ABUSING THE CONCEPT OF HUMAN DEVELOPMENT

Unfortunately there is a danger that the idea of human development might be perverted by donors and some multilateral institutions. IFIs, most notably the IBRD after the Wapenhans Report but also for example the IDB, have started to re-orient their activities perceptibly to financing projects without clear economic returns, that is without an income stream in foreign exchange sufficient to cover debt service, which are activities to which defenders of human development would subscribe. Examples are the financing of institution building, which should facilitate democratic participation by the people or, even more in line with essential human development, investments in the social sector such as in basic education. An example of the latter is a local language school for indigenous children in Mexico financed by the IBRD. This is no doubt a socially highly recommendable project that serves human development priorities and deserves to be financed. However financing such activities by loans, particularly by IFI loans, is not a viable way of doing so. Such projects may very often have 100 per cent local content, which is good for local development, but they, as well as for instance institution building, cannot and should not earn foreign currency income directly. For example one can hardly expect poor indigenous children in Mexico to pay school fees in US dollars. Nor does an improved legal system release an immediate stream of US dollars.

Nevertheless these loans have to be repaid with interest in foreign exchange. Institutional changes, such as the reorganization of the legal system within a country or reforms in the course of democratization should thus not be financed by loans, particularly not on the expensive terms of 'development finance'. While such changes are no doubt important for a sound framework of future development, democratic participation and human development, they do not generate foreign exchange income directly and will have to be serviced out of the budget. In countries where debt service already puts heavy strains on the government, new loans that do not earn their own amortization and interest service are bound to worsen the country's debt situation further. If undertaken on a larger scale they will increase the debt burden of a country dramatically. Particularly for countries still suffering from considerable debt pressures and unable to honour large percentages of contractually due payments on time this must have highly negative economic consequences, especially at the 'near-market' interest rates usual with the IBRD or regional development banks. Therefore such urgently needed projects must be financed by other means, preferably by grants. If the evolution of democratic institutions or human development is really as important to donors as their rhetoric claims, they should be prepared to finance these commendable activities. As economic theory holds that the willingness to pay reveals an actor's true preferences, this would also be an opportunity for donors to prove the honesty of their concern for the poor or for values such as democracy or the rule of law.

The fact that the evaluation of such activities is particularly dependent on what the OED called subjectivity of assessment or perceptions difficult to explain fully, as well as the Wapenhans Report's findings, should be a further caveat. As these projects are by definition not expected to cover their costs but to have long-run benefits for the whole economy which cannot be properly gauged at the moment, the results can be substantially 'improved' – and the rate of unsatisfactory projects 'reduced' – by inexplicably positive assessments. The fact that few or no hard economic data exist and the monetary equivalent of the effect of, say, primary education covering a larger share of the population or a more democratic system on the whole economy cannot be objectively established may prove extremely 'helpful' in this respect. It gives evaluators enormous leeway in defining 'success', which is likely to compound with the effects of lacking financial accountability. Without drastic changes of present structures the mechanisms forcing the poor to pay for IFI inefficiency are likely to be further strengthened. Focusing loans and credits by multilateral institutions on these activities may be abused as a means to hide their inefficiency, simply because the effects of these particular projects, necessary as they are, cannot be measured objectively on a monetary scale. Thus the danger of being challenged on the grounds of efficiency would be virtually overcome by IFIs. Although even the gravest shortcomings do not lead to reactions by their shareholders at present, this evolution would further decrease the likelihood of changes in their management culture to the better. The urge to survive, described so well for bureaucracies by Parkinson, would win again.

This imminent danger, as well as the real attitude of OECD donors manifested in their deeds which are in sharp contrast to their words, bodes ill for SCs and particularly for the poor. There is reason to believe that, if and as far as the concept of human development might be taken up by donors at all, it is not unlikely to be abused for the purpose of promoting donors' interests, very much like political conditionality. An increased amount of projects in sectors classified as falling under 'human development' along the lines of the OECD described above but without benefits to the poor might be forthcoming. In the worst case these activities could even hurt vulnerable groups.

At present though, it is at least as likely that the $30 to 40 billion a year for human priority activities demanded by the UNDP will not be forthcoming, even if this could be achieved wholly by restructuring budgets, that is without any new money. The costs of eliminating malnutrition, one of the main targets on the UNDP list, may serve to show how little would be needed to alleviate hunger. The IBRD (1980, p. 61) calculated that 'redirecting only about 2 percent of the world's grain output to the mouths that need it' would be sufficient. Compared with other outlays it would not be costly to feed the victims of transitions and global changes. Unfortunately this little is unlikely to be forthcoming.

14. The future of aid: proposals for change

Aid and development finance are currently ridden by numerous faults: money has been spent on useless prestige projects (by donors as well as by recipients), on the military, on bailing out commercial banks or IFIs, to achieve political objectives and in many inefficient ways. Quite often intended objectives have not been achieved or failed projects made many people worse off. All these factors have contributed to 'aid fatigue' and some critics conclude that one should get rid of aid.

Concurring with Paul Streeten (1994a, p. 125), we think that a better and more adequate conclusion is to get rid of the faults and to evolve mechanisms that improve the quality of aid and development finance. With this conclusion in mind previous Chapters have continuously suggested improvements or shown our support for proposals such as the UNDP's 20:20 compact. This Chapter focuses on some important proposals for improvements. Because of its importance for future development co-operation, the issue of whether aid is presently shifting to the former Eastern bloc, is also tackled. Large shifts from South to East would threaten to undermine the financial basis of proper development co-operation.

Naturally one has to expect that the ideas presented will not be popular with donors and IFIs, as they run counter to several important interests within the development business. But this is a good reason to popularize them. Doing so we let ourselves be guided by Jan Tinbergen's dictum quoted in Chapter 4, that the idealists of today often turn out to be the realists of tomorrow.

COMBINING EMERGENCY AND DEVELOPMENT AID TO A NEW AID PARADIGM

Within total aid, emergency aid for disasters has come to play an increasingly important role while within this increasing emergency aid, the share of aid absorbed by manmade disasters (wars, conflicts, ethnic cleansing) has been constantly increasing as compared with natural disasters. Emergency aid raises very different problems from normal development aid – it often requires quick action without the time for careful project analysis, it requires massive action, much of the aid is in the form of direct supply of commodities (especially food aid) and much of the emergency aid is channelled through NGOs. Thus emergency aid is not easily combined with normal development aid in one and the same institution.

Emergency aid in cases of war and conflict also raises specific political problems. Normally aid is channelled through governments, but in the case of war and conflict the government is one of the participants in the conflict or may even be the perpetrator of ethnic cleansing. This raises special problems for multilateral UN programmes which are supposed to operate through governments, but somewhat less for NGOs. It even raises military problems since the aid supplies may have to be protected. Hence in cases such as Bosnia and Somalia emergency aid is closely linked with UN peacekeeping operations. In extreme cases, such as Somalia, there may be no organized government at all to deal with, in which case the aid donors assume the functions of a *de facto* government.

There is little doubt that the rapid increase in emergency aid has been at the expense of normal development aid. Total aid budgets have been declining rather than increasing, certainly in real terms and as percentages of donor GNPs. It is true that emergency aid with its special urgency and appeal to humanitarian instincts also helps to tap additional resources for funding, for instance through appeals by NGOs or special contributions to UN actions. But the fact remains that development aid is under threat, especially since the diversion to emergency aid coincides with the new threat of aid-diversion to Eastern Europe and the former Soviet Union. Hence much thought is now being given to how to link emergency aid with development aid. This idea, also known as the relief-development continuum, points to the possibility of preventive action as the first step to make emergency less likely to happen, then to combine the actual relief action as much as possible with development work, for example by not only feeding refugees in refugee camps but also by organizing food for work projects such as road building or other infrastructure projects useful for further development in their own or in another country. Next would come the phase of reconstruction and rehabilitation which again can be organized to be useful for subsequent development, for example after an earthquake previously wooden houses can be replaced by better structures which can withstand earthquakes better and raise housing standards generally. Finally the next 'normal' development programme, after peace has been restored or after the effects of a natural disaster have been overcome, could pay special attention to reducing vulnerability to future disasters, for instance by favouring drought-resistant crops in areas vulnerable to drought. It should be aimed at building local capacity and drawing on local knowledge. In this way emergency aid and development aid would be combined and complementary to each other. This aid paradigm is superior to the conventional paradigm in which disasters are treated as separate interruptions of the development process during which all 'normal' aid would be suspended.

COPYING THE SUCCESS OF THE MARSHALL PLAN: REGIONAL CO-OPERATION AND SELF-MONITORING

In Chapter 4 we described the strong effects of the Marshall Plan on aid and North-South relations, also pointing out the difference between reconstruction efforts after a war and long term development. Unfortunately two of the Plan's characteristic and successful features, which could easily have been copied, were never considered by Northern donors *vis-à-vis* the South. These are the clear intention of promoting regional co-operation among recipients by joint assessments of needs and joint requests, and the principle of self-monitoring by recipients. Since other features of Marshall aid were emulated by development aid, the above is difficult to explain unless one accepts the view that the relatively democratic and open structures that the US encouraged Western Europe to develop were at odds with Northern donor governments' intentions to use development aid to their own narrow political and economic advantage. Here the Marshall Plan still has something to teach.

To overcome the problems of aid fatigue, lack of 'ownership' by recipients but also sometimes of mutual distrust, an emulation of these principles of Marshall aid is advocated. Countries could group themselves on a geographical basis or, if more advisable, according to other, economic criteria. Regions would not necessarily have to be constituted following present continental borders but one continent might contain two or more regions. Regions might contain countries from two continents, for instance crossing the continental border between Asia and Africa. Paul Streeten (1994a, p. 126), who also sees emulation of the Marshall Plan as one possibility to improve present aid strategies, illustrates possible regional groupings: 'The East African countries, or members of ASEAN, or a group of Latin American countries could inspect each other's performance.' Self-monitoring groups, for instance in Sub-Saharan Africa (SSA), could focus on the specific needs and problems of their regions, which will often diverge from those of other regional groupings. In the case of SSA both contacts established within the ACP group and existing regional organizations could provide a starting point.

Among the different regions it is SSA which is most in need of a major and comprehensive aid action on the dimensions of the Marshall Plan. Presently SSA is in danger of becoming marginalized and left completely out of the mainstream of global development. This situation would not only be economically harmful for the global economy, it would also be politically and socially unsustainable and a sure recipe for war and conflict which might affect other regions. The regional monitoring and co-operation among the recipients would be of particular importance to SSA.

SSA is split up among a large number of often economically very weak states with arbitary boundaries cutting across natural and demographic units. Improved regional co-operation is an absolutely essential pre-condition for economic improvement in SSA. The scope for this is large. For example, Yeats (1990) has shown that SSA countries were overcharged by 20 per cent or more for their imports compared with world market prices because of factors such as insufficient bulk and market knowledge. A common procurement agency, based on regional co-operation would therefore result immediately in considerable savings of foreign exchange. The development of better transport links throughout the continent is another pre-condition for improvement – as advocated by the former Austrian Chancellor Bruno Kreisky (1980; 1983). This can only be done efficiently on a regional basis. Existing regional institutions, such as the African Development Bank, could be strengthened by channelling Marshall Plan type aid though them, although this would presuppose major reforms in many of these institutions, not least the African Development Bank. Furthermore the present conflict over shares, voting rights and political control in the AfDB has to be resolved.

This process of self-monitoring and joint requests to the donor community should and could be further enhanced by integrating NGOs into the process. Present institutional contacts between official donors and NGOs could serve as a starting point. Public discussions including affected people, open information policies and thus strong transparency should be encouraged.

This structure would change North-South relations radically. The present situation of largely unhampered donor power would give way to a much more open, transparent and democratic structure of development co-operation, which would go beyond the concept of partnership within the first Lomé treaty, before the backswing towards 'normal' donor-recipient relationships occurred. This would not mean the end of any donor influence but this influence would be counterbalanced. The pursuit of narrow donor self-interests would become next to impossible because of the participatory and people-centred nature of this model of new and improved Marshall Plan procedures. It would fulfil all demands of good governance, democracy and transparency presently voiced by donors in a democratic and transparent way. Finally it would use a model whose ability to foster growth and whose success have already been proved. Since practically all industrialized country donors are already organized in the DAC (and the OECD), an important pre-condition for donor co-ordination is already met. Regarding SCs, grouping could also take already existing regional co-operation and integration efforts into account, but would not need to do so.

STRUCTURAL ADJUSTMENT PROGRAMMES AND REGIONAL ECONOMIC CO-OPERATION IN AFRICA

Virtually all African countries have Structural Adjustment Programmes, most of them are subject to IMF stabilization programmes and IBRD Structural Adjustment Programmes (here combined as SAPs). At the same time, as the recent Nairobi Conference on an Imperative Agenda for Africa has emphasized, there is a clear need and many opportunities for intensified regional and continental co-operation within Africa. This raises the question of how the SAPs can in principle be reconciled or combined with such intensified regional co-operation. Naturally SAPs themselves would have to be reformed substantially as well.

It is not difficult to think of SAPs and regional co-operation as intrinsically opposed to each other. The SAPs are negotiated on a country-by-country basis without any specific provision for assessing the impact of a SAP for country A on its neighbours and regional partners B, C and D. There are signs that the IBRD is becoming aware of this limitation of the country-by-country approach. This applies in particular to the fallacy of composition which is involved when each country is induced to increase exports and thus to compete in the world market with other countries, including regional partners, exporting the same commodities. The same fallacy of composition can apply to devaluation and other elements of SAPs. In that way SAPs can be obstacles to regional co-operation and set potential regional partners against each other.

Similarly the SAPs may be said to be antagonistic to regional co-operation in that their basic philosophy is that of integration into a free-trading global economy. Regional arrangements, at least if they take the form of movements towards free trade areas, customs unions or common markets, inevitably contain an element of discrimination and inward-looking, not easily reconciled with principles of outward-looking global non-discrimination. Regional organization is permitted, subject to certain conditions. In any case more specific acts of regional co-operation (falling short of free trade areas) such as establishment of transport links, planned distribution of industries, joint import procurement or export marketing would not be subject to any restrictions under GATT or WTO rules.

While the fallacy of composition is well known and the BWIs are themselves beginning to take more account of the repercussions of SAPs on other countries and on the global economy, there is another aspect of SAPs which should be modified in the interests of regional co-operation. Under the system of country-by-country negotiations a project or activity which benefits several neighbouring countries simultaneously will not receive sufficient weight in an approved SAP. Only the benefit accruing directly to country A, subject to the SAP negotiation, will be counted; benefits accruing to neighbouring country B or neighbouring countries B, C, D and E, will be disregarded – at least they are not the direct concern of the negotiations for the SAP of country A. The same applies in reverse when SAPs are negotiated for countries B, C, D and E. In technical economic terms such regional benefits represent externalities which should be included in overall cost-benefit calculations but fall outside the scope of national SAPs. There is clearly a need for some kind of mechanism or arrangement either to modify or supplement national SAPs so as to take account of such regional externalities.

What form should such modification take? Here we are entering unknown territory. But however speculative, it seems important to list and explore a number of possibilities. The most far-reaching suggestion obviously would be to abandon the country-by-country basis of SAP negotiations and to negotiate regional (or even global Third World) SAPs. In this form such a proposal would appear somewhat Utopian at the present time, conflicting as it does with principles of national sovereignty and the constitution of multilateral institutions with their membership limited to national governments. It would also conflict with the specific and differing needs and situations of individual countries which call for separate individualized programmes. (Critics might well observe that in any case the present individual country programmes are not highly specific since they tend to contain similar types of measures inspired by the common ideology of the Washington Consensus.)

However there are milder ways to introduce regional externalities into SAPs which may be less Utopian. One such possibility would be for representatives of regional groupings to be present and heard during the national SAP negotiations, for example SADC would be represented in SAP negotiations for Zimbabwe or Zambia and ECOWAS in negotiations for Nigeria or Ghana. Another possibility would be for regional co-operation programmes to be prepared prior to national SAP negotiations and to be separately approved and financed so that the national SAPs can then be negotiated on a strictly country-by-country basis without offending regional externalities. One could imagine a revitalized African Development Bank being enabled to approve and finance such additional regional programmes (although in the interests of co-ordination there may be advantages in having the supplementary regional programmes approved and supported by the same institution also involved in the national SAPs). The very least one would suggest is that regional co-operation projects and policies should be specifically included in SAPs and that countries should get credit for positive acts of regional co-operation in the same way as for reducing budget deficits, reducing rates of inflation, reducing subsidies or promoting exports. Perhaps separate additional support could be earmarked for, and made conditional upon, promoting regional co-operation – preferably monitored by the regional organization itself.

A Structrual Adjustment negotiation on a regional basis, or with a regional element, would strengthen the current very weak bargaining position of African countries in relation to the BWIs. Regionally, the African side would be bigger actors. They would also be 'price takers' to a lesser degree. They could look at the joint effects of export expansion and avoid at least some problems of the fallacy of composition. A joint industrial policy in which regional partners agree to specialize in different industries or activities would increase the domestic market and thus make the countries more creditworthy in relation to financing those selected industries. In fact a regional market would be able to remove some of the market imperfections and hence make liberalization and market-friendly policies more plausible – an argument which should certainly appeal to the BWIs!

In any regional grouping there would almost certainly be losers as well as winners. The argument for regional co-operation is that on balance this is a positive sum game where benefits exceed costs and losers could be compensated while still leaving the winners better off than before. Such compensation payments, which would oil the wheels of regional co-operation and remove the political and social obstacles in the way of reaping the benefits of regional co-operation, would be a good investment and there seems no reason why such compensation payments could not themselves be financed as part of the SAP.

Support for regional co-operation in Africa is, at least in theory, encouraged and supported by aid donors, both bilateral and multilateral, as well as in the policy recommendations of the BWIs. If there is a genuine political will to make a reality out of this rhetorical support and convert benign neglect into active support, then ways and means of incorporating such support in SAPs would not be too difficult to devise. Certainly on an experimental basis some of the suggestions made in this paper could be practised. This need not interfere with the major proposition that the impetus for regional co-operation must come from the African countries themselves. They would also have to take the initiative in seeing that SAPs (and other forms of external support) are suitably adjusted to fit in with an endogenous movement towards regional co-operation.

ALLOCATING AID ACCORDING TO THE HUMAN DEVELOPMENT INDEX

Paul Streeten (1995) proposed that aid should be given according to the Human Development Index (HDI), which combines longevity, GDP per head and knowledge. The criterion proposed is the difference between expected future values of the HDI (discounted at some agreed social discount rate) with and without aid. Past performance is seen as a potentially useful guide to assess future performance. The result shows an expected or potential improvement and aid should go to the greatest potential improvers. Since the HDI is an average not sensitive to difference between rich and poor, men and women or neglected ethnic groups, additional weight should be given to specific HDIs covering these groups. Similarly additional weight could be attached by multiplication for countries which do not practise torture, which apply the rule of law and so on. Finally reform-minded governments should be helped over transitional difficulties caused by reforms which pose additional burdens on their budgets and administrations. 'Human adjustment assistance' should be used so that countries taking positive steps towards human development do not suffer a short term and transitional deterioration of their HDI.

Streeten remarks that donors might wish to attach additional political weights depending on their preferences for or against countries. This is a realistic but dangerous addition as it would largely destroy the usefulness of this or any other index.

To restrict subjectivity Streeten proposes international monitoring by institutions trusted by both sides, recommending three alternatives: an emulation of the Marshall Plan model of self-monitoring by recipients, a mutually agreed council of wise persons or a genuine global secretariat with loyalties to the world community. He points out that this last point was not reached by existing organizations such as the IBRD or UN agencies.

While this form of public and international control would guarantee greater objectivity if the institution functions in a transparent way, the counterfactual nature of the difference between expected values is a problem. Therefore we should like to propose a change in the criterion from which calculations start. Instead of counterfactual values, which are problematic even if the past is taken into account, it appears to be preferable to direct aid exclusively according to past performance. A necessary exception would be a country where the government has changed radically and so recently that no (meaningful) record exists.

Aid can either be directed to countries with low HDIs which are not improving, provided that they are the result of insufficient resources and aid will be used to improve human development, or good performers get more aid. If one wishes to connect aid and human development in this way there are two important criteria of performance. First SCs achieving high improvements in their HDIs should be encouraged with more aid. Second countries with both high HDIs and low per caput GNPs should be helped to improve their economic capacities.

Streeten's idea differs from the 20:20 compact because it is not confined to financing essential human development targets. Other aid, for instance ODA aimed at improving the economic fabric of a country, export possibilities or local production without a direct link to human priorities, should be given more generously to good performers as well. Successful projects strengthen economic capacities to finance further improvements in human development.

While it is highly commendable to support countries working on improving the welfare of their citizens, not all aid should be allocated according to HDI criteria. People living in countries ruled by regimes violating human rights also have a right to receive help. By not giving any aid to people in such countries the population, particularly the poor, would suffer twice. In such cases though the government is not a partner in development co-operation. Aid must go to projects benefiting the population directly. Unfortunately the amount of aid that can be given under such circumstances would be smaller than in the case of co-operating governments.

DEBT RELIEF – INTERNATIONAL CHAPTER 9 PROCEEDINGS

Aid has frequently been abused to bail out private banks, IFIs and donors themselves for too many years. In such cases it has been given with the main objective of keeping creditors afloat rather than mainly promoting economic development. Nevertheless donors recognize it as aid. Unless the debt problem is solved, this abuse is bound to go on. Debt relief is both necessary to free resources for development and to remove the disincentive to private economic activity posed by arrears of unserviceable debts.

The case for debt relief has become very strong following the Mexican fiasco in 1995, when the optimistic claim that the debt crisis was over, at least for Latin American countries with renewed 'market access', became untenable. The $50 billion price tag for the stabilization of Mexico also proved convincingly that the costs of further debt crises could be very high. On the other hand all banks – even US money centre banks – have meanwhile provided for their remaining exposure to SCs. The debatable argument of the 1980s that debt reduction would lead to a crash of commercial banks and to an international financial crisis has long ago lost any initial validity it might have had. The need to find a permanent and viable solution to the debt problem makes itself felt again in a most forceful way.

This need was also seen by G7 governments and politicians. The option of some kind of international bankruptcy was discussed informally before the Halifax Summit of June 1995. In contrast to the 1980s, when it was initially proposed, international insolvency is seen with more sympathy in 1995.

Shortly after the Mexican crash the Chairman of the Federal Reserve System, Alan Greenspan, suggested an international insolvency as an appropriate mechanism to settle the debt problem. The *Financial Times* reported that US Treasury Secretary Robert Rubin said he carefully avoided the term 'international bankruptcy court' but that some procedures to work out the debt obligations of debtors were needed. In an article in the *Wall Street Journal* of 10 April 1995 Rep. Jim Leach, the Chairman of the House Banking and Financial Services Committee, recommended international insolvency proceedings: 'What is needed today is a Chapter 11 [insolvency of firms] process for the global financial system, a technique to keep nation states and their people from the impoverishing implications of insolvency.' Mentioning the little known Chapter 9 proceedings [for debtors with governmental powers, so-called municipalities] briefly, he specifically emphasized its basic understanding that (local) government must continue to function. US Chapter 9 is therefore particularly well suited for sovereign debtors. Its essential elements are participatory, fair, democratic and economically viable procedures safeguarding human dignity. In short, it would embrace all the principles advocated and proposed by the donor community under the heading of political conditionality.

Nevertheless Northern governments are not keen to introduce a solution so obviously in line with their own preaching. International insolvency was not mentioned at the Halifax G7 meeting. Interestingly the German government opposes any insolvency proceedings particularly strongly, although Germany itself benefited from very generous debt relief in the 1950s. The London Accord halved the present value of Germany's foreign debt in a *de facto* insolvency, putting the country on the road to reconstruction and economic success. Furthermore Indonesia was given the same treatment at the end of the 1960s (Raffer 1990a) with active support from the German government, which also went along in the case of Poland. Germany's present opposition to treating other countries in the same way it was treated by its own creditors is therefore somewhat peculiar. It is difficult to see Germany's cited moral and economic reasons as perfectly honest arguments.

DAC governments considering any form of insolvency proceedings for sovereign debtors want the IMF to act as the bankruptcy court. This is a very dangerous and ill-advised proposal. First the IMF, as well as all other IFIs, is itself a creditor. Furthermore it is controlled by a majority of creditors. This would remain so even if the Fund stopped lending to SCs and all its own claims were settled before proceedings started. According to any decent legal system and in fact the principle of the rule of law itself, this contradicts the requirements of a fair, equitable and impartial procedure.

Second, present Structural Adjustment policies have not been able to achieve any lasting positive results, although the IMF started adjustment policies (see

Chapter 12) soon after 1973. In the case of Mexico, IFI policies since 1982 have brought about an even bigger debacle than the crises of the 1980s. Applying the most basic principles of a market economy to the IFIs themselves would make a discontinuation of these policies mandatory, particularly so as even IFIs agree that they have created great hardship.

Debtor countries' debt services have to be brought in line with their abilities to pay under present, protectionist conditions, while safeguarding a minimum level of human dignity for the poorest. The fairest and economically most sensible way to do so would be the internationalization of Chapter 9 of US insolvency laws. As this idea, initially proposed in 1987, was elaborated in detail elsewhere (Raffer 1990a) the essential elements of this solution with a human face are presented briefly. It deals with debtors having governmental powers and protects those affected by the composition plan, giving them a right to be heard. Both the indebted municipality's employees and taxpayers expected to pay more have the opportunity to object. Creditors are to receive what can be *reasonably* expected under the circumstances and humane living standards of people living in the indebted municipality are protected.

The essence of this kind of debt relief, which contrasts vividly with the treatment debtors with governmental powers receive at present, recommends itself as a solution to the international debt crisis. Chapter 9 insolvency combines necessary debt relief in general with the flexibility demanded by individual cases, accommodating the case-by-case approach within a general framework. It could be applied internationally at once with very minor changes. Thus a neutral court of arbitration – as is usual in international law – would have to replace national courts to avoid decisions influenced by national interests of creditor or debtor countries. The interests of the population affected by the plan could be defended by trade unions, grassroots organizations, religious or non-religious NGOs, or international organizations such as UNICEF. This right to be heard in fair and equitable proceedings and the possibility of describing the expected effects on the poor in public would certainly have mitigating effects, contributing to an adjustment with a human face. Besides, the arbitrators would have to take particular care to ensure that a minimum of human dignity of the poor population in the debtor country is safeguarded – exactly as the court would do in a US Chapter 9 insolvency case. This law has been successfully applied within the US for decades and there is no reason why it should not be applied to sovereign debtors. It differs very strongly from the solution allowing the IMF to function as the court.

Where the removal of protectionist barriers can be expected to lead to higher export revenues, a trade-off between more repayments and less protection or higher debt reduction without reduced protection is necessary. Strictly symmetrical treatment of all creditors including IFIs is necessary as a means to increase allocative efficiency.

Unquestionably a need for reform within debtor countries exists. These reforms, monitored by the council of arbitrators – or if the Marshall Plan model of self-monitoring were adopted for SCs, by an appropriate body within this framework – should adjust the debtor to the real international environment, not to a textbook illusion of 'free markets'. Realistic strategies have to drop the BWIs' predilection for one-sided liberalization by those countries that can be forced to do so. Import substitution should be encouraged where economically viable to form the basis of future economic diversification. Monitoring by the arbitrators, agreed upon in the plan, could help to overcome the problem of petrifying protection. Protection should allow domestic industries to compete with imports and should be reduced as domestic industries become more efficient. The real experiences of successful East Asian countries (as opposed to the IBRD description of them) would be highly useful even though adapting rather than copying would be required. The Japanese perception that development strategies must take a country's specific characteristics and history into account must serve as the basis of pragmatic economic policies.

The introduction of Chapter 9 insolvency would encourage private lenders to make loans basically if repayments could be expected from proceeds. Debts which have to be serviced out of the budget would and should remain the exception. Commercial lenders would stop lending if previous loans were not put to efficient use, as they would be sure to lose their money eventually. Briefly put, if international insolvency procedures had existed in the 1970s the burden of debt would be much lower, and maybe there would not even be a debt crisis.

FINANCIAL ACCOUNTABILITY OF DONORS

Reducing official bi- and multilateral debts by an international Chapter 9 insolvency would automatically introduce an element of financial accountability of donors and IFIs. Accumulated bad projects financed by loans or a string of unsuccessful programmes would eventually lead to insolvency reducing these creditors' claims. As donors and particularly IFIs control the use of loans, this would be a highly positive result. While the importance of decisions by donors and IFIs may vary from country to country as well as over time, it has always been particularly strong in the poorest countries. Lack of local expertise to participate appropriately in decision making as well as high dependency on aid inflows are the reasons. Using a term coined by Svendsen (1987, p. 27) we may refer to debts accumulated by such countries as 'creditor-determined' or (mainly) the result of creditors' decisions. The present practice of letting recipients pay for failures of their creditors is particularly unjustified in these cases.

As there is no sufficient proof that present Structural Adjustment or IMF programmes work, while there is substantial evidence of their negative effects (even IFIs agree, for instance, that the poor were hurt considerably or that the effects on capital formation endanger future development), they should be discontinued. Strictly logically it does not matter whether programmes do not work because of failures and inconsistencies, which appears to be the case (see Chapter 11), or because IFIs cannot make them work in SCs, as documented by their failures (see Chapter 12). There is no economically valid point in funding something that does not work but harms. Discontinuing programmes would also have the doubly beneficial effect that aid presently used to repair damages done by them would be free to be used in an economically better way. Present Structural Adjustment should be replaced by an international Chapter 9 insolvency and necessary and adequate reforms should be effected within this framework.

Discussing financial accountability, one need differentiate between programmes and projects. As it is practically impossible to determine the fair share of one or more IFIs in failed programmes, Chapter 9 insolvency procedures provide a clear and simple solution, monitored by independent outside experts as suggested in Chapter 11. IFIs should lose the same percentage of their claims as other creditors. In SCs with high IFI involvement, which have been forced to orient their policies according to IFI 'advice' for quite some time, this is particularly necessary and justified. As the shares of multilateral debts are relatively higher in the poorest countries, protecting IFIs from losses is at the expense of particularly poor clients, often highly dependent on solutions elaborated by IFI staff.

As a consequence the IMF could either be dissolved or redirected to other tasks unconnected to development. Proposals to merge the Bretton Woods twins into one institution or to take the Fund out of the development business have already been made, so this is not a wholly new idea.

Although an improvement, symmetrical treatment is not a satisfactory solution to the problem of financial accountability of donors and IFIs. In the case of projects accountability must go further. As errors can often be isolated and proved with less difficulty, donors and IFIs should be liable for damage done by them in the same way private consulting firms are liable to their clients. The present practice of 'IFI-flops securing IFI-jobs' (Raffer 1993, p. 158), to some extent also valid for donors, must stop.

Economically viable projects that earn their amortization and interest payments pose no problem. If a project goes wrong it is necessary to determine financial consequences (ibid.). In the simplest case borrower and lender(s) agree on a fair allocation of costs. If they do not, the solution used between business partners or transnational firms and countries in cases of disagreement could be applied: the decision of a court of arbitration. This concept is well known in the field of international investments. If disagreements between transnational firms and host countries can be solved that way there is no reason why disputes between donors or IFIs and borrowing countries could not be solved by this mechanism as well.

A permanent international court of arbitration – different from insolvency arbitration mentioned above, but composed in the same way – would be ideal. If necessary this court might consist of more than one panel. It would decide on the percentage of the loan to be waived to cover damages for which the IFI is responsible. The right to file complaints should be conferred on individuals, NGOs, governments and international organizations. As NGOs are less under pressure from IFIs or member governments their right to represent affected people is particularly important. The court of arbitrators would of course have the right and the duty to refuse to hear apparently ill-founded cases. The need to prepare a case meticulously would deter abuse. The possibility of being held financially accountable would act as an incentive for donors and IFIs to perform better and protect the poor from damage resulting from ill-conceived projects.

Last but not least it must force donors and IFIs to respect human rights when financing projects, enabling victims of aid projects to receive damage compensation. Quite often people living on land wanted for development projects are expropriated without proper or even any compensation. Forced resettlements occur to make room for dams, highways or harbours, but also for BWI conferences. The Morse Commission concluded 'that the abuses in Sardar Sarovar were not an isolated exception, particularly with respect to the mistreatment of thousands of forcibly resettled rural poor: "The problem besetting the Sardar Sarovar Projects are more the rule than the exception to resettlement operations supported by the Bank in India"' (Rich 1994, p. 252).

According to Cernea (1988, p. 44) about 40 IBRD projects 'will cause the relocation of at least 600 000 people in 27 countries' during 1979–85. He warns however that 'the number of people needing to be resettled is *chronically underestimated*' (ibid., p. 45, emphasis as original). The author concedes that forcibly resettled people often get a raw deal, which allows the project to be implemented more cheaply. If they receive any compensation it is often inadequate and leads to impoverishment, particularly so in the case of dams. Cernea cites the destruction of productive assets, higher morbidity and mortality, ecological disaster and the destruction of social structures as effects of development projects with compulsory resettlement. Susan George (1988, p. 158) reports that people resisting resettlement under the huge Indonesian *transmigrasi* project were crushed by security forces. In several countries people unwilling to clear their land for large development projects were killed. While NGOs blamed police or military death squads, governments did not find any proof for such accusations.

While IFIs and donors keenly preach human rights or respect of private (especially foreigners') property they have not seen great problems in financing projects violating these values, particularly so when the victims were indigenous people. The right of victims to make donors accountable for what they facilitate is needed to improve the lot of the poor, whose human rights and sometimes lives are too often considered unworthy of respect by their governments as well as their governments' public financiers.

Financial accountability would thus be beneficial to donors and IFIs themselves. It would give their staffs a good argument against pouring money into regions just because of lending targets, as well as against political interference by important politicians or shareholders including demands to bail out other creditors. Projects and programmes actually financed under these conditions of accountability would therefore have a much better success rate and more positive impacts on development.

The root of the problem, non-accountability and the systemic failures it causes, would be eliminated. Bilateral donors have already acknowledged the necessity of debt relief for quite some time by reducing official debts. IFIs, by contrast, still do not. Naturally it would cost IFI shareholders something to clean up the failures of the past but there is no more reason to spare IFI owners than any other shareholders of a firm. However as Mexico proved convincingly, a big bail out costs money as well. If development banks cannot survive being financially accountable, dissolving them would be the economically indicated solution because no project at all is preferable to a costly flop – at least for those who have to pay for it. If subject to economic scrutiny and damage compensation claims the amount of ODA might, and IFI activities will, strongly decrease to fewer but economically more viable projects. Considering the increasing involvement of IFIs in Eastern Europe and the former Soviet Union the problem of efficiency and accountability becomes even more important. Pouring money there just to meet regional targets would certainly not be indicated.

FINANCING INSTITUTIONAL REFORMS AND SOCIAL AGENDA BY GRANTS

The close scrutiny of how loans are used, which would result from implementing the proposals made above, does not mean an end of concessional lending. Nor does it mean the end of financing social agenda or projects in the poorest countries. In the case of concessional interest rates debt service can be covered with relatively lower income streams. As shown in the last Chapter, institution building, social agenda and projects for the poor must be financed by grants unless a recipient is sufficiently liquid, which is however extremely unlikely in the case of most SCs.

IS AID DIVERTED TO THE EAST?

To what extent are the fears of traditional ODA recipients justified that resources otherwise available to them might be shifted to the post-communist countries? Strong Western interest in these Countries and Territories in Transition (CTTs) or Central and Eastern European Countries/ Newly Independent States (CEECs/NIS) made SCs fear that DAC donors might remember the old English proverb 'nere is my kyrtyl, but nerre is my smock' [near is my kirtle, but nearer is my smock]. If aid to CTTs were recognized as ODA, as has been suggested, donors could maintain their ODA levels while shifting their money along with their interest.

Discussions on whether to subsume official aid to CTTs under ODA started immediately after the demise of the Eastern bloc and interest varied widely among DAC members according to their economic and political interests. Australia allocated slightly more than $5 million to CTTs in 1992 and 1993, or 0.00 per cent of GNP, the US 0.02 per cent on average during 1991–93 and Japan less than 0.01 per cent, well below the DAC average of 0.04 during 1991–93. By contrast Germany's disbursements were 0.13 per cent in 1993 (0.16 and 0.17 in 1991 and 1992 respectively), not counting transfers to the former GDR. Austria – traditionally rather ungenerous to SCs – took the first rank, averaging above 0.2 per cent during the three years 1991–93 (OECD 1995, p. 85). The DAC total of 'official aid' to the East was around $7 billion annually since 1991 according to the latest *Chairman's Report 1994* (ibid.), but substantially higher according to the *Report 1993* (OECD 1994). For 1992 for example this difference is more than $1 billion. Politically motivated debt relief to Poland was one major part of some Western countries' aid. Keen to help Russian soldiers leave, Germany was a major source of flows to Russia at the beginning of the 1990s.

So far DAC donors opposing an inclusion of CTT aid in ODA have more or less prevailed. The present compromise differentiates between Part I and Part II aid recipients. Part I comprises SCs as well as some NIS. These are Armenia, the Kyrgyz Republic, Georgia, Uzbekistan, Azerbaijan, Turkmenistan, Kazakhstan and Albania. One might argue with some conviction that countries such as Kazakhstan would have been listed as recipients long ago had they not been part of the Soviet Union. Part II recipients are all other CTTs, including Russia, Hungary or the Czech Republic. Furthermore some few SCs were graduated to Part II status as from 1996 by the DAC: the Bahamas, Singapore, Brunei, Kuwait, Qatar and the United Arab Emirates. 'Official aid' and 'flows of financial resource' to Part II – CEECs/NIS are officially not 'development assistance', recorded separately but in the same way as ODA. 'Official aid' is defined by exactly the same wording as 'ODA' (see Chapter 1), except that 'developing countries' is replaced by 'recipient countries' (OECD 1994, p. 131). But language has already been blurred. The Chairman's Overview of the *Report 1993* called 'concessional development assistance' to the East explicitly a 'new demand on development co-operation' (OECD 1994, p. 5). This *Report* included these data for the first time in an Annex.

Statistical separation is of course irrelevant to the question whether funds are actually being re-routed to the East. Naturally donors claim that aid to the CTTs is additional. A closer look at DAC statistics shows the following evolution of the two types of aid expressed in percentages of DAC GSP:

	1986	1987	1988	1989	1990	1991	1992	1993
Official Aid	–	–	–	–	0.01	0.04	0.04	0.04
ODA	0.35	0.34	0.34	0.32	0.33	0.33	0.33	0.30

ODA has shown a slightly falling trend for more than three decades. Increasing after Western Europe's reconstruction to a peak of 0.54 per cent of DAC GSP in 1961, it dropped afterwards, oscillating around 0.35 per cent during the 1970s and 1980s (OECD 1985, p. 335). The relatively steep fall from 1992 to 1993 is the strongest argument for a shift of aid to the East, particularly as aid to CTTs has remained constant. However special factors contribute to this drop. First, US ODA dropped sharply by one-quarter, from 0.20 to 0.15 per cent of GNP. This accounted for 40 per cent of the $4.9 billion reduction of total DAC ODA. It might well be connected with the end of the Cold War but much less with aid to CTTs, although it increased from 0.01 to 0.02. Second, German ODA expressed as GNP percentages fell monotonously during the 1990s, from 0.42 in 1990 to 0.37 in 1993. Between 1992 and 1993 it decreased by $629 million, roughly 13 per cent of the decrease of the DAC total. In this case shifts of resources to CTTs and to the so-called 'new states' (*Neue Bundesländer*, the former GDR) seem to explain the evolution of ODA quite well. Third, Italian ODA fell by more than $1 billion, accounting for 22.08 per cent of the DAC's decrease, but its aid to CTTs decreased also from 0.03 to 0.02. Fourth, Sweden's ODA fell by $691 million, a further 14.14 per cent of the decrease in the DAC total. While ODA fell from 1.03 to 0.98 per cent of GNP, aid disbursements to CEECs/NIS remained stable at 0.15, after they had tripled between 1991 and 1992. On the other hand 1992 was an exceptional year: in 1990 and 1991 ODA was 0.91 and 0.90 per cent respectively. The remaining tenth is accounted for by several other donors, such as Finland, Canada and Norway. Finland however halved its aid to CTTs between 1991 and 1993. Canada reduced it from 0.05 to 0.01 per cent of GSP. Norway increased it relatively generously from 0.02 in 1991 to 0.07 in 1992 and 0.08 in 1993. Finally Japan's ODA fell from 0.30 to 0.26 per cent of GNP between 1992 and 1993 although it increased slightly in current dollars due to the appreciation of the yen.

Data published so far would hardly support the thesis of a clear general shift from South to East. Germany or the EU budget (see Chapter 7) seem to be exceptions apparently proving the rule. The OECD (1994, p. 128) described official aid quite pithily: 'disbursements of concessional assistance continue to lag far behind the large commitments announced at international conferences'. Great expectations were aroused when Centrally Planned Economies were about to shake off communism and have apparently influenced evolutions. But generous promises soon gave way to less generous reality, possibly so when they had served their purpose. The enormous 'peace dividend' expected to be available as aid to both East and South failed to materialize. Both 'kyrtyls' are less 'nere' to donors than the smock of national budgets. The end of the Cold War as such seems to have had greater negative effects on SCs for the moment than any shift of resources to the East. This does not of course mean that such shifts will not occur in the future.

Bibliography

Adler, John (1952), 'The Fiscal and Monetary Implication of Development Programs', *American Economic Review, Papers & Proceedings*, May, pp. 584ff.

African Development Bank (1994), *The Quest for Quality – Report of the Task Force on Project Quality for the African Development Bank*, April.

Agata, Masahiko (1994), 'Financing Projects for Energy Efficiency', summary of a paper presented at an International Energy Agency sponsored conference in Mexico, March 1994 (mimeo).

Arab Banking Corporation (1990), *The Arab Economies, Structure and Outlook*, third rev. edn.

Asian Development Bank (1994), *Report of the Task Force on Improving Project Quality*, January.

Ayres, Robert L. (1984), *Banking on the Poor, The World Bank and World Poverty*, Cambridge (Mass.): MIT Press.

Balogh, T. (1970), 'Multilateral *v.* Bilateral Aid', in J. Bhagwati and R.S. Eckaus (eds), pp. 203ff, (originally published in 1967: *Oxford Economic Papers*, **19**, (3), pp. 328ff).

Bauer, P.T. (1976), *Dissent on Development*, London/Cambridge (Mass.): Weidenfeld and Nicholson/Harvard UP.

Beckmann, David (1986), 'The World Bank and poverty in the 1980s', *Finance & Development*, **23**, (3), pp. 26ff.

Bhagwati, J. (1970), 'The Tying of Aid', in J. Bhagwati and R.S. Eckaus (eds), pp. 235ff.

Bhagwati, J. and R.S. Eckaus (eds) (1970), *Foreign Aid*, Harmondsworth: Penguin.

Bloch, Julia Chang (1991), 'A U.S.-Japan Aid Alliance?', in S. Islam (ed.), pp. 70ff.

Bossuyt, J., G. Laporte and G. Brigaldino (1993), *European Development Policy after the Treaty of Maastricht – The Mid-Term Review of Lomé and the Complementary Debate*, Maastricht: European Centre for Development Policy Management.

Bradlow, Danny (1995), 'The Panel's Investigation of the Arun Dam in Nepal', The American University, Washington DC, 8 March, (mimeo).

Bratton, Michael (1989), 'The politics of government NGO-relations in Africa', *World Development*, **17**, (4), pp. 569ff.

Brezinski, Horst (1986), 'The Relations between the Democratic People's Republic of Korea (DPRK) and the Council of Mutual Economic Assistance (CMEA) and its Members', *Journal für Entwicklungspolitik*, **2**, (2), pp. 93ff.

Cassen, Robert et al. (1986), *Does Aid Work? Report to an Intergovernmental Task Force*, Oxford: Clarendon Press.

Cathie, John (1982), *The Political Economy of Food Aid*, Aldershot: Gower.

Cernea, Michael C. (1988), 'Involuntary Resettlement and Development', *Finance & Development*, **25**, (3), pp. 44ff.

Chenery, Hollis et al. (1974), *Redistribution with Growth*, London etc: Oxford UP.

Chenery, Hollis (1989), 'Foreign Aid', in J. Eatwell, M. Milgate and P. Newman (eds), *Economic Development – The New Palgrave*, London and Basingstoke: Macmillan, pp. 137ff.

Christoffersen, Leif E. (1978), 'The Bank and Rural Poverty', *Finance & Development*, **15**, (4), pp. 18ff.

Clay, Edward (1994), 'The Decline of Food Aid: Issues of Aid Policy, Trade and Food Security', in R. Prendergast and F. Stewart (eds), pp. 186ff.

Commission (1992) [of the EU], 'Development Cooperation Policy in the Run up to 2000: The Consequences of the Maastricht Treaty', SEC (92) 915 fin.

Commission Européene (1994), 'Texte F, Exportations de viande bovine de la Communauté européenne en Afrique occidentale', Communication de M. Marin, Brussels, 29 April 1994 [SEC(94)754/2].

Cornia, G.A., R. Jolly and F. Stewart (eds) (1987), *Adjustment with a Human Face*, two vols, Oxford: Oxford UP.

Crockett, Andrew (1982), 'Issues in the use of Fund resources', *Finance & Development* **19**, (2), pp. 10ff.

Elliott, Charles (1987), 'Some Aspects of the Relations Between the North and South in the NGO Sector', in Ann Gordon Drabek (ed.), pp. 57ff.

Emmanuel, Arghiri (1976), 'La "stabilisation" – alibi de l'exploitation internationale', *Revue Tiers-Monde*, **17**, (66) April–June, pp. 257ff.

Erler, Brigitte (1985), *Tödliche Hilfe, Bericht von meiner letzten Dienstreise in Sachen Entwicklungshilfe*, Freiburg i.B.: Dreisam Verlag, (an English translation *Lethal Aid: Report on My Last Assignment as a Foreign Aid Official*, bound mimeo., available at the IDS library, University of Sussex).

European Parliament (1992), *Report of the Committee on Development and Cooperation on Structural Adjustment in the Developing Countries*, 4 February 1992, Rapporteur: Mr Eugenio Melandri, PE 155.077/fin.

Farrington, John and Anthony Bebbington (1993) with Kate Wellard and

David J. Lewis, *Reluctant Partners? Non-Governmental Organizations, the State and Sustainable Agricultural Development*, London and New York: Routledge.

Fernandez, Aloysius P. (1987), 'NGOs in South Asia: Peoples Participation and Partnership',in Ann Gordon Drabek (ed.), pp. 39ff.

Fishlow, Albert and Catherine Gwin (1994), 'Overview: Lessons from the East Asian Experience' in Fishlow et al. (1994), pp. 1ff.

Fishlow, Albert et al. (1994), *Miracle or Design? Lessons from the East Asian Experience*, Washington DC: Overseas Development Council.

Friedeberg, Alfred S. (1975), 'The Lomé Agreement: Co-operation Rather than Confrontation', *Journal of World Trade Law*, **9**, (6), pp. 692ff.

Friedman, Milton (1970), 'Foreign Economic Aid: Means and Objectives' in J. Bhagwati and R.S. Eckaus (eds), pp. 63ff, (original in *Yale Review*, vol.47, pp. 24ff).

GATT (1980), *International Trade 1979/80*, Geneva: GATT.

GATT (1994), *International Trade, 1994, Trends and Statistics*, Geneva: GATT.

George, Susan (1988), *A Fate Worse than Debt*, Harmondsworth: Penguin.

German, T. and J. Randel (1994), 'The European Union' in J. Randel and T. German (eds), *The Reality of Aid 1994*, London: Actionaid.

Gerster, Richard (1989), 'How to Ruin a Country: The Case of Togo', *IFDA-Dossier* **71**, (May/June), pp. 25 ff.

Gerster, Richard (1994), 'Monitoring Swiss Participation in the Bretton Woods Institutions', presentation on the occasion of the workshop '50 Years Bretton Woods' in The Hague, 12 September 1994 (mimeo).

Goldin, Ian, Odin Knudsen and Dominique van der Mensbrugghe (1993), *Trade Liberalisation: Global Economic Implications*, Paris/Washington DC: OECD/IBRD.

Goldman, Marshall I. (1967), *Soviet Foreign Aid*, New York etc: Praeger.

Gordon, Drabek, Ann (ed.) (1987), *Development Alternatives: The Challenge for NGOs*, Supplement to *World Development*, vol.15.

Goto, Kazumi (1992), 'The Management of Japan's International Contribution: A Case of Overseas Aid', in Ippei Yamazawa and Akira Hirata (eds), pp. 55ff.

Goto, Kazumi (1994), 'Japan's Aid Policy and Institutions', in ODI (ed.), pp. 8ff.

Gotur, Padma (1983), 'Interest rates and the developing world', *Finance & Development*, **20**, (4), pp. 33ff.

Gurtner, Bruno (1994), 'Monitoring Swiss Participation in the Bretton Woods Institutions', *Swiss Coalition News*, **2**(September), pp. 2ff.

Hanabusa, Masamichi (1991), 'A Japanese Perspective on Aid and Development' in S. Islam (ed.), pp. 88ff.

Hancock, Graham (1989), *Lords of Poverty*, London: Mandarin.

Hardy, Chandra (1994) 'The Case for Multilateral Debt Relief for Severely Indebted Countries', International Development Training Institute, Washington DC (mimeo).

Haselbach, Arne (1981), *Bruno Kreisky's Drive for a Large-Scale Economic Solidarity Programme with Developing Countries*, Vienna Institute for Development, Occasional Paper 81/3.

Hayter, Teresa (1987), 'Is Reform of the World Bank Possible?', in Bruno Kreisky and Humayun Gauhar (eds), *Decolonisation and After, The Future of the Third World*, London: South Publications, pp. 95ff.

Healy, Derek (1991), *Japanese Capital Exports and Asian Economic Development*, Paris: OECD.

Helleiner, G.K., G.A. Cornia and R. Jolly (1991), 'IMF Adjustment Policies and the Needs of Children', *World Development*, **19**, (12), pp. 1823ff.

Hewitt, Adrian (1987), 'STABEX and Commodity Compensation Schemes: Prospects for Globalisation', *World Development*, **15**, (5) (special issue on primary commodities ed. by A. Maizels) pp. 617ff.

Hirono, Ryokichi (1991), 'Japan's Leadership Role in the Multilateral Development Institutions', in S. Islam (ed.), pp. 171ff.

IBRD (1976), *The World Bank, Questions and Answers*, Washington DC: IBRD.

IBRD (1980), *World Development Report 1980*, Washington DC: IBRD.

IBRD (1987), *World Development Report 1987*, Oxford etc: Oxford UP.

IBRD (1989), *World Development Report 1989*, Oxford etc: Oxford UP.

IBRD (1990), *World Development Report 1990*, Oxford etc: Oxford UP.

IBRD (1992), *Effective Implementation: Key to Development Impact, Report of the World Bank's Portfolio Management Task Force*, Washington DC: IBRD.

IBRD (1993), *The East Asian Miracle: Economic Growth and Public Policy*, New York: Oxford UP.

IBRD (WDT) (1988), *World Debt Tables 1988–89, External Debt of Developing Countries*, vol. I, *Analysis and Summary Tables*, Washington DC.

IBRD (WDT) (1992), *World Debt Tables 1992–93, External Debt of Developing Countries*, vol. I, *Analysis and Summary Tables*, Washington DC.

IBRD (WDT) (1993), *World Debt Tables 1993–94, External Debt of Developing Countries*, vol. I, *Analysis and Summary Tables*, Washington DC.

IBRD/IDA (1993), 'The World Bank Inspection Panel', Resolution No. 93–10; Resolution No. IDA 93–6, 22 September.

IDB (1993), *Managing for Effective Development – Report of the Task Force on Portfolio Management for the Inter-American Development Bank*, October.

IMF (1992), *Private Market Financing for Developing Countries*, World Economic and Financial Surveys, December.

IMF/WEO, *World Economic Outlook*, Washington DC, October (various years).

Islam, Shafiqul (1991a), 'Introduction', in S. Islam (ed.), pp. 1ff.

Islam, Shafiqul (1991b), 'Beyond Burden Sharing: Economics and Politics of Japanese Foreign Aid', in S. Islam (ed.), pp. 191ff.

Islam, Shafiqul (ed.) (1991), *Yen for Development*, New York: Council on Foreign Relations Press.

Jansen, Eirik G. (1979), 'Choice of Irrigation Technology in Bangaldesh: Implications for Dependency Relationships between Rich and Poor', *The Journal of Social Studies*, **5**, pp. 61ff.

JEXIM (1993), 'The "Funds for Development" Initiative', Export Import Bank of Japan (mimeo).

Joint Economic Committee (1982), *USSR: Measures of Economic Growth and Development 1950–1980*, studies prepared for the use of the Joint Economic Committee, Congress of the United States, 8 December, (97th Congress, Second Session), Washington DC: US Government Printing Office [volume prepared by the CIA].

Jolly, Richard (1991), 'Adjustment with a Human Face: A UNICEF Record and Perspective on the 1980s', *World Development*, **19**, (12), pp. 1807ff.

Kaiser, Walter (1986), 'Die Entwicklungshilfeleistungen der Sowjetunion in den OECD-Publikationen', *Journal für Entwicklungspolitik*, **2**, (2), pp. 32ff.

Kajese, Kingston (1987) , 'An Agenda of Future Tasks for International and Indigenous NGOs: Views From the South', in Ann Gordon Drabek (ed.), pp. 79ff.

Kanesa-Thasan, S. (1981), 'The Fund and adjustment policies in Africa', *Finance & Development*, **18**, (3), pp. 20ff.

Kinoshita, Toshihiko (1993), 'The end of the Cold War and Japan's financial contribution to international development', in S. M. Murshed and K. Raffer (eds), pp. 115ff.

Kohama, Hirohisa (1995), 'Japan's Development Cooperation and Economic Development in East Asia', in I. Takatoshi and A.O. Krueger (eds), pp. 201ff.

Kono, Yoshihiko (1994), 'Japan's Aid to East Asia and Its Impact on Development', in ODI (ed.), pp. 12ff.

Kramer-Fischer, Dorit (1981), 'Ein Neuer Marshallplan für die Dritte Welt. Der österreichische Vorschlag zu einem verstärkten Ressourcentransfer', *Österreichische Zeitschrift für Politikwissenschaft*, **10**, (2), pp. 139ff.

Kreisky, Bruno (1980), *Massive Transfer of Resources and the Development of Infrastructure*, Vienna Institute for Development, Occasional Paper 80/1.

Kreisky, Bruno (1981), *The McDougall Memorial Lecture 1983*, Vienna Institute for Development, Occasional Paper 81/3.

Kuznets, Simon S. (1955), 'Economic Growth and Income Inequality', *American Economic Review*, **45**, (1), pp. 1ff.

Kwack, Sung Yeung (1986), 'The Economic Development of the Republic of Korea, 1965–1981', in Lawrence Lau (ed.), *Models of Development*, San Francisco: ICS Press, pp. 65ff.

Lenin, W.I. (1973), 'Über unsere Revolution (Aus Anlaß der Aufzeichnungen N. Suchanows)', in W.I. Lenin, *Werke*, vol. 33, 5th edn, Berlin: Dietz, pp. 462ff.

Lipton, Michael and John F.J. Toye (1990), *Does Aid Work in India? A Country Study of the Impact of Official Development Assistance*, London: Routledge.

Marin, Manuel (1990a), 'The Convention "is of paramount political importance for the Community"', *The Courier*, **120**, (April–May), pp. 8f.

Marin, Manuel (1990b), 'Lomé IV – the scope of a new Convention', ibid., pp. 12ff.

Marx, Karl (1967), *The Capital*, edited by F. Engels, 3 vols, New York: International Publishers.

Maurizio, Roberto (1983), 'IFAD – A New Tool for Agriculture', *Politica Internazionale* (English Edition), **3**, (1), pp. 105ff.

Meyer, Carrie A. (1992),'A Step Back as Donors Shift Institution Building from the Public to the Private Sector', *World Development*, **20**, (8), pp. 1115ff.

Meyer, Klaus (1980), 'The Second Lomé Convention, the European Community and the North-South Dialogue', *The Courier*, **61**, (May–June).

Ministry of Foreign Affairs (of Austria) (1989), *Dreijahresprogramm der österreichischen Entwicklungshilfe 1990 bis 1992 (Fortschreibung)*, Vienna: BM für Auswärtige Angelegenheiten.

Mosley, P., J. Harrigan and J. Toye (1991), *Aid and Power, The World Bank and Policy Based Lending*, two vols, London: Routledge.

Murshed, S. Mansoob and Somnath Sen (1995), 'Aid Conditionality and Military Expenditure Reduction in Developing Countries: Models of Asymmetric Information', *The Economic Journal*, **105**, (429), pp. 498ff.

Murshed, S. Mansoob and K. Raffer (eds) (1993), *Trade, Transfers and Development, Problems and Prospects for the Twenty-First Century*, Aldershot: Edward Elgar.

Murtada Mustafa, Mohamed El (1983), 'Development Planning, Urban Labour Markets and International Migration in the Sudan', in P. Oesterdieckhoff and K. Wohlmuth (eds), *The Development Perspectives of the Democratic Republic of Sudan, The Limits of the Breadbasket Strategy*, München/ Köln/ London: Weltforum Verlag, pp. 277ff.

Myrdal, Gunnar (1970), *The Challenge of World Poverty, A World Anti-Poverty Program in Outline*, London: Allan Lane, The Penguin Press.

Myrdal, Gunnar (1985), 'Relief instead of Development Aid', *Journal für Entwicklungspolitik*, **1**, (1), pp. 4ff, (Swedish original in *Ekonomisk Debatt*, 8/1980).

Nowzad, Bahram (1982), 'Debt in developing countries: some issues for the 1980s', *Finance & Development*, **19**, (1), pp. 13ff.

Nurkse, Ragnar (1952), 'Some International Aspects to the Problem of International Development', *American Economic Review, Papers & Proceedings*, (May), pp. 571ff.

Nuscheler, Franz (1994) 'Japan als "aid leader", Neue Entwicklungen in der japanischen Entwicklungspolitik', (mimeo).

ODI (Overseas Development Institute) (ed.) (1994), *Japan's Aid and the Developing Countries*, London: Chameleon Press.

OECD (1970), *Development Co-operation, Efforts and Policies of the Members of the Development Assistance Committee,Review 1970*, Paris: OECD.

OECD (1973), *Flow of Resources to Developing Countries*, Paris: OECD.

OECD (1977), *Development Co-operation, Efforts and Policies of the Members of the Development Assistance Committee, Review 1977*, Paris: OECD.

OECD (1980), *Development Co-operation, Efforts and Policies of the Members of the Development Assistance Committee, 1980 Review*, Paris: OECD.

OECD (1981), *Development Co-operation, Efforts and Policies of the Members of the Development Assistance Committee, 1981 Review*, Paris: OECD.

OECD (1982), *Development Co-operation, Efforts and Policies of the Members of the Development Assistance Committee, 1982 Review*, Paris: OECD.

OECD (1983), *Aid from OPEC Countries*, Paris: OECD.

OECD (1984), *Development Co-operation, Efforts and Policies of the Members of the Development Assistance Committee, 1984 Review*, Paris: OECD.

OECD (1985), *Twenty-Five Years of Development Co-operation – A Review, 1985 Report*, Paris: OECD.

OECD (1988), *Development Co-operation, Efforts and Policies of the Members of the Development Assistance Committee, 1988 Report*, Paris: OECD.

OECD (1992), *Development Co-operation, Efforts and Policies of the Members of the Development Assistance Committee, 1992 Report*, Paris: OECD.

OECD (1993), *DAC Orientations on Participatory Development and Good Governance*, Paris: OECD [OCDE/GD(93)191].

OECD (1994), *Development Co-operation, Efforts and Policies of the Members of the Development Assistance Committee, 1993 Report*, Paris: OECD.

OECD (1995), *Development Co-operation, Efforts and Policies of the Members of the Development Assistance Committee, 1994 Report*, Paris: OECD.

OECD (GDF, various years), *Geographical Distribution of Flows to Developing Countries – Disbursements, Commitments, Economic Indicators*, Paris: OECD.

OECF (1994), *Annual Report 1994*, Tokyo: OECF.

OED (Operations Evaluation Department) (1989), *Project Performance Results for 1987, A World Bank Operations Evaluations Study*, Washington DC: IBRD.

Ohlin, Goran (1966), *Foreign Aid Policies Reconsidered*, Paris: OECD.

Okuda, Hidenobu (1992), 'Japanese Two-Step Loans: The World Bank Approach and the Japanese Approach', in Ippei Yamazawa and Akira Hirata (eds), pp. 87ff.

Ozawa, Terutomo (1989), *Recycling Japan's Surpluses for Developing Countries*, Paris: OECD.

Page, John (1995), 'Comment', in I. Takatoshi and A.O. Krueger (eds), pp. 221ff.

Pearson, L.B. (1969), *Partners in Development: Report of the Commission on International Development Cooperation*, New York: Prager.

Pickett, James and Hans Singer (eds) (1990), *Towards Economic Recovery in Sub-Saharan Africa, Essays in Honour of Robert Gardiner*, London and New York: Routledge.

Pierre-Charles, Gérard (1972), 'Dominación y dependencia', in M. Monteforte Toledo (ed.), *Centro América I, Subdesarollo y dependencia*, C. México: Universidad Nacional Autónoma de México, pp. 348ff.

Pisani, Edgard (1985), 'Giving tangible expression through frank and fair dialogue to the hopes raised by the new Convention', *The Courier*, **89**, (January–February), p. 15.

Polak, J.J. (1991), *The Changing Nature of Conditionality*, Essays in International Finance No. 184, International Finance Section, Department of Economics, Princeton University NJ.

Prebisch, Raúl (1949), 'El desarrollo económico de la América Latina y algunos de sus principales problemas', *El Trimestre Económico*, **XVI**, (3), (Julio–Sept.), pp. 447ff, (English version published by UN-ECLA in 1950).

Prendergast, Renee and Frances Stewart (eds) (1994), *Market Forces and World Development*, London and Basingstoke/ New York: Macmillan/ St.Martin's Press.

Price Waterhouse (1992), *Study on the Causes of Delay in the Implementation of Financial and Technical Cooperation – Final Report*, November, (accounting number: 6.ACP.RPR.472) (mimeo).

Raffer, Kunibert (1986), 'Siphoning-Off Resources from the Periphery: The Relevance of Raúl Prebisch's Thinking for the Eighties', *Development & South-South Cooperation*, **II**, (3), (Special Issue: 'Homage to Raúl Prebisch'), pp. 100ff, reprinted in H.W. Singer, N. Hatti and R. Tandon (eds) (1991), *Aid and External Financing in the 1990s*, (New World Order Series, vol.9), New Delhi: Indus Publishing, pp. 583ff.

Raffer, Kunibert (1987), *Unequal Exchange and the Evolution of the World System, Reconsidering the Impact of Trade on North-South Relations*, London and Basingstoke/ New York: Macmillan/ St. Martin's Press.

Raffer, Kunibert (1989), 'A Critique of the Socialist Countries' Theory and Practice of the New International Economic Order', in B.H. Schulz and

W.W. Hansen (eds), *The Soviet Bloc and the Third World – The Political Economy of East-South Relations*, Boulder etc: Westview, pp. 91ff.

Raffer, Kunibert (1990), 'Trade in Agrarian Products and Services: How Free Should it Be?', in H.W. Singer, N. Hatti and R. Tandon (eds), *Trade Liberalisation in the 1990s*, (New World Order Series, vol. 8), New Delhi: Indus Publishing, pp. 851ff.

Raffer, Kunibert (1990a), 'Applying Chapter 9 Insolvency to International Debts: An Economically Efficient Solution with a Human Face', *World Development*, **18**, (2), pp. 301ff.

Raffer, Kunibert (1992), 'The Effects of Oil Prices on Peripheral Net Importers: A Crude Estimate with Special Reference to LDACs', in K. Raffer and M.A.M. Salih (eds), pp. 13ff.

Raffer, Kunibert (1993), 'International financial institutions and accountability: the need for drastic change', in S.M. Murshed and K. Raffer (eds), pp. 151ff.

Raffer, Kunibert (1994a), 'Is the Debt Crisis Largely Over? – A Critical Look at the Data of International Financial Institutions', in R.M. Auty and J. Toye (eds), *Challenging Orthodoxies*, London and Basingstoke: Macmillan (forthcoming).

Raffer, Kunibert (1994b), 'Disadvantaging Comparative Advantages: The Problem of Decreasing Returns', in R. Prendergast and F. Stewart (eds), pp. 75ff.

Raffer, Kunibert (1994c), '"Structural Adjustment", Liberalisation, and Poverty', *Journal für Entwicklungspolitik*, **10**, (4), pp. 431ff.

Raffer, Kunibert (1995a), 'Good Governance, Accountability, and Official Development Co-operation: Analysing OECD-Demands at the Example of the IBRD', in E.M.G. Denters, K. Ginther and P.J.I.M. de Waart (eds), *Sustainable Development and Good Governance*, Dordrecht etc: Martinus Nijhoff.

Raffer, Kunibert (1995b), 'The Impact of the Uruguay Round on Developing Countries', in F. Breuss (ed.), *The World Economy after the Uruguay Round*, Vienna: Service Fachverlag, pp. 169ff.

Raffer, K. and M.A.M. Salih (eds) (1992), *The Least Developed and the Oil-Rich Arab Countries, Dependence, Interdependence or Patronage?*, London and Basingstoke: Macmillan.

Randel, Judith and Tony German (1993), 'Prospects for the Poorest? International Aid in the 1990s', in J. Randel and T. German (eds), pp. viiiff.

Randel, Judith and Tony German (eds), (1993), *The Reality of Aid 1993 – An Independent Review of International Aid*, London: Actionaid.

Reichmann, Wilhelm (1988), *Die Verschuldung der Dritten Welt 1970–1983, Entwicklung und Ursachen der Krise in den Finanzbeziehungen zwischen Norden und Süden*, Frankfurt a.M. etc: P. Lang Verlag.

Republic of Trinidad and Tobago, Ministry of Finance and the Economy

(1989), *Trinidad and Tobago's Government's Relationship with the International Monetary Fund 1988*, January, (mimeo).

Rich, Bruce (1994), *Mortgaging the Earth, The World Bank, Environmental Impoverishment and the Crisis of Development*, London/ Boston: Earthscan/ Beacon Press.

Riddell, Roger C. (1987), *Foreign Aid Reconsidered*, Baltimore/ London: J.Hopkins UP/ J. Currey.

Rix, Alan (1980), *Japan's Economic Aid*, New York: St. Martin's Press.

Rosenstein-Rodan, Paul N. (1981), *The New International Economic Order, Relations between the Haves and the Have-Nots (North-South)*, University Lecture, Boston University.

Saran, Ram and Panos Konandreas (1991), 'An Additional Resource? A Global Perspective on Food Aid Flows in Relation to Development Assistance', in Edward Clay and Olav Stokke (eds), *Food Aid Reconsidered: Assessing the Impact on Third World Countries*, London: Frank Cass, pp. 37ff.

Schatz, Klaus W. and Frank Wolter (1982), 'International Trade, Employment and Structural Adjustment: The Case Study of the Federal Republic of Germany', *ILO Working Paper* 2–36/WP 19 WEP (October).

Schneider, Bertrand (1988), *The Barefoot Revolution: A Report to the Club of Rome*, London: Intermediate Technology Publications, (French original, Paris: Fayard, 1985).

Seers, Dudley (1979), 'Introduction: The Congruence of Marxism and Other Neoclassical Doctrines', in *Toward a New Strategy of Development. A Rothko Chapel Colloquium*, New York and Oxford: Pergamon Press, pp. 1ff.

Sen, Amartya K. (1981), *Poverty and Famines: An Essay on Entitlement and Deprivation*, Oxford: Clarendon Press.

Sengupta, Arjun (1988), 'What is to be done with the Japanese Surplus?', *Finance & Development*, **25**, (3), pp. 24ff.

Serfas, Alexander (1987), *An der Schwelle zum Industrieland: Die wirtschaftliche Entwicklung Südkoreas 1963–1983*, Frankfurt a.M. etc.: P. Lang.

Shihata, Ibrahim F.I. (1982), *The Other Face of OPEC, Financial Assistance to the Third World*, London etc: Longman.

Singer, H.W. (1950) 'The Distribution of Gains between Investing and Borrowing Countries', *American Economic Review, Papers & Proceedings*, **XL**, pp. 478ff.

Singer, H.W. (1989), 'Lessons of Post-War Development Experience 1945–1988', *IDS-Discussion Paper* no. 260, Sussex: IDS.

Singer, H.W. (1994), 'Tinbergen and International Policy Making', paper presented at a special commemorative conference on the work and impact of Jan Tinbergen on 17 December 1994, Erasmus University, Rotterdam (forthcoming in the Proceedings Volume edited by Piet Terhal).

Singer, H.W. and Sumit Roy (1993), *Economic Progress and Prospects in the Third World*, Aldershot: Edward Elgar.

Singer, H.W. and D.J. Shaw (1995), 'A future food aid regime: implications of the Final Act of the GATT Uruguay Round', paper presented at the DSA Annual Conference, Dublin, 7–9 September 1995 (mimeo).

Smillie, Ian (1993), 'Changing Partners: Northern NGOs, Northern Governments', in I. Smillie and H. Helmich (eds), pp. 13ff.

Smillie, Ian and Henny Helmich (1993a), 'Japan', in Ian Smillie and H. Helmich (eds), pp. 177ff.

Smillie, Ian and Henny Helmich (eds) (1993b), *Non-Governmental Organisations and Governments: Stakeholders for Development,* Paris: OECD [bilingual book; English and French].

Spraos, John (1983), *Inequalising Trade? A Study of Traditional North/South Specialisation in the Context of Terms of Trade Concepts*, Oxford: Clarendon Press.

Stauffer, Thomas R. and F.H. Lennox (1984), *Accounting for Wasting Assets, Income Measurement for Oil and Mineral-Exporting Rentier States*, OPEC Fund Pamphlet Series No. 25, Vienna.

Stewart, Frances (1991), 'The Many Faces of Adjustment', *World Development*, **19**, (12), pp. 1847ff.

Streeten, Paul (1993), 'From growth via basic needs, to human development: the individual in the process of development', in S. M. Murshed and K. Raffer (eds), pp. 16ff.

Streeten, Paul (1994), *Strategies for Human Development*, Copenhagen: Handeslshøskolens Forlag.

Streeten, Paul (1994a), 'A New Framework for Development Cooperation', in *Benessere, equilibrio e sviluppo, Studi in onore di Siro Lombardini*, a cura di T. Cozzi, P.C. Nicola, L. Pasinetti, A. Quadrio Curzio, con la collaborazione di G. Marseguerra, Vol. I, Milano: Vita e Pensiero, pp. 111ff.

Streeten, Paul (1995), 'Some Unsettled Problems in International Cooperation' in A.R. Khan and A. Abdullah (eds), *State and Development Policy: Essays in Honour of Professor Rehman Sobhan* (tentative title; forthcoming).

Svendsen, Knud Erik (1987), *The Failure of the International Debt Strategy*, CDR Research Report no.13, Copenhagen.

Takatoshi, Ito and Anne O. Krueger (eds) (1995), *Growth Theories in Light of the East Asian Experience*, Chicago and London: University of Chicago Press.

Takayanagi, Akio (1993), 'Japan', in J. Randel and T. German (eds), pp. 32ff.

Tetzlaff, Rainer (1980), *Die Weltbank: Machtinstrument der USA oder Hilfe für die Entwicklungsländer?*, München and London: Weltforum Verlag.

Tinbergen, Jan (1962), *Shaping the World Economy, Suggestions for an International Economic Policy*, New York: 20th Century Fund.

Tinbergen, Jan (1990), 'The Optimal Amount of Development Assistance', in Pickett and Singer (eds), pp. 169ff.

Tinbergen, Jan (1990a), *World Security and Equity*, Aldershot: Edward Elgar.

Toye, John (1994), 'Memorandum to the Foreign Affairs Committee of the House of Commons, Session 1993–94', London: HM Stationery Office.

Tseng, Wanda (1984), 'The effects of adjustment', *Finance & Development*, **21**, (4), pp. 2ff.

UN (1995), *World Economic and Social Survey 1995*, New York: UN.

UNCTAD (1983), 'UNCTAD VI – International financial and monetary issues, Item 11 – Policy Paper', TD/275 (26 January 1983).

UNCTAD (1987), *Financial Solidarity for Development, Development Assistance from OPEC Members and Institutions to Other Developing Countries*, New York: UN.

UNCTAD (1988), *Financial Solidarity for Development, Development Assistance from OPEC Members and Institutions to Other Developing Countries 1982–1986, 1988 Supplement*, New York: UN (TD/B/C.3/226).

UNCTAD (1994), *Trade and Development Report, 1994*, New York and Geneva: UN.

UNDP (1992), *Human Development Report 1992*, New York etc: Oxford UP.

UNDP (1993), *Human Development Report 1993*, New York etc: Oxford UP.

UNDP (1994), *Human Development Report 1994*, New York etc: Oxford UP.

Uvin, Peter (1993), '"Do as I Say, Not as I Do": The Limits of Political Conditionality', *The European Journal of Development Research*, **5**, (1) (June), pp. 69ff.

Uvin, Peter (1994), *The International Organization of Hunger*, London: Kegan Paul.

van der Laar, Aart (1980), *The World Bank and the Poor*, Boston etc: M. Nijhof.

Wade, Robert (1994), 'Selective Industrial Policies in East Asia: Is *The East Asian Miracle* Right?', in Fishlow et al. (1994), pp. 55ff.

Warren, Bill (1979), 'The Postwar Economic Experience of the Third World', in *Toward a New Strategy for Development. A Rothko Chapel Colloquium*, New York and Oxford: Pergamon Press, pp. 144ff.

Watkins, Kevin (1995), *The Oxfam Poverty Report*, Oxford:Oxfam,.

White, Howard (1993), 'Aid, investment and growth: what prospects in the 1990s?', in S.M. Murshed and K. Raffer (eds), pp. 99ff.

Wolf, Ch. (1960), *Foreign Aid: The Theory and Practice in Southern Asia*, Princeton: Princeton UP.

Yamazawa, Ippei and Akira Hirata (eds) (1992), *Development Cooperation Policies of Japan, United States, and Europe*, Tokyo: Institute of Developing Economies.

Yanagihara, Toru (1992), 'Policy Based Lending and Japanese Policy', in Ippei Yamazawa and Akira Hirata (eds), pp. 77ff.

Yanagihara, Toru and Anne Emig (1991), 'An Overview of Japan's Foreign Aid', in S. Islam (ed.), pp. 37ff.

Yeats, Alexander (1990), 'Do African Countries Pay More for Imports?', *Finance & Development*, **27**, (2), pp. 38ff.

Index